# EVANGELIZED
# AMERICA

~ WILLIAM ASHLEY SUNDAY ~

# EVANGELIZED AMERICA

*By* GROVER C. LOUD

BOOKS FOR LIBRARIES PRESS
FREEPORT, NEW YORK

First Published 1928
Reprinted 1971

INTERNATIONAL STANDARD BOOK NUMBER:
0-8369-5990-6

LIBRARY OF CONGRESS CATALOG CARD NUMBER:
70-169770

PRINTED IN THE UNITED STATES OF AMERICA

## DEDICATION

*To the Reverend Frederick Harrison Corson, a minister of the Methodist Episcopal Church, this book is dedicated. From his pulpit in a little New Hampshire community came messages that strengthened his people and widened their vision. A great liberal, he wrought a finer conception of God and with it an ennoblement of man. He took evolution as scientific truth and dealt with no dualism.*

*He joined men in the fields and sat down by their workbenches to talk with them about life as it is. He went to bedsides of pain and to homes where death had brought sorrow, taking with him the hope and the understanding that imparted a benediction of peace.*

*He stirred the ambition of youth toward greater usefulness. He opened the way for many to go to college and stimulated many more to seek out their own self-education. The author of this book acknowledges his own deepest gratitude to this Soldier of God, this man among men.*

*His eyesight failed him in his last days, but the light of his soul burned brighter. He grew with his faith to the end.*

*He did not believe in revivals.*

# TABLE OF CONTENTS

# LIST OF ILLUSTRATIONS

# FOREWORD

## I

As every evangelist will hark back to the hour in which he was "called to preach," so the writer of this book is moved to record how his "call" came. It was around a fireside in Gramercy Park in the house where once dwelt Edwin Thomas Booth, by windows that looked across to the site of the New York home of Colonel Robert G. Ingersoll.

But the shades of the great actor and the agnostic orator had nothing to do with the beginning of the book. A publisher was in search of an author and a newspaper man had brought him one who had made his name as a master of research, a thinker and a writer. The candidate said something more than his qualifications was needed, something he did not possess and could not acquire.

The conversation drifted into the very channel of the projected book. Gradually all became aware that they were listening to the newspaper man. He knew the revival because he had felt its power. He had heard Sankey sing and he knew the words, the melodies of a hundred hymns that have stirred the hearts of succeeding generations in the resurgent spirit of the American revival.

He recalled the burning denunciations, the militant commands, the tender pleadings of evangelists great and obscure, in thronged tabernacles and in wayside tents. He had seen a city shaken, a college caught up in a tumult of emotion greater than that stirred by "the big game," and a rural community so overwhelmed that its inhabitants feared destruction before the dawn of another day.

All his life he had been drawn to the revival, whether of Methodists, Pentecostalites, Adventists, devotees of the Burning Bush, or no denomination in particular or all denominations in one tidal wave of evangelistic fervor.

He had observed certain constant elements indigenously American in the rise and fall of the spiritual waters and had differentiated between the outer depths and the surf on the shoals. And yet in his own heart he believed that in this fathomless sea of faith, without beginning, without end, lay the only hope of peace for a restless, unsatisfied world.

The newspaper man had ceased speaking. All were contemplating the dying embers of the fire. The master of research broke the silence by abruptly saying: "You are the one to write this book." And the publisher added: "You must."

The newspaper man demurred. Though every night of his life for years he had pitted all his mental and nervous energy against a flood of news from all over the world, the aggregate of which would dwarf an eighteenth-century novel, he hesitated at venturing into the creation of a book that in a hundred thousand words or so would tell the story of the incessant evangelizing of America.

But in the end he accepted the assignment. He knew that all the heart and imagination he possessed would be at the service of his pen.

## II

Then came the months of assaying what others had already written on the subject. The newspaper man began to realize the gingerbread nature of pretentious bibliographies. Every book he tackled had one of these. He even compiled one of his own only to find that one day he was compelled to cease wasting his time, and that of his eventual reader, and to plunge in straightway and begin to write.

He soon discovered that only rarely had the critical function been exercised, that his predecessors in the field had taken houselot subdivisions of it and then, intruding their own honestly biased appraisal of men, doctrines and events, had, with a few notable exceptions, lapsed finally into the indiscriminate and the superficial.

Denominational histories, individual biographies, especially such incisive studies as that of Dwight L. Moody by Gamaliel Bradford, periodic and sectional accounts, of which one of the best was Catherine Cleveland's "Great Revival in the West, 1797–1805," contributed in a measure restricted by a standard of values set by the comprehension of the whole. Psychological analyses, like those of William James and Sydney G. Dimond helped toward a generous understanding of the springs of action underlying the revival.

But despite a few ambitious attempts, among which might be mentioned Beardsley's "History of American Revivals," Headley's "American Evangelists," Thompson's "Times of Refreshing," and the works of Davenport, Goss and Torrey, there was no sweep of the entire two centuries of American evangelism. And above all, there was no objective, journalistic record of the onward marches, with the inevitable strategic retreats, in the militant conquest that began on this continent in the days of Jonathan Edwards and is being carried on into a future beyond prophecy.

To supply this need is the sole justification for adding one more book in a world where "of making many books there is no end; and much study is a weariness of the flesh."

To those who have experienced personally the power of the revival this book would recall their great hour, the forces that lay behind it and the circumstances that make it akin to the timeless, limitless manifestations invoked by others wearing the mantle of Elijah.

To those who have only observed the typical revival, whether with indifference, antagonism or sympathy, this book would bring a realization that all the tributaries of evangelism in this country from the early Colonial sources to the present day flow into one continuous stream whose varying watermark, higher or lower, records the molding of lives, for better or worse, in every generation.

The preachers pass in review, from stalwart saints to mountebanks of Mammon. Between are the self-anointed egotists expounding their own dogma and the mesmeric exhorters kindling the fires of their hell in the minds and even the bodies of those under their sway.

The circumstances that pushed these men forward, or of which some took advantage, in the rolling up of one evangelistic movement after another, and the "messages" they delivered, all converge upon the multitudes who heard them in clearings of the wilderness, under canvas by village roadsides, beneath the open rafters of a city tabernacle or amid the splendor of a temple dedicated to the prophet of the hour.

Of these things this book will tell and it is concerned with no more than the telling. It is the work of a journalist who knows no other way.

G. C. L.

# EVANGELIZED
# AMERICA

# CHAPTER I

## WHAT IT IS TO BE CONVERTED

At the Cross, at the Cross
Where I first saw the Light
And the burden of my heart
Rolled away—rolled away!
ISAAC WATTS, 1674–1748.

WHEN the "Fire" has descended and circled through the "Camp," consuming guilt and fear and shame and hate, purifying and then exalting as it spreads from one human consciousness to another till at last the single mind of all is ablaze in one intense sacrificial flame, behold the American revival is come.

All things of earth have melted away. The heavens have opened and where there was darkness there now is light, where there was uncertainty there now is security, where there was conflict there now is peace. The sense of freedom is complete, the assurance of understanding perfect. This is at once individual and collective. It is conversion, the fruit of the revival.

Perhaps the trapdoor of a hell had been lifted, perhaps the floodgates of divine love had been loosed. The sacerdotal strategy for the winning of souls may have been on the level of gross sensationalism or on the plane of finely-wrought emotional appeal. The conversion may have been the mere triumph of the evangelist or one genuinely dedicated to the God invoked by a despairing being who found ultimate and absolute relief in self-surrender. It may have been for the moment or for a lifetime.

In retrospective analysis the evangelist discriminates and speaks of the "truly converted." Such, Jonathan Edwards tells us, have been conscious of two states, "a state of condemnation," in which they are even "willing to be damned," and "a state of justification and blessedness" regenerated by supernatural power. More than a century later, Dwight L. Moody pleaded with men to "let the will of God be done" in them as it had been in him, challenged the manner of their living and believing, and, in "inquiry meetings" when preaching was over, broke down the barriers to faith by taking the load of sin's consciousness from their minds.

Throughout all the evangelizing of America, however, underlying both pulpit plea and resultant response, there is one fundamental ruling motive—the ever-welling yet constantly frustrated human impulsion to escape. It is the insatiable longing of the race for peace away from conflict, for quietude away from restlessness. It is the highly individualized desire to burst the bonds of earth and it brings men and women to the mercy seat or down the sawdust trail in the alluring hope of a vision into the hitherto impenetrable Beyond with security for all eternity as the reward.

Salvation from hell has always meant escape from the perpetual human predicament. When Jonathan Edwards and George Whitefield were kindling America's first great revival fires in the third and fourth decades of the eighteenth century, they were preaching in the shadow of the primeval forest where the danger of savages and wild beasts had not yet become remote. It was along a new and still more hazardous frontier that James McGready carried the Gospel torch at the dawn of the nineteenth century in the camp meetings of Kentucky and Ohio where the phenomena of conversion reached the most poignant stage of all revival history. In the writhing of body and torturing of mind the "redeemed soul" was visibly wrenched from the clutches of "the world, the flesh and the Devil."

Each revival movement has been progressive to a peak of saturation or satiation. Not that any part of the country was ever fully "redeemed," but that people would no longer be able to endure the sustained tension and the crusading energy would burn itself out. A decline in spiritual responsiveness would follow the revival, sometimes lasting for years. Then at the lowest point of the pessimism consequent upon apathy or disillusion, the revival was reborn and with it another of the cycles of revivalism that have characterized the American way of getting religion, losing it and finding it yet again.

Even when the fruits of a revival were preserved in the forming of a new denomination, like the Methodists under the Wesleyan apostles, Francis Asbury and Dr. Thomas Coke, who took root in the post-Revolutionary despair of the struggling young nation and spread to its uttermost fringes along the Gospel trails of such circuit riders as Peter Cartwright, still it has been found necessary in succeeding generations as altars grew cold to return to the primal evangelical spirit. It was in the second century after Roger Williams founded Providence on their faith that the Baptists were led by Jacob Knapp and Jabez Swan to make one of the greatest extensions of the fold of those who symbolize their salvation by total immersion. Swan baptized ten thousand with his own hands.

Then again, denominations have clashed in the fury of

the revival, sundering families and rending whole communities in doctrinal warfare. The attack has been even carried into open meeting, as when demon-chasing Presbyterians pursued Asbury's disciple, Benjamin Abbott, whose visions encompassed both the Devil and the Christ. Though the churches have gained in membership from a revival, in notable instances they have lost adherents through the schisms it engendered, bringing forth the Campbellites, Thomas and Alexander Campbell's flock that seceded from the Baptists in the Tennessee evangelistic tornado of the early nineteenth century, and later William Miller's Adventists and the Pentecostalists riven from the Methodist ranks, each one proclaiming its monopoly on the sole means of grace.

More often, however, the evangelist in America has disregarded denominational lines or has subordinated them to his own conception of a larger purpose embodied in an all-inclusive message. Whitefield never relinquished his ties with the Church of England, though his preaching from Carolina to Maine doubtless made more eventual Methodists than Episcopalians and his staunch Calvinism certainly added to the Presbyterians.

"Are you a Christian?" was the incessant question that Moody hurled at vast assemblages as well as at individuals throughout his ministry and he poured his converts into all churches. But some of his successors have taken a cue from certain of the exhorters of the early days and have been actually subversive of contemporary ecclesiastical authority, drawing thousands into the revival whirlpool and then leaving them stranded after it has subsided.

Every evangelist has started with his own conversion. Besides being his call to preach it is also his principal theme. Over and over again he tells of his personal regeneration through supernatural power manifesting itself in unmistakable ways at a definite time and place. And for all who hear him he lays down the fundamental premise that they too must be born again by faith alone and, like him, must be so conscious of it that the soul-shaking change convinces the messengers and witnesses for God in the very hour of redemption.

Pentecost repeats itself in the midst of the evangelized. They indeed become all of one mind and their tongues are loosened. And the first desire of those whose "burdens have rolled away" is to bring others to share their experience. All become potential evangelizers. Each one seems to have heard the command to "go into all the world and preach the gospel to every creature."

And so the revival spirit spreads. Neighbors gather in fervent home prayer meetings under the spell of the preaching of Edwards. Laymen carry the word of Wesley and Whitefield into the byways. Volunteers throw out Ira Sankey's "life line." "Workers" lead the hesitant down Billy Sunday's "sawdust trail."

At first God's eye is on Northampton or His hand is laid upon Boston or the Presence dwells in a forest clearing in Kentucky or the Holy Ghost descends in a tabernacle at Chicago. Soon all sense of locality is lost and the saved set out to evangelize the whole world. It has always been so. And it has always come to a climax in which physical and mental power to endure the strain has become exhausted and the revival tide has ebbed only to roll in again and yet again in timeless succession.

This rise and fall of the revival constitutes a sequence of definite cycles of which the outstanding are the Great Awakening of 1740, the Kentucky camp meetings of 1800, the Miller preparation for the Second Advent in 1843, the post-panic waves of repentance in 1857 and 1907 and the Moody movement reaching its heights in the 80's.

Before the Great Awakening, revivals that were styled "ingatherings" and "harvests" of souls were sparsely chronicled in Massachusetts and Connecticut, beginning as early as 1679 at Northampton and recurring in 1683, 1696, 1712 and 1718. Similar "stirrings" were recorded at Hartford in 1696, at Taunton in 1795 and at Windsor in 1721, and the earthquake that shook New England in 1727 evoked widespread inquiry for a time concerning the way to salvation.

Following Moody and Sankey, only one evangelistic team can be considered comparable with them—Chapman and Alexander. This is conceded by the younger Gypsy Smith, who, in widening the field of his father in the South, has come to be recognized as a rationalizing force for better living as distinct from sensational pulpiteers.

In the latter days the itinerant spectacular individual evangelist has come to the fore, of whom the chief exemplar is William Sunday. With "big top" or rough-hewn tabernacle, Billy and his imitators borrow from Barnum in drawing their crowds and take a leaf from modern big business in selling salvation.

There are those who maintain perpetual motion evangelistic plants in centers calculated to attract people from afar. Aimee Semple McPherson has dedicated her own Angelus Temple with its stage settings and radio masts in Los Angeles to the idea of continuous performance. Frank Norris of Texas and John Roach Straton of New York City make every service in their Baptist edifices a revival throughout the year and keep the yeast of religion in constant ferment.

And modern evangelism pays material dividends. Billy

Sunday exacts his cash guarantee in advance. Mrs. Mc-Pherson packs in five thousand, hangs out the "Standing Room Only" sign and her collection plates are weighed down with greenbacks.

Be it said for the pioneer evangelists that their thoughts were not of this world but of the future of eternal souls they earnestly yearned to snatch from a hell and assure of a heaven which were very real to them. Some of the lesser revival periods in the two-century span came about from the inspiration of a single man, like Charles G. Finney, the Congregationalist lawyer, who turned to a client on the morning his case was set for trial and said: "Deacon B., I have a retainer from the Lord Jesus Christ to plead His cause and I cannot plead yours!"

Other revival seasons were purely denominational in character. And still others, which seemed to chroniclers to have been spontaneous, can be traced to the same cause—reaction from spiritual stagnation. In 1831 a revival swept over fifteen hundred towns with more than 100,000 persons added to the churches and then followed a decline, intensified by the disillusion in the failure of the Second Coming in 1843, that reached its lowest point on the eve of the great religious upheaval of 1857.

And here appears a mainspring of the American revival that cannot be neglected. It has been said that the 1857 revival came without a human herald, prearranged plan or purpose, a revival without a revivalist. But it was economic pressure that then forced the people to their knees. A financial crash had shaken the money centers of the world. All confidence was undermined. Industry stood still. Bewildered and fearful, men turned back to religion and prayed to God not only to save their souls but also to restore their credit.

It was the same after Wall Street floundered in 1907 and men surged to hear Alexander's vast choirs sing "All Other Ground Is Sinking Sand" and to heed Chapman's plea to fill again the vacant pews of the churches. It was the old, old urge to escape from that perplexity which transcends time and space in the annals of humanity.

For all the converted have been refugees. They have been saved not so much from the terrors of hell as from things as they are or at least as they only too rationally seem to be. The acute realization of the human predicament has given substance to the preaching of a hell that ceased to be theoretical and became something to be reckoned with.

The discrepancy between desire and destiny has confronted man since the dawn of his intelligence when his primal ancestor recoiled from the fury of the elements or in a calm night gazed in awe upon the star-studded sky and wondered what it was all about, whence it came and whither it led. The reasonings of scientists and philosophers have only deepened the mystery and made man the more conscious of his ignorance and helplessness. The physical world remains at once beautiful and sinister, and, if Godless, utterly indifferent to the intricate, subtle, sensitive mind of mankind that would thus appear to be superfluous and negligible upon one of the countless planets of an infinite universe.

In the misty beginnings, man invented gods to compensate this sterile void and devised rites for their propitiation. With time came theologians developing theological systems and doctrines and dogmas to support them. The simplest of these was Israel's "Jehova our God is One." Jehova made all and dealt directly with his creation.

But with the passing of centuries, despite evangelists

like Elijah and Isaiah, Jehova became aloof from Israel or Israel lost contact with Jehova. The Sadducees banished hope of immortality and the Pharisees fell back upon the barren formality of the Scriptural law. The imperial masters in distant Rome mocked the gods of their ancestors and darkness fell upon the world.

In the midst of all this despair the Man of Galilee was born and with Him the new hope that lives on through two thousand years. Apart from the doctrinal complexities woven about Him, one thing is plain. He brought God back to man and man back to God. And He did this by inculcating the conviction that the Power which was "mindful of the sparrow's fall" was the refuge and strength of every individual human being.

It was the first revival. Or perhaps it is *the* revival and all the revivals that have come since and have been like it are only continuous manifestations of the same fundamental elements—the decadence of hope and personal inspiration, the advent of a new light, and the exaltation of the individual. Again and again, it is the way of escape, escape from things as they are, escape from self. And finding that is what it is to be converted.

# CHAPTER II

## THE VOICE IN THE WILDERNESS

The morning light is breaking,
The darkness disappears;
The sons of earth are waking
To penitential tears.

INDIVIDUALISM, economic, social and political, inspired the conquest of the new world. It reasserted itself time and again against mass crystallization in every consolidating of the frontier and in the eventual rise of industrialism. Its persistency has made America the peculiarly fertile field of evangelism.

For one dynamic force actuating the first American religious revival and the constant element pervading the continuity of its spirit even to this day is this individualism challenging submergence in prescribed conformity, insisting upon the necessity of a personal experience and assuming the personal right to receive and proclaim a special understanding of God and His past, present and future relations with man.

In a broad sense, then, this revival is a revolt against the neglect or suppression of the individual by formal ecclesiasticism, against the aloofness and inertia of authoritatively established practice, against the failure of the Church so to reach and convict the individual mind that moral as well as religious sanctions generally have lost their force. Its fire burns against the icy wall of a frozen faith.

~ JONATHAN EDWARDS ~

The revival, in fact, is not so much directed against irreligion as against somnolent indifference, stubborn willfulness or repressed spiritual energy. It would awaken, overcome and inspire, giving voice to the inarticulate, guidance to the derelict and a feeling of personal participation to all.

Moreover, the evangelist comes to sweep away all sense of security among churchmen relying upon the mere performance of good works and the usual observance of ordained rites to get them into their Heaven. Indeed the first concern of the pioneer savers of souls was to make every living human being supremely aware of the imminent danger of a literal Hell!

This was the theme of Jonathan Edwards when at Northampton, Massachusetts, in 1734 he heralded the "Great Awakening" that was to spread the smell of brimstone from backslidden Puritan New England to the comfortably-cushioned consciences of the Colonists of New York, New Jersey, Pennsylvania and the South.

"Justification by faith alone" was what Edwards preached, Edwards the forerunner who prepared the way for George Whitefield in the wilderness, Edwards the original turnkey of the Gates of Hell in the New World.

"God has laid Himself under no obligation, by any promise, to keep any natural man out of hell one moment," he thundered. "The bow of God's wrath is bent, and the arrow is made ready on the string, and justice bends the arrow at your heart, and strains the bow, and it is nothing but the mere pleasure of God, and that of an angry God, without any promise or obligation at all, that keeps the arrow one moment from being drunk with your blood."

Then the excruciation:

"The God that holds you over the pit of hell, much as one holds a spider or some loathsome insect over the fire, abhors you and is dreadfully provoked.

"You hang by a slender thread, with the flames of divine wrath flashing about it, and ready every moment to singe it and burn it asunder, and you have no interest in any mediator, and nothing to lay hold of to save yourself, nothing to keep off the flames of wrath, nothing of your own, nothing that you have ever done, nothing that you can do to induce God to spare you one moment!"

Even so was the consciousness of guilt of original sin that no man could exculpate by his own works laid upon the third and fourth generations, who had banked the fires of the faith brought to the shores of New England by their Puritan forefathers.

For Edwards was of the Puritan tradition that never suffered either the godly or the ungodly to rest but made all life an unending Sabbath in which the righteous by self-examination and supplication yearned for saintliness and the unrighteous perforce had to listen and be taxed to support the preaching that damned them eternally. And Edwards was in revolt against the consequences of the softening of the ancient rigorous code through the promulgation of the so-called "Half-Way Covenant," adopted by the Boston Synod in 1660 and upheld by Solomon Stoddard, his venerable grandfather and colleague in the Northampton pulpit.

Stoddard favored admitting the unconverted to participation in the Lord's Supper, even regarding Holy Communion as a converting ordinance, and urged granting to the unregenerate the right to have their children baptized. His liberalizing influence survived and spread in spite of the reaffirming in 1679 of the original Cam-

THE VOICE IN THE WILDERNESS

bridge Platform that laid down the rights, duties and practices for the governance of the united Puritan Church and State, drawing the line of the saved and the unsaved in according the privileges of church membership and civil suffrage but compelling all to attend meeting, be taxed to support both parson and magistrate and be subject to their discipline.

This reinvoking of the Cambridge Platform by what was known as the Reforming Synod, at Boston, in the main called for strict accountability by profession of faith, but most of those added to the rolls of the churches at this time were Half-Way Covenanters who merely renewed their conditional vows and remained content with the privileges thus secured without pressing onward toward "full salvation."

And so it came about that the very evils that the Reforming Synod set itself to check sprang up anew to choke out the "Vine planted in the Wilderness." The listed sins included the decadence of the Sabbath, profanity and irreverent behavior; backbitings, censures and litigations among professing Christians whose godliness declined; pride, extravagance and lustfulness in dress, intemperance and tavern haunting; mixed dancings, gaming and idleness; dishonesty and covetousness; neglect of baptism, church fellowship and means of grace, and, above all, refusal to repent.

Accentuating all this were economic unsettlement with the accumulation of debt, political disruption in such events as the loss of the old charter of Massachusetts, and religious dissension as evidenced by the seizure of the Old South Meeting House in Boston for Episcopal services and the tumult over the witchcraft delusion in Salem. Unquestionably there was a general lapse in public morals and a spiritual desolation as the combined clerical and magisterial sanctions loosed their grip on New England.

Essentially, the whole downward movement that gathered impetus during the first three decades of the eighteenth century was the utter relaxation of the individual responsibility exacted by the pristine Puritan Church. The generosity of Stoddard's extension of the Half-Way Covenant, paradoxically, left to the Church only the austere formalism which had been a fault of its absolute sway. Personal religious incentive, once compelled, was now neglected till it was almost lost.

Then the prophet came to Northampton, once a stronghold of the theocratic régime and now bearing witness to its decline as the old-time "ingatherings" became feebler and farther apart till the revival power all but died away and none hardly knew what it was to be converted. Amid the gathering shadows of this year of 1727, Jonathan Edwards received his charge. Upon the youth of twenty-four were laid in token of ordination the hands of Solomon Stoddard, his revered grandfather, whose pulpit he was to share for two years before death ended the labors of the patriarch at the age of eighty-six.

Whatever of good was bestowed or whatever of havoc was wrought by the ministry that began this day can be accounted for in the mainsprings of the life of the young preacher who seems to have been anointed for his calling from his birth.

Jonathan was the fifth child and the only son of the family of eleven born to the Reverend Timothy Edwards and the daughter of Solomon Stoddard, "a woman surpassing her husband in native understanding." It was his mother that endowed Jonathan with brains. She was a remarkable woman for her day in that she would not be hurried into becoming a professor of religion, for, though the wife of a parson, she did not join the Church till Jonathan was twelve years of age.

At this time, however, Jonathan was writing letters to refute the idea of the material nature of the soul. Ever since the age of four he had been continually engaged in looking into his little mind and forming resolutions against faults he discovered lurking there, setting forth once a determination "never to do, be or suffer anything in soul or body but what might tend to the glory of God; to live with all my might while I do live; never to speak anything that is ridiculous or a matter of laughter on the Lord's Day, and frequently to renew the dedication of myself to God."

Thus the sermons upon which his ancestors had fed nourished the growing prophetic consciousness. All his inherited instincts, training and surrounding conditions molded this young Samuel who so long as he lived was to be "lent to the Lord."

Moreover, the very nature of his work was constantly before him, for East Windsor, Connecticut, the town of his nativity, was shaken throughout his youth by revivals of remarkable power and frequency. Rowelled from the pulpit, the lad was always confronting himself with self-accusations, with the meaning of human existence and a sense of littleness and sinfulness within it, and with the awful nearness of God, with His wrath and its consequences.

No wonder he became, like so many other evangelists, including Whitefield and Wesley and Asbury, a sort of spiritual hypochondriac. His delicate, nervous constitution, taken with the tendency to asceticism, made him a sort of habitual invalid. His whole life was given to moral introspection, "counting the spiritual pulse," as his own diary abundantly discloses. His career conforms to this rule which one commentator on revivalists has given:

"A gently complaining and fatigued spirit is that in which evangelical divines are very apt to pass their days.— There is an air of invalidism about most religious biographies."

A portrait of Edwards in his maturity reveals the man and the preacher. The forehead is high and unfurrowed. The eyes are calm and steady, bespeaking patience and resolution. The mouth is prim as that of a maiden lady and just as likely to be positive in the utterance of unswerving convictions.

The essential characteristics mirrored in this countenance were already strongly possessed by the boy of thirteen when he entered Yale College, where he was graduated four years later. Then, after two years of theological study, he preached for eight months in a newly organized church in New York, returning to Yale to be a tutor till the Northampton call came.

By nature religious rather than philosophical, Edwards began his apprenticeship to his grandfather by living alone, studying thirteen hours a day, abstaining from all amusements and any excess of food and rarely visiting the parishioners. After a few months of this stern regimen, a third woman came into his life. First there had been his mother and then his sister Jerusha, seven years his junior and also very devout, to whom he was tenderly attached. Now the Nemesis of Northampton took unto himself a wife.

The bride was Miss Sarah Pierrepont of New Haven, the seventeen-year-old daughter of a professor of moral philosophy at Yale. Her mother was a descendant of

Thomas Hooker, the founder of the Church in Connecticut. Edwards had known her since she was thirteen when he himself wrote of her: "She is spiritual to exaltation and ecstasy."

Throughout their lives together, her mind reflected his and, reinforcing his convictions, sustained him in his chosen course. This good woman also bore him eleven children, and of the ten who reached maturity, one daughter became the mother of Aaron Burr, soldier of the Revolution, Vice President of the United States, survivor of the duel in which Alexander Hamilton was fatally wounded and, though acquitted, one of the few Americans ever to be tried for treason to their country.

But the preaching progenitor of this high adventurer and dreamer of an empire knew only one realm of exploration and that was the Kingdom of God. He held himself aloof from the things of this world and from his exalted pinnacle of moral grandeur and purity he called the sinful sons of men to an accounting with the Justice of Heaven.

From childhood Edwards had rebelled against the Calvinistic doctrine of God's sovereignty and to him at first it seemed horrible "that God should choose whom He would and leave the rest eternally to be tormented in hell." But before he ascended the pulpit he had become actually happy in the acceptance of this dogma and he spent his life urging it upon others as their only hope.

His profound spiritual nature lent force to his extraordinary talent as a logician in expounding the thesis of original sin, the conception of a revengeful God and the conclusion that hell was the just desert of the greater part of the human race.

From the outset of his preaching at Northampton he

was a powerful controversialist and in him positive predestinarian Calvinism triumphed over "Arminianism,"
that belief, given to the world in the last of the sixteenth
century by Jacob Arminius, the Dutch divine, which held
that "a sincere though necessarily imperfect obedience
to the will of God would bring saving grace."

It was against this "heresy" that Edwards went up to
battle when the death of Solomon Stoddard in 1729 left
him alone in the pulpit of Northampton. It meant to him
every kind of reaction against Calvinism. It was the loosely
applied term of "Bolshevism" in the mouths of the present-
day stalwarts of the established political and economic
order.

Arminianism, to its followers, stood for toleration, free
inquiry, reason, democratic methods in Church and State,
in short, liberalism. But to Edwards and the strict Cal-
vinists it was a word for disapproval, contempt and condemnation, an all-inclusive repository for the vices, social
depravities, love of freedom and the world and presumptuous assertion of personal independence that characterized
America of the eighteenth century.

It was the Arminianism of the Methodists that eventually split John Wesley and George Whitefield. And it was
the spirit of Arminianism that led to the American
Revolution. Accepting freedom of the will and the spiritual capacity of man, it first asserted faith in humanity
and then advanced the concept of human liberty and
equality.

So Arminianism went beyond its theological sense and
became the expression of universal democracy. The Calvinistic doctrine of the sovereignty of God was probably
a reflection of monarchism, the belief that "the king can
do no evil." It was the spiritual version of the divine right

of kings. Opposed to this, Arminianism might be called the faith of the people claiming the right to rule themselves. From royal absolutism came the doctrine of human depravity; with the rise of democracy came the doctrine of man's moral capacity.

Jonathan Edwards invested the deity with diabolical regal attributes in the execution of "divine justice." He made the Devil the agent of God, seducer of the children of Adam on earth and jailer of their hell forever after. Though he called the Devil "one of the greatest blockheads and fools in the world," he assigned him a rôle second only to that of God Himself from the disruption of Eden to the peopling of America with the purpose of "luring men and women away from the Gospel." And thus to him Satan was the original Pilgrim Father, the true pilot of the Mayflower.

For five years Edwards pleaded in vain against the perversity of his generation, which, while groping toward the democratic ideal, had fallen into moral laxity, economic confusion and religious indifference. To him it was the work of the Devil, who even boldly "invaded God's house and had prevailed against two revivals." And to him it was a manifestation of Arminianism which "about this time made a great noise in this part of the country."

But the condition of affairs needed no theological definition. It was there. It was real. The Faith of the Fathers had almost lost its hold. Yonder in Boston Increase Mather in bitterness of spirit had cried: "O New England, thy glory is departing!"

Into the last days of 1734 that darkness deepened as it will before the dawn. Then Jonathan Edwards took his stand. For then it was that the young preacher of Northampton heard the challenge: "Watchman, what of the night?" and gave answer, saying: "The morning cometh!"

And the first light was the glare of the fires of hell, rekindled round the pulpit of Jonathan Edwards and burning brightly in the skies above Northampton. It was the beacon that signalled the Great Awakening, the first all-American revival.

# CHAPTER III

## THE EDWARDEAN HELL

Depth of mercy, can there be
Mercy still reserved for me?
Can my God His wrath forbear,—
Me the chief of sinners spare?
CHARLES WESLEY, 1708–1788.

JONATHAN EDWARDS did not ask his people, and the countless others to whom his words were carried as the "message" spread, if they were saved; he sternly told them and grimly convinced them that they were not. He burned into the souls of men, women and even children the fear and horror of everlasting punishment and he justified it to them. He spoke little of heaven, he cared nothing for this world, but he certainly knew his hell.

Northampton was compelled to contemplate a boundless, plumbless sea of fire, undiminished yet unconsuming throughout eternity. Every feelingful fiber of the sinful human frame, in an unabated state of living combustion, was doomed to fry forever. This was the just desert of the "bulk of mankind," part of the divine plan to satisfy divine justice, the inescapable penalty of being born upon a planet fashioned in six days for a race whose progenitor manifested their unanimous ingratitude and rebellion in his own.

Not for one moment did Edwards spare these "sinners

in the hands of an angry God." All their ritual, all their prayer, all their charity could not take from them the predestined fate of the "bulk of mankind" inheriting the corruption and condemnation of Adam. The posterity of the gardener of Eden, that all-inclusive "public person" with whom Jehova dealt so explicitly regarding one tree in earth's first orchard, had sinned with him, had fallen with him and must share his hell.

"God aims at satisfying justice in the eternal damnation of sinners," Edwards dinned into believing ears.

"You have never loved God, who is infinitely glorious and lovely, and why then is God under any obligations to love you, who are all over deformed and loathsome as a filthy worm, or rather a hateful viper?

"Seeing you thus disregard so great a God, is it a heinous thing for God to slight you, a little, wretched, despicable creature; a worm, a mere nothing and less than nothing; a vile insect that has risen up in contempt against the Majesty of heaven and earth?

"The glory of God will be of greater consequence than the welfare of millions of souls!"

Children—some of whom went home from the services shrieking through the streets of the town by night and one of whom at the tender age of four years is written down as having been converted—children were not exempt from the great damnation.

"As innocent as children seem to be to us," Edwards said, "yet, if they are out of Christ, they are not so in God's sight, but are young vipers and are infinitely more hateful than vipers and are in a most miserable condition, as well as grown persons; and they are naturally very senseless and stupid, being born as the wild ass's colt, and need much to awaken them."

~ "A PROPER PRESBYTERIAN PRAYER-MEETING" ~

(From an Old Engraving)

Nor was this all. The pulpiteer of divine justice went on to heaven with the elect and with them looked down into the roaring pit below. All bowed to the inexorable will of the Eternal and even rejoiced in it. "Parents," he said, "will sing hallelujahs as they see their children driven into the flames where they are to lie roasting forever."

None of this was metaphorical to Edwards. His theology was literal. The woman was conjured from the rib, the snake did talk with her and at his bidding she did nibble the apple that corrupted the mother of mankind with the consciousness of carnality. And the hell to pay for this disobedience was so terribly real that sinners struck down in Northampton felt its heat.

The revival became epidemic, "like a distemper" its contemporary critics said, only instead of putting people to flight it drew them into its convulsive throes. Overwhelmed by its power, they swooned, fell into trances, beheld visions like those of delirium tremens and babbled incoherently of things beyond mortal ken.

Emerging from the first stage of fear and anguish, the "victorious" ones exulted in their own damnation as Edwards lashed them into acknowledgment of the triumphant justice of God. But some went insane. This extremity did not worry Edwards, who calmly said:

"We cannot determine how great a calamity distraction is, considered with all its consequences, and all that might have been consequent if the distraction had not happened; nor indeed whether, thus considered, it be any calamity at all, or whether it be not a mercy, by preventing some great sin."

Doubtless the zealous evangelist was thinking of the Scriptural injunction to pluck out the offending eye. On this score one wretched man tried to cut his throat and set the example for many others, some of whom, it is not recorded how many, succeeded in ending their lives.

Of one suicide it was said that he was so concerned about his soul that he "durst entertain no hope." And it was added that "after this multitudes in this and other towns seemed to have it strongly suggested to them and pressed upon them to do as this person had done as if somebody had spoken to them, saying: 'Cut your own throat! Now is a good opportunity! Now! Now!'"

Those who survived the prescribed course of conversion, however, did find peace,—peace in the acceptance of the judgment of God and resignation to the disposal of God. For Edwards conceded that those "elected from eternity according to God's good pleasure" would be saved.

The choice was all God's. His liberty in making it was "perfect" and "just," an attribute of His "complete sovereignty." He could inflict damnation on the instant or defer it. But He also aimed "to satisfy His infinite benevolence by the bestowment of a good infinitely valuable because eternal." There was no appeal to His justice, which only condemned, but this had to be admitted as a prerequisite to an appeal to His mercy through Christ.

But it was not so much the love of God as the wrath of God that went out on winged words day and night from the pulpit of Northampton from the first of January to the last of May, 1735, and spread to South Hadley, Deerfield, Hatfield, West Springfield, Longmeadow, Enfield, Hadley Old Town and Northfield, the eventual home of Dwight L. Moody.

On to Connecticut the widening fire of the Edwardean hell advanced. Its consuming power was first felt in Windsor. It was "remarkable" at East Windsor and "wonderful" at Coventry. "Similar scenes" were enacted at Lebanon, Durham, Stratford, Ripton, Guilford, Mansfield, Tolland, Hebron, Bolton, Preston, Groton, Woodbury and New Haven where the tumult invaded the quiet stately halls of Yale.

Even so the message sped, finding an echo or at least a parallel in the New Jersey "awakening" under William and Gilbert Tennent. In Northampton Edwards alone gathered three hundred converts in half a year, converts whom he had led through the fiery ordeal to the depths of all-engulfing despair. Then they knew their hell. Then they felt their hell. And then they found their God.

These "legal distresses," Edwards says in his retrospective "Narrative of Surprising Conversions," were succeeded by a "special and delightful manifestation of the grace of God—a comfortable and sweet view of a merciful God." In fact, he remarks that in some converts "the first sight of their just desert of hell, and of God's sovereignty with respect to their salvation, and a discovery of sufficient grace, are so near that they seemed to go, as it were, together."

The first recorded redemption is that of a young woman of Northampton, quaintly described as having been "notorious as a leader in scenes of gayety and rustic dissipation." It may be that her worst offenses were playing a good hand at euchre or dancing a lively step in a quadrille. Edwards further vouchsafes that she was "one of the greatest company-keepers in town" and even this might have meant merely that she was willing to take the arm of too many a gallant and often was "seen" home after nine o'clock curfew.

Be all this as it may, Edwards say of this Magdalenian maid:

"When she came to me, I had never heard that she had become in any way serious, but by the conversation I had with her it appeared to me that what she then gave an account of was a glorious work of God."

Humble and penitent as the young lady was, the divine had fears that "the work of conversion in a person of such a character would give it a bad name."

"But the event was the reverse to a wonderful degree," he declares. "The news of it seemed to spread like a flash of lightning upon the hearts of the young people all over the town and many others. Many went to talk with her concerning what she had met with, and what appeared in her seemed to be to the satisfaction of all that did so."

In other words, the tale of the once naughty miss was tremendously interesting—especially the confession and then the descent into damnation—as it brought her through the fire to the mercy seat. It was an experience to be shared, paralleled, and improved upon and it was even so.

One woman of a quiet rational family, whose education had been opposed to such evangelical "enthusiasm," became converted. She was "much wrought up and read her Bible almost constantly to find relief for her distressed soul," Edwards tells us.

"Her terror was great that she had sinned against God and for three days she trembled in fear of His wrath. Then a calmness came over her when she felt that she had discovered Christ. Two days later her soul was filled with distress for Christless persons and she wanted her brother to carry her from house to house to warn sinners. (The brother would not thus oblige her.) She had many extraordinary discoveries of the glory of God, sensing Him in the wind blowing in the treetops and the growing of fields."

Then there was little Phoebe Bartlett, four-year-old daughter of William Bartlett of Northampton, who followed her brother of eleven to the altar of Edwards. She went to the family closet for prayer six or seven times a day. Of her own accord she discoursed upon her unsuccessful search for God, say, "Yes, I am afraid I shall go to hell." After long weeping she finally began to smile and cried out "The Kingdom of Heaven is come to me!"

Back to the closet for more prayer and then she emerged proclaiming that she loved God more than she did any of her family or anybody or anything else and was no longer afraid of going to hell. From that moment onward she kept a strict Sabbath and even longed for the day to come when she could hear Edwards preach. Edwards tells of it and digresses to recount how once she ate some plums taken from a tree without the permission of the owner. She retained her aversion for that fruit for a long time.

And so the work of salvation went on, day to day, week to week, month to month, in the church and in private home spontaneous prayer-meetings, with weeping for distress and more weeping for joy. It was "as a sound of going in the tops of the mulberry trees," "as an outpouring of the spirit," or "as a troubling of the waters."

"The noise among the dry bones waxed louder and louder," the preacher tells us. "Concern about eternal things became universal. The minds of the people were taken from things of the world.

"It was then a dreadful thing to lie out of Christ, in danger every day of dropping into hell; and what people's minds were intent upon was to escape for their lives and to fly from the wrath to come."

The zenith was reached in Northampton and the surrounding region toward the close of May, 1735. Physical power to endure the excitement became exhausted and nerves sought repose. But it was only a natural lapse. The fire smoldered with ever and anon a breath of a glow till it burst loose again when George Whitefield blew his bellows over New England in 1740.

Edwards wrote his "Thoughts on the Revival in New England in 1740" as a sort of sequel to his "Surprising Conversions" of 1735. The passing of the revival grieved him. He writes in 1744 of "the very melancholy state of things in New England." Speaking of the "vast alteration" within two years, he says:

"Many high professors are fallen, some into gross immoralities, some into a rooted spiritual pride, enthusiasm and an incorrigible wildness of behaviour, some into a cold frame of mind showing great indifference to things of religion."

But the good Jonathan ultimately became reconciled, writing, in 1751, concerning "true converts" that "the proportion may perhaps be more truly represented by the proportion of the blossoms on a tree which abide and come to mature fruit to the whole number of blossoms in the spring."

His Northampton parishioners were not so complacent. For four and twenty years they had let him call them "vipers, vile insects and firebrands of hell" and had let him dangle them over the roaring flames of the bottomless pit. They endured through the rise and wane of two revivals and still the herald of holiness kept on sermonizing to save. Then the long-suffering congregation declared it had had enough.

The church vote on "whether they still insisted upon

Mr. Edwards's dismission from the pastoral office over them" was two hundred to twenty. The overt cause was his conscience-bidden refusal to admit the "unconverted" to the communion table. But there was more to this quarrel that culminated in so overwhelming a verdict.

The record is neither complete nor clear. It was said that "excitement was caused in families by fear of exposure." Whether this "exposure" was directly threatened from the pupilt or was coming from the public confessions of converts laying their burdens upon the altar, was not told. At any rate, it seems that so long as Edwards was content to deal with sin in general terms no one took offense, but when he undertook to apply his epithets where they were individually felt, this was taken for "incivility," to say the least.

It was also said that "evil ways had crept in to an alarming extent among the young people who listened to his preaching." Just what these "evil ways" were, was not specified, any more than were the sins of that young woman whose conversion was of the first fruits of the 1735 revival.

The virtue and sincerity, the power and eloquence of the preacher were unquestioned. But the results of his ministry cost him his pastorate—the falling away of the majority of the converts in the wake of the revivals, the nervous disorders, insanity and suicides. Then came erosion of the morals of youth in the midst of the theological thunders and the turning of the hearts of the people against the apostle of condemnation.

It was finished. The Prophet of Northampton whose burning words had set the New World afire now could complete the response of the Watchman in Isaiah—"The morning cometh—*and also the night!*"

And so, deprived of his pulpit, rejected by his own people, Jonathan Edwards went out to those who in his eyes were in darkness. Behold him a missionary to the Indians at Stockbridge. There is something at once pathetic and comic in his going up against the tradition of this wild offspring of Adam. It was an offering of the Puritan Heaven for a few and the Edwardean Hell for the many in place of the Happy Hunting Ground.

How much Edwards dwelt upon the future state of his aboriginal parish is not exactly known. But one by one the braves and their families vanished into the forest and at the end of two years the preacher discovered that they had all gone and once more he was relieved of his charge, this time without a vote of record.

Though he had made no headway in the conversion of the Indians, he had exemplified to them what justice meant on earth by freeing them from exploitation and oppression. And during his sojourn at Stockbridge he had found time to write a treatise on "Freedom of the Will," in which he said that "the term 'Calvinistic' is, in these days, among most, a term of greater reproach than the term 'Arminianism,'" and another treatise on "Original Sin" that remarked the "strange progress within a few years" of hostility to this doctrine.

Jonathan Edwards had ceased to be the crusading pulpiteer and had settled down to be a true philosopher of religion. His reward for this came too late. At the close of the year 1757, he was called to the presidency of the college at Princeton, the earthly seat of Presbyterianism in America. Three months later, on March 22, 1758, at the age of fifty-five, he died of an inoculation for smallpox.

In his latter days, Edwards arrived at a clearer understanding of the work he began amid the overwhelming

tumult of clashing doctrines. Had he lived to see Arminianism lost as a theological boundary line and to feel the
stirring of the new consciousness of human rights that
inspired the prayer of those who knelt round Elder Clark
on Lexington Green on that April morning of 1775, he
would have preached the truer Calvinism—that the birth
anew through grace consecrated life to God through service to brother men.

The evangelistic message of Jonathan Edwards still lives
and church edifices have deen dedicated in his name. He
preached it without thought of material reward or personal glory. His own earnest belief in it, his own concern
for those who heard it, impelled him.

Long since, his God of wrath has become a God of love
and the fires of his hell have receded. But down through
the years, now faint, now strong, yet never ceasing, has
come the voice of him who awakened America to its first
great revival and, in the words of the prophet of old—
"Repent ye, for the Kingdom of Heaven is at hand"—
opened the way for all the sons of men to discover and
declare the faith that is in them.

# CHAPTER IV

## PENTECOSTAL CONSECRATION

Come, Holy Spirit, Heav'nly Dove,
With all Thy quick'ning pow'rs;
Come shed abroad a Savior's love,
And that shall kindle ours.
ISAAC WATTS, 1674–1748.

WHILE Jonathan Edwards was crying in the wilderness preparing the way of the Lord and making His paths straight, the Day of Pentecost was fully come in the ancient capital of the mother kingdom, even in Fetter Lane in London Town, where the Holy Ghost descended upon the "chosen few" who were to bear the Word over sea and land and bring their brother men out of their darkness and into the light of the Great Awakening of 1740.

It was there in the Moravian Chapel, built in 1738 and afterwards attacked and dismantled by rival religionists, that the gift of at least one fiery tongue was bestowed upon John Wesley and George Whitefield as they knelt on that memorable day of 1739. And it is from this solemn hour that posterity must date the beginning of their message to a "lost and ruined world."

Strange was the neighborhood for a pervasion of the Presence. It was not a lane of fetters chaining felons or martyrs. Chaucer in his day called it "Faitours Lane," and to him a faitour was a "lazy, idle fellow." Others extended the meaning to include "pretenders, impostors,

32

~ GEORGE WHITEFIELD ~

vagabonds and fortune tellers." Still another early usage
was "Fewtars Lane," a fewtar being a "loafer and a nui-
sance."

Running out from Fleet Street to Holborn, paralleled
by Chancery Lane and nigh unto Mitre Court, Bolt Court
and Wine Office Court, Fetter Lane once was fringed by
cottages and gardens. Here dwelt Praisegod Barebones and
his brother Damnéd Barebones, in a house later occupied
by the Royal Society under the presidency of Sir Isaac
Newton.

Over in Chancery Lane, home of the Inns of Court and
the Temple dedicated to the majesty of the secular law,
Izaak Walton sold hosiery, when he was not cogitating the
art of angling, and Drayton began his profane sonneteer-
ing. Boswell trailed Dr. Johnson in Mitre Court and Bolt
Court and Goldsmith joined them at the Cheshire Cheese,
the hostelry of Wine Office Court. Among the printers
and publishers of Fleet Street, that thoroughfare of immortal tavern sign-boards, was William Hone, the free
thinker, who dared issue his "Everyday Book" from No.
56.

Such were the environs of Fetter Lane, first the covert
of vagabonds, then the dwelling place of Roundhead zealot
and Cavalier poet, then the haunt of scientist, philosopher, lexicographer, scribbler and reveller. Here it was that
the Heavens opened and the Holy Ghost came down.

It was the first recorded Methodist "watch-night" meet-
ing. Gathered there in the House of the Lord in Fetter
Lane as zero hour neared for the year of 1739 were the
Wesley brothers, John and Charles, George Whitefield,
and Benjamin Ingham, all charter members of the Oxford
Holy Club, of which more shall be told presently. Messrs.
Hall, Kinchin and Hutchins are also mentioned as being

among the leaders of the sixty brethren at the love feast.

"About three in the morning, as we were continuing instant in prayer," John Wesley writes, "the power of God came mightily upon us, insomuch, that many cried out for exceeding joy, and many fell to the ground. As soon as we had recovered a little from that awe and amazement at the presence of His Majesty, we broke out with one voice: 'We praise Thee, O God; we acknowledge Thee to be the Lord!'"

This occurred about eight months before Whitefield sailed for his conquest of sin in America and only eight weeks after his return from his first voyage thence on a spiritual reconnaissance when he had discovered the two guiding stars of his life ever after.

One was the necessity of his preaching the English world, particularly its colonial domains, into regeneration, and the other was the need of the "Orphan House" in Georgia which supplied him with a permanent appeal for funds.

To accomplish both of these aims he had to abandon the time-honored tradition of holding a settled pastorate and wander far and wide, sometimes bringing down on his head objurgation for "invading" the pulpits of others and sometimes, barred from churches, forced to preach the Word in the open fields. Thus he became the first of the long line of itinerant evangelists who have followed him to this day.

II

Whitefield began his work-a-day life as a bartender at the age of fifteen in the Bell Inn, in the city of Gloucester, where he was born on December 16, 1714, the youngest of a family of seven comprising six sons and one daughter.

His great grandfather, a rector in Wiltshire, had two sons, Samuel, who succeeded to the pastorate, and Andrew, who lived upon an estate as a private gentleman. The eldest of Andrew's fourteen progeny was Thomas, the father of George. After being "bred to the employment" of a Bristol wine merchant, Thomas married Mrs. Elizabeth Edwards and was proprietor of the inn at Gloucester till his death when George was only two years old.

Six years later the widow again tried marriage and the worst said of it was that it was "unhappy" for her and an "affliction" to her family. Their circumstances so far declined that when George was fifteen he had to leave school and assist his mother in the public house. In his words, he "put on a blue apron, washed mops, cleaned rooms and became a professed and common drawer."

This was not all that might have befallen him. For while making progress in the Latin classics at the public school of St. Mary de Crypt he had discovered and developed his innate powers of eloquence and had taken a strong liking to play-acting. An early active conscience saved him from the theater, however, and brought him to remorse and penitence for hating instruction and for stealing from his mother's pocketbook.

His menial toil at the inn lasted about a year. In between setting up drinks and making beds he carried to fruition his boyhood searchings of the soul and ventured within the boundary of his life's calling by composing three sermons. They went unpreached but somehow they provoked Providence. Soon after an elder brother took over the inn, friends opened to George Whitefield a servitor's place at Pembroke College, Oxford.

In the year 1734 when Whitefield at the age of eighteen entered Oxford, he found the seat of learning also a place of moral danger still sunk in the lethargy consequent upon the ejection of the two thousand non-conformists from the Church and seeming "to care less for conformity than for character." Shocked by the impiety of fellow-students and beset by "temptations," he drew himself apart from worldly men.

Soon he found that he need not be alone in his diligence for the pursuit of righteousness. He discovered and joined himself unto that nucleus of young men that was to give Methodism to the world. These fifteen formed themselves into a "society for mutual improvement and edification" with religion the chief concern. John Wesley, then a Fellow of Lincoln College, Charles Wesley, his brother, and William Morgan, of Christ Church, Benjamin Ingham, of Queens, Robert Kirkham of Merton were the original sponsors. Whitefield was won to them by his intercession with Charles Wesley for a pauper who attempted suicide.

They drew up rules to guide themselves in self-examination, prayer and meditation to make themselves acceptable to God; they pored over the Scriptures word by word in the original Greek; they received the Lord's supper every week, kept all the fasts of the ancient Church and sought holiness through rigorous self-denial. Other Oxonians derided them as "Bible-bigots," "Bible-moths" and "Sacramentarians." They were known also as the "Holy Club" and the "Godly Club," but one of their irreverent critics, remarking their living by rule, gently called them "Methodists."

### III

#### CONVERSION

Conversion was the requisite for full participation in this sacred union and each member, alone with his God, had to initiate himself. Whitefield's initiation almost cost him his life, but in it he came upon his inspiration for bringing his thousands to the Throne of Grace.

For forty days he fasted and deprived himself of all comforts till, "overwhelmed with horrible dread," all power of meditation, or even thinking, was taken away, his whole soul was barren and dry and his sensations were like those of a man "locked up in iron armor."

"Whenever I knelt down," he says, "I felt great pressure both on body and soul and often prayed under the weight of them till the sweat came through me. Whole days and weeks I spent lying prostrate on the ground in silent or vocal prayer."

He chose the worst food, coarse bread and sage tea, when he ate any at all, he put on a patched gown, dirty shoes and woollen gloves and ceased powdering his hair to humble his spirit. Shivering with cold, he would kneel under the trees of Christ Church Walk in silent devotion till the Great Bell called him in for the night. He would expose himself to winter rigors till his hands turned black.

At the end of this Lent he was too weak to stand and had to take to his bed where he lay ill for seven weeks under the care of a physician. In the seventh week the Light came for which he declares he has reason "to bless God through the endless ages of eternity."

In the final hour of his agony, when nothing availed to allay "an uncommon drought and noisome clamminess" in his mouth, it came to Whitefield that Christ himself had cried out "I thirst!" when His sufferings were nearly over. Thereupon Whitefield, who admitted that his self-inflicted flagellations were to imitate the Messiah and to escape the snares of Satan, gave way to utterance of these very words: "I thirst! I thirst!"

At once the "weight of sin" was lifted, the "Spirit of mourning" was taken away, and his soul was filled with the "pardoning love of God." Hour on end afterward he could not cease from singing psalms. Gradually his joy became "more settled" but it "abode and increased" throughout the rest of his life.

While convalescing at Gloucester from the effects of his spiritual struggle, Whitefield read and prayed over the Scriptures, line by line, word by word, laying the doctrinal foundations of his whole preaching thesis. First there was "free grace"; second, the necessity for being "justified only by faith in the sight of God"; third, the "new birth" through conversion, and fourth, the exclusive saving of the "elect," the point which later divided him from John Wesley.

## IV

Thus fortified, George Whitefield began. He prayed with the poor in the byways, he prayed with the prisoners in jail and he prayed alone. Word of his faith and works came to Bishop Benson of Gloucester who offered to ordain him a deacon though at the age of twenty-one he was two years under the usual requirement.

It was on June 20, 1736, a year after Jonathan Edwards had started stoking to steam up religion in New England, that the Bishop laid his hands upon the new disciple who was to travel farther in the name of his Lord than any other throughout all time.

"I gave myself up to be a martyr for Him who hung upon the Cross for me," Whitefield said of his ordination. "When I went up to the altar, I could think of nothing but Samuel's standing, as a little child, before the Lord, with a linen ephod."

The very next Sunday he preached his first sermon in the Church of St. Mary de Crypt at Gloucester where he had been baptized. It was on "The Necessity and Benefits of a Religious Society," reciting the blessings of mutual exhortation as against "revellings and banquetings," all in severely logical firstly to thirdly style. Whitefield says "some mocked yet most seemed struck and fifteen were driven mad." A perusal of his manuscript, however, discloses neither cause for ridicule nor provocation to insanity. It was quite regular and many a substantial churchman could sleep through it in any age.

After receiving his bachelor's degree at Oxford, Whitefield preached in various charges from the Tower chapel in London to a rural parish in Hampshire, with a progressive growth in the number and fervor of his auditory till the name of the young divine of twenty-two had so spread that when he determined to go to Georgia on an errand of the Lord in 1737 weeping multitudes accorded him a triumphant farewell, the first of seven that marked each of his embarkations for the New World.

It seems that the Wesleys had invited him to Georgia. Charles wrote an impassioned poem to him beginning: "Servant of God, thy summons hear!" and John asked: "What if thou art the man to come over and help us?" John had been having his troubles with magistrates after barring from the communion table the former Sophia Christina Hopkey, whose troth with him had been broken and who now was the wife of another man.

The call across the sea thrilled religious England as much as it did Whitefield himself. From Gloucester to

Bristol the people thronged the churches and followed him through the streets. The "enthusiasm" pained the staid regular clergy, who branded Whitefield a "spiritual pick-pocket" and closed their doors to him. But his star kept on rising and was riding high when he preached his vale-dictory, solemnly adjuring the sobbing penitents that they "might see him no more." He never forgot this postscript upon subsequent departures for America and it was always effective.

While Whitefield's ship lay off the Downs awaiting a favorable wind, John Wesley's vessel came in from America. The departure of Whitefield weighed on Wes-ley's soul. He prayed and sought Scriptural guidance and finally resorted to the casting of a lot under divine bless-ing—a measure by which he made many of his momentous life decisions—and the drawing was against Whitefield's setting forth. Wesley sent word. Then it was Whitefield's turn at supplication. He sensed an answer to his prayer and determined to sail on.

It was not till the end of January, 1738, that the evangel craft cleared and then she had to call at Gibraltar with troops, Whitefield's shipboard "redcoat parish." Those troopers ceased from swearing, listened to preaching and even allowed themselves to be catechized. On the open At-lantic the skipper was converted and all "bad books and playing cards were cast into the sea." A contagious malig-nant fever scourged many into serious reflection and Whitefield, though himself stricken, crept over the decks administering medicine and saving both souls and bodies.

Whitefield landed at Savannah on May 5, taking leave of the ship's company in a flood of tears. He received re-spectful treatment from the magistrates who had been at odds with Wesley and promptly plunged into his work.

It was a torrid summer. The sun-baked earth burned his feet and in the comparative cool of the nights he inured himself to future hardships by learning to sleep on the ground. The while he was preaching about the colony and exhorting from door to door, he developed his plan for the Orphan House that was first conceived by Governor Oglethorpe and Charles Wesley. He made it his own project and it proved to be his talking point to the end of his days. The redeemed were provided with a conscience fund and surely the breadwinner of the fatherless was worthy of his own pittance wherewithal to be sheltered, clothed and fed on his holy mission.

Anxious to complete his own preparations, Whitefield sailed back to England on September 6 and, on January 14, 1739, he was ordained a priest of the Established Church. The Georgia Trustees offered him the "living" at Savannah. He refused it but accepted a grant of five hundred acres for his beloved Orphan House. His eyes were fixed on America. He had no patience with settling down in a comfortable pastorate. He had the primal apostolic call. That is what took him to Fetter Lane and thence to preach in the fields.

Those Fetter Lane meetings with the Wesleys and the others were to Whitefield what "third heavens" were to Paul, one commentator says, and became the "school of his spirit in which he caught the holy and heroic impulse to challenge the Scribes and Pharisees." Church doors swung shut in his face. Bishops turned cold to his "enthusiasm." And then Whitefield forsook the righteous and went out among sinners.

"I thought it might be doing the service of my Creator," said Whitefield, "Who had a mountain for his pulpit and the heavens for a sounding board and Who, when His gospel was refused by the Jews, sent His servants into the highways and hedges."

So he went out from Bristol into barbaric Kingswood, the habitat of savage miners, brutalized by unmitigated toil, despised outcasts who had never known the amenities of church-going and who had stones and staves as well as jeers and gibes for the first preacher to dare to come among them. Barred from the sanctuary, he raised a cross upon a hillside in the midst of a glowering mob. Thus of him it was written:

> Whitefield preached to colliers grim—
> Bishops in lawn sleeves preached at *him*.
> —AUSTIN DOBSON,
> "The Ballad of Beau Brocade."

From a scant ten score of surly ruffians the Kingswood congregation grew to twenty thousand singing souls. The swelling chorus of their hymns could be heard for two miles and the voice bearing the tidings to them is said to have carried almost half as far.

"Having no righteousness of their own to renounce," Whitefield wrote of them, "they were glad to hear of a Jesus Who came not to call the righteous but sinners to repentance."

He told of the "white gutters made by their tears which fell plentifully down their black cheeks as they came out of their coal pits" and rejoiced that "hundreds and hundreds were brought to full conversion."

John Wesley, with the power that was to inspire the Methodist militants to go out to "make the world his parish," took up the battle of the Lord on the Bristol front while Whitefield swept on to greater and yet greater triumphs at Moorfields, Kennington Common and Blackheath on the fringe of London whose multitudes poured out to hear him.

The preparation was completed. Given to view the promised land on his first voyage to America, consecrated and reconsecrated at Fetter Lane, tried by fire at Kingswood, brought to the fulness of spiritual puissance under the firmament in the shadow of London, this "Luther of the Great Awakening" was ready for his life. Across the Atlantic this time he would go knowing what to do and how to do it.

With upwards of one thousand pounds amassed for his Orphan House, Whitefield and his friend, William Seward, with a company of eight men, a youth and two children, set sail on August 14, 1739. But he did not land in Georgia to take up the task of an almoner. Instead the ship bore him to Philadelphia where the miracle of Moorfields was to be multiplied a hundredfold. Another Boanerges went ashore to claim the New World for his God.

## CHAPTER V

## THE GREAT AWAKENING

There is a fountain filled with blood
Drawn from Immanuel's veins,
And sinners plunged beneath that flood
Lose all their guilty stains.
WILLIAM COWPER, 1731–1800

AMERICA'S evangelist had come. Philadelphia was the threshhold and the gates were flung open wide. No meeting house could contain the people or circumscribe the spirit that responded to the man and the message he was to spread from the craggy coast of Maine to the sandy shores of Carolina for thirty years till death should ride with him the last march on the Gospel trail.

Night after night, while the chill winds of November blew over them, the thousands massed in Market Street where the Court House steps became the pulpit of George Whitefield. His voice could be heard on the distant Jersey shore. His every word could be clearly understood aboard craft at the river wharves. And under the spell of his eloquence penitents knelt in windrows upon the cobble stones crying out what they should do to be saved.

The impress upon Philadelphia made by Whitefield on this and subsequent visits was both deep and lasting. All denominations were quickened. Mrs. Hannah Hodges, in her memoirs published at Philadelphia in 1806, tells of public worship continuing twice daily and thrice and more

44

~ CHARLES WESLEY ~

on the Sabbath for a year afterward. The effect of White-field's eloquence upon Benjamin Franklin, the calm ration-alist philosopher, is a striking indication of what must have been borne in upon the minds of others. It seems that interspersed with rebirth through saving grace Whitefield from the very outset put his Orphan House to the fore.

"I did not approve of the design," said Franklin, "but as Georgia was then destitute of materials and workmen and it was proposed to send them from Philadelphia at a great expense, I thought it would have been better to have built the house at Philadelphia and brought the children to it. This I advised, but he was resolute in his first proj-ect, rejected my counsel and I, therefore, refused to con-tribute.

"I happened, soon after, to attend one of his sermons in the course of which I perceived he intended to finish with a collection, and I silently resolved he should get nothing from me. I had in my pocket a handful of copper money, three or four silver dollars and five pistoles in gold. As he proceeded, I began to soften and concluded to give the copper; another stroke of his oratory made me ashamed of that and determined me to give the silver, and he fin-ished so admirably that I emptied my pocket into the col-lector's dish, gold and all."

At this same sermon Franklin tells of a member of his club who, aware of possible susceptibility, had taken the precaution to attend with empty pockets. Overwhelmed at the climax, he applied to a neighbor, a placid Quaker, evi-dently the only one present not caught with the tide, to lend him some money for a gift.

"At any other time, friend Hopkins, I would lend to thee freely," was the reply, "but not now, for thee seems to me to be out of thy right senses."

Whitefield, inwardly strengthened by this initial success, pushed on to New York. On the way he preached at Neshaminy, the site of the Log College of the Tennents that afterwards became Princeton University, New Brunswick and other New Jersey towns. He joined himself in spirit with William and Gilbert Tennent and their patriarchal father and Samuel Blair who were to be his collaborators and "waterers of the seed he planted in the wilderness."

At New York, his own church was closed to him by the Commissary and it is recorded that he was disappointed with the results attained in the Rev. Mr. Pemberton's Presbyterian church in Wall Street. It was not until Whitefield's return in the fall of 1740 that New York really "awoke" at his bidding. Back through Philadelphia, with scores following him out of that city, Whitefield went southward to erect his Orphan House in Georgia.

Across Maryland and Virginia he preached to immense congregations. At Charleston, South Carolina, began the hostility of Commissary Garden which only grew more bitter in later years but the Independent Church was opened to Whitefield and great numbers of people wept under the conviction laid upon them. They even drew the preacher back from his boat when he was departing and had another sermon on the shore.

The Rev. Josiah Smith, pastor of the Independent Church, at this time wrote a stirring defense of Whitefield that stands out against the criticism that followed, especially in New England.

"How awfully did he discharge the artillery of heaven upon us!" read the account, "pointing the arrows of the Almighty at the hearts of sinners while he poured the

balm upon the wounds of the contrite. So Saint Paul
would look and speak in a pulpit!"

In another visit to Charleston Whitefield put the Last
Judgment in nautical terms for an audience of seafaring
men. His pulpit became the deck of a ship overwhelmed
by a tempest.

"Our masts are gone!" he shouted amid the storm he
had stirred up. "The ship is on her beam-ends! What next?
What next?"

"The long-boat!" the mariners spontaneously replied.
"Take to the long-boat!"

This maritime note in evangelism had an echo in the
succeeding century when singing thousands joined Ira
Sankey in throwing out his lifeline. Again it came in the
moving hymn of P. P. Bliss—"Let the Lower Lights Be
Burning, Send a Gleam Across the Wave!" And yet again
in Charles H. Gabriel's "Sail On! Sail On!"

From Charleston, Whitefield went by boat to Savannah
where, on March 25, 1740, he laid the first brick of the
Orphan House, naming it Bethesda, or "House of Mercy."
Already forty children were being cared for by Mr. Haber-
sham in a hired house, and sixty workmen also had to be
fed. Whitefield turned to the North for needed funds,
preaching twice and three times a day as he travelled for
the next two months.

Renewing the revival in Philadelphia, he saw a church
formed of his converts from the open fields with Gilbert
Tennent as pastor. Exhausted by the heat upon his journeys he had to be lifted thrice a day into the saddle, but
he gloried in it, telling of the singing as his party rode
through the woods and of the fires by night to keep away
wild beasts. On June 5, he got back to Savannah with

two thousand five hundred dollars and more orphans and a great reunion service was "dissolved in tears."

Till the end of August he braved the oppressive weather preaching constantly to great crowds about Georgia and in Charleston. Then two eminent Boston divines, Messrs. Colman and Cooper, pressed him to redeem the lost sheep of the Puritan pasture. Whitefield's sloop landed him at Newport, Rhode Island, on September 14.

It was the Sabbath. Balky winds so delayed the ship that when Whitefield got ashore morning services were already in progress. He slipped quietly into a pew and worshipped humbly with the rest. But at the close a Mr. Bowers came to him and, calling him by name, invited him home. There the first citizens of the town eagerly waited upon him. They convinced him that New England was "ripe unto a harvest of souls."

Forthwith, Whitefield faced the Episcopal pastor and argued down the godly man's fear that the itinerant's preaching would be "disorderly," invoking the apostolic injunction in defense of heralding the new birth in Rhode Island. Whitefield won entry into the pulpit and exhorted till Wednesday, the Legislature adjourning to hear him and the Court rising for the same purpose when he passed through Bristol on his way northward.

In one of these sermons he sternly upbraided the pious smugglers among the leading churchmen, saying: "What will become of you who cheat the King of his taxes?" It is set down that this made them look at one another in consciousness of guilt. It was a direct linking of mundane sovereignty with the Throne on High, the very source of the divine autocracy preached by Edwards, then Whitefield and then the satellites of Whitefield. But they who went down to the sea in ships from Newport were to do even worse by the King before Whitefield had lain five years in his tomb.

At eight o'clock on the morning of Thursday, September 18, 1740, Boston welcomed the evangelist. Four miles from town the son of Governor Jonathan Belcher and a party of clergymen met Whitefield on the road and escorted him into the capital of the colony. But for a large funeral that compelled the attention of the foremost citizens an impressive delegation would have marched in with him. Funerals, however, especially those drawing wide public recognition, were always helpful to evangelizing. Edwards used several to peculiar advantage.

Whitefield was ill upon arrival. It was a recurrence of the affliction that constantly haunted him. His heart was low, his body was weak. The next day the trouble passed; in waking he "perceived fresh emanations of divine light break in upon his soul." The refusal of the Episcopal pulpit did not deter him. He began at once preaching daily in the other meeting houses of the town, including Benjamin Colman's in Brattle Street, Joseph Sewall's Old South, Joshua Gee's Old North and "the Old Brick" of Thomas Foxcroft and Dr. Charles Chauncey in Cornhill Square near the Old State House.

Whitefield says he preached to about six thousand at the Old South. If he did, the miracle of the loaves and fishes was overshadowed. The closest packing of pews and aisles would admit no more than two thousand five hundred to three thousand. This brings into question Whitefield's lifetime habit of giving estimates of the numbers that received his message.

The Rev. Thomas Prince reckoned that about three thousand attended Whitefield's first service in Boston, at the Brattle Street Church, and that seems reasonable.

Whitefield himself thought that about thirty thousand heard his farewell sermon on Boston Common, but the newspapers of the day put the crowd at two thousand three hundred. Whitefield tells of seven thousand listening to him under the elms of Harvard Yard when he took it out on the students of Harvard College for reading "bad books," on theology and on the tutors for not praying with their charges. These corrupted intellectuals, "the sons of the prophets in all New England," as Whitefield called them, must have had reinforcements from across the Charles River and, even so, the ancient quadrangle has never since endured the tread of so many feet at one time.

Still, as one contemporary writer says, one can be charitable and accept the enthusiastic preacher's computations with "abatement." Two things are certain: more than a hundred were added to the rolls of the Old South Church alone under the quickening of the revival and the meeting house of the Rev. Samuel Checkley in Summer Street got so overcrowded that panic ensued with leaping from the galleries and windows and trampling that killed five persons and injured many others.

There were crowds and there were results and probably the greatest manifestations were under the open sky on Boston Common. There, as in Philadelphia's Market Street and London's Moorfields, the evangelist and the evangelized seemed to be drawn closer to one another and, together, to the Power beyond the stars yet down among men.

Look out upon the people so close-packed that one could step from head to head. See the twinkling of myriad lanterns. Feel the kindred spirit that makes all listen as if for eternity. Hear the words that awake a century and call it back to timeless things. The hour is late, but the preacher is saying: "I would speak till midnight, yea, I would speak till I could speak no more, so might it be a means of bringing you to Jesus."

With the commanding tones of a bell in clearness and all the modulations of an organ in variety and sweetness, the voice of this "Orpheus of the Pulpit" rings with the final vibrant appeal:

"Come, all of you, come and behold Him stretched out for you; see His hands and feet nailed to the Cross; oh, come, come, my brethren, and nail your sins there too; come, come and see His side pierced. There is a fountain open for sin and for uncleanness; oh, wash, wash and be clean!

"Come and see His head crowned with thorns, and all for you. Can you think of a panting, bleeding, dying Jesus and not be filled with pity towards Him? He underwent all this for you.

"Come unto Him by faith; lay hold on Him; there is mercy for every soul of you that will come unto Him. Then do not delay; fly into the arms of this Jesus and you shall be made clean in His blood."

"I may never see your faces again," says the preacher, pausing on every word. "But at the Day of Judgment I will meet you. There you will bless God that ever you were moved to repentance or else this sermon, though in a field, will be as a swift witness against you.—Repent!— Repent!"

A strange sound is borne upon the still night air. It is the low mourning of thousands. A multitude is melted. Here a cry, there a cry and countless voices raised in prayer. "The Spirit of the Lord was upon them all," Whitefield said again and again of those scenes on Boston Common. It was upon him too. Drenched through, spent, exhausted, deathlike, he would sink down sobbing in the arms of friends. "That place was a Bethel," he declared, "and the Gate of Heaven."

Day by day the power of the revival increased. Governor Belcher came weeping to Whitefield's chamber and begged prayer for himself and his people. One preacher rejoiced to hear Whitefield call man "half a devil, half a beast." Crowded auditories taxed the capacity of the churches in Boston and in the towns along the preaching journey that Whitefield took through Marblehead, where one man was "struck down by the Word," Ipswich, Newburyport and Portsmouth to York.

Every service in every place yielded not pence but pounds for the Orphan House, which Whitefield never forgot the while he was pleading for repentance. His journal faithfully keeps an account of every contribution. One service on Boston Common brought in two hundred pounds (about one thousand dollars) from fifteen thousand purses. On Tuesday, October 7, he got an ovation at Brattle Street Church upon appearing alive to refute a rumor that he had suddenly died of poison. The next day, a little child having died after lisping that it was going to see "Mr. Whitefield's God," the preacher pleaded that babes should lead their parents to Christ and collected four hundred forty pounds at the New North Church.

On Thursday Whitefield made his first attack upon the clergy of New England, opening up a controversy that was to make trouble for him the rest of his days and set a precedent for itinerant evangelists in all the years to come. Preaching at the Old South on Christ's colloquy with Nicodemus, he denounced an "unconverted ministry." He laid down the dictum that all who ascended the pulpit should have experienced the conversion for which he set the standard.

"The generality of preachers talk of an unknown and unfelt Christ," he said. "The reason why congregations have been so dead is that they have had dead men preaching to them. The Lord will choose vessels made meet by operations of the Holy Spirit for His sacred use. I would not lay hands [in ordination] on an unconverted man for ten thousand worlds."

It was in this mood, as he himself afterward admitted, of being "puffed up" by his great success in New England that he wrote the famous sharp rebuke to John Wesley for "Arminianism" which was the entering wedge in the life-long breach between them. At the top of the wave of triumphant Calvinism, Whitefield had no patience with the Wesleyan widening of the approach to a heaven dedicated by dogma to the elect.

Whitefield left Boston with this same critical attitude. Praising the Lord for the "glorious work begun," he laid strictures upon the inhabitants for being "too much conformed to the world" and for having too much "pride of life."

He denounced the "mixed dancings and frolickings" prevalent in New England and the "jewels, patches and gay apparel commonly worn by the female sex." He also expressed fear of the Bostonian tradition, that many should "rest in head knowledge." Nevertheless, he concluded that the people of Boston were "dear to my soul, greatly affected by the Word, very liberal to my dear orphans, and I promised to visit them again."

The parting was at the high tide of the Great Awakening. It was a tide of tears. Whitefield so wept with the

throng which followed him to his lodgings from the farewell service on the Common that he had to break off in
the midst of his last prayer. Governor Belcher, constantly
giving way to his emotions, went with Whitefield as far as
Worcester, spurring him to stir up the clergy and spare
none. Whitefield preached to thousands all along the over-
land route to Northampton, confessing that the Governor
had heartened him to it.

Then the prophets met and wept together before the
Lord. They also argued. Edwards warned Whitefield
against "impulses." The forerunner spoke from bitter experience, but this Elisha would have none of it. He wore
his own mantle and was conscious of its folds. And
yet Whitefield preached mightily from the pulpit of
Northampton and, dwelling in the home of Edwards,
hailed his host as a "son of Abraham" and the good woman
by his side as a "daughter of Abraham." With the old fire
relighted on the altar of Northampton, the sacristan of
salvation went on to New Haven and New York.

Mingled with his proclaiming the necessity of the new
birth at Springfield, Suffield, Windsor and New Haven,
Whitefield pressed his insistence upon ministers going
through this transformation before they could preach
Christ aright. Many parsons heard and great offense was
given. The students of Yale College were told of the
"dreadful ill consequences of an unconverted ministry"
and they responded with forty pounds for the Orphan
House. Another weeping Governor was grateful for re-
freshings in the way, but President Clapp of Yale saved
something against a later day when he took Whitefield to
task for those self-same "impulses" which had brought the
caution from Edwards.

It was one of these "impulses" that led him across the

boundary into New York, causing him to declare that the Lord had filled his heart to "wrestle" with the Almighty for the inhabitants of another Nineveh. This time in Pemberton's meeting house the Spirit of the Lord "came down like a mighty rushing wind and carried all before it."

This was in the first week of November, 1740. Though New England had borne the brunt of the Great Awakening, it had remained for New York to exalt the evangelist to the zenith of his conscious power. Wall Street for the moment become the Fetter Lane of the New World.

"Shrieking, crying, weeping and wailing were to be heard in every corner," Whitefield said, "men's hearts failing them for fear and many falling into the arms of their friends. My soul was carried out till I could scarce speak any more."

"Fast flowing divine manifestations" shook the "frail tabernacle" of his body and followed him to his couch. He prayed alternately with friends sitting round the bedside with strong cries and "pierced by the eye of faith even within the veil."

The "Spirit" went with him out from New York southward, the emotional force within him gaining momentum from his contact with Jonathan Barber and James Davenport, the Long Island itinerants who were to carry the revival to then unexpected excesses. Whitefield was already pointing the way, however, when at Baskingridge he let a weeping boy of eight years preach in his stead as one inspired by the Holy Ghost.

"God displayed His sovereignty and out of an infant's mouth came perfecting praise," said Whitefield. "Fresh persons dropped down and the cry increased for more and more."

Across New Jersey, now witnessing the presence of Christ in a crowded barn, now exhorting from a scaffold outside a jail, now in the as yet roofless new church of the Tennents, always to "thousands on thousands melting under the power," Whitefield pushed on to Reedy's Island whence he sailed December 1 for Savannah and Charleston to take ship for England.

In the seventy-five days between his landing in Rhode Island and his arrival at Reedy's Island, he had preached one hundred and seventy-five times in public, not to count private occasions, on a journey of eight hundred miles. And seven hundred pounds accrued in money and goods for the unforgettable orphans.

"Never did God vouchsafe me such assistance," said the evangelist. "Never did I see such a continuance of the Divine Presence in the congregations to whom I preached. All things concur to convince me that America is to be my chief scene of action."

Whitefield was right in his prediction. Though London built him a tabernacle and the power of his eloquence was felt throughout the British Isles, swaying such men as David Garrick, the brilliant actor of Drury Lane, Viscount Bolingbroke, the adviser of Kings, the Earl of Chesterfield, immortalized as a man of fashion, and David Hume, the Scottish philosopher, yet it was in America that his life found its greatest usefulness in perpetuating and extending the effects of the Great Awakening even unto death in the service of his God.

In the Fall of 1741, upon his return to England, Whitefield, by deliberate resolution, married Mrs. Elizabeth Burwell James, a widow about ten years his senior. He said of her: "She has been a housekeeper for many years, once gay, but for three years past a despised follower of the

Lamb of God." However true that may have been, she certainly was neglected, remaining almost out of mention till her death from a fever in August, 1768. She accompanied her husband on at least one of his voyages to America, for a writer in the Boston Evening Post in November, 1744, upbraided the evangelist with his wife's non-attendance at a certain revival meeting. It was afterwards proved that she was present.

Whitefield records delivering his wife's funeral sermon and then turns to his own concerns in the same item, telling of bursting a vein by overexertion amid "glorious gospel gales." Of their only child, a son who died in infancy in February, 1744, he voices disappointment that another Whitefield could not have been raised to be a preacher!

In October, 1744, Whitefield, on his third voyage to America, landed at York, Maine, and proceeded to Portsmouth, New Hampshire. Gravely ill, he was believed nigh to death. Suddenly he cried out to his doctor: "My pains are suspended. By the help of God I will go and preach and then come home and die." The people listened to him as if to a dying man. He spoke "expecting to be launched into eternity before morning and with the invisible realities of another world open to view" and achieved an effect that was "worth dying for a thousand times."

Gradually he recovered, but on all his preaching journeys he was subject constantly to such sinkings, with retching, perspiring, and even hemorrhages. It was at Portsmouth that another dramatic episode occurred. A chimney fire seen through the church windows caused the alarm to be spread that the Last Judgment had indeed come. In a torrent of eloquence Whitefield drew the parallel while a bucket brigade doused the blaze.

By his exhortations in the Spring of 1745, Whitefield helped Colonel Pepperell recruit the successful expedition against Louisburg. Then he preached his way southward after declining the offer of a great permanent tabernacle in New England. Brief excerpts from his letters reveal his work and strength of purpose:

"Aug. 26, 1746 . . . The door for my usefulness opens wider and wider. I love to range in the American woods and sometimes think I shall never return to England any more."

"June 4, 1747 . . . I have omitted preaching one night to oblige my friends that they may not charge me with murdering myself, but I hope yet to die in the pulpit or soon after I come out of it."

"June 23 . . . Since my last I have been several times on the verge of eternity. At present I am so weak that I cannot preach. It is hard work to be silent, but I must be tried in every way."

"Sept. 11 . . . We saw great things in New England. The flocking and power that attended the Word was like unto that seven years ago. Weak as I was and have been, I was enabled to travel ELEVEN HUNDRED MILES and preach daily."

In the Spring of 1748 he spent close to three months in Bermuda for his health, but kept at work, preaching daily —once from a boat to throngs that fringed the shores of St. George's Bay. He raised one hundred pounds and this time admits that all did not go to his orphans but some "enabled me to make such a remittance to my dear fellow yoke as may keep her from being too much beholden in my absence." This is also one of his very few references to his wife, whom he soon rejoined.

Whitefield spent the winter of 1751–52 in America

and returned a fifth time for a year's stay in 1754 with twenty destitute little recruits for the Orphan House. On a two thousand mile circuit, he preached in Carolina, Georgia, Philadelphia, New York and New England.

In one of his sermons he made use of an electrical storm that was terrifying his auditors, calling the lightning "a glance from the angry eye of Jehova" and the crashing thunder "the voice of the Almighty" and finally, with the clearing, pointing to the rainbow as witnessing the love of Him that bended it.

The sixth missionary voyage was in 1763 and he doubled on the old trails for two years. Then came the last crossing. In a touching farewell sermon in England he preached upon Jacob's Ladder, likening God's care of Jacob, pillowed upon stones in a strange land, to the divine watchfulness over the evangelist far from home. Sailing in September, 1769, he went to Savannah and his beloved Bethesda, there to cry hallelujahs over the success of the orphan house. The Georgia Assembly praised him for what he had done, but he exclaimed: "Let the name of George Whitefield perish if God be glorified!"

Again he turned to "gospel ranging" during the Summer of 1770, averaging about one hundred miles a week as he swung over the old route northward through Philadelphia and New York to New England, the scene of his last labors. The following chronology of his preaching in the last two months of his life discloses the final measure of his devotion:

Aug. 4–8, Newport, R. I.  Aug. 15–18, Boston
"  9–12, Providence  "  19, Malden
"  13, Attleboro, Mass.  "  20–25, Boston
"  14, Wrentham  "  26, Medford

| | | | |
|---|---|---|---|
| Aug. 27, Charlestown | Sept. 14–16, Too ill to |
| "   28, Cambridge | preach |
| "   29–30, Boston | "   17–19, Boston |
| "   31, Roxbury Plain | "   20, Newton |
| Sept. 1, Milton | "   21–22, On way East. |
| "   2, Roxbury | "   23–25, Portsmouth, |
| "   3, Boston | N. H. |
| "   5, Salem | "   26, Kittery, Maine |
| "   6, Marblehead | "   27, York, Maine |
| "   7, Salem | "   28, Portsmouth, N. |
| "   8, Cape Ann | H. |
| "   9, Ipswich | "   29, Exeter, N. H. |
| '   10–11, Newburyport | "   30, Died at dawn, |
| "   12–13, Rowley | Newburyport, Mass. |

One of the great concourse of people who heard the last sermon in the open fields at Exeter reported that White-field was so weak that he had to pause to get strength to lift up his voice and after a few minutes said: "I will wait for the gracious assistance of God, for, I am certain, He will assist me once more to speak in His Name."

And towards the end of two hours of preaching the evangelist seemed aware that this was the last time as he said:

"I go to rest prepared. My sun has risen and by aid from Heaven has given light to many. It is now about to set— but no, it is about to rise to the zenith of immortal glory. I have outlived many on earth, but they cannot outlive me in heaven. Oh! thought divine! I shall soon be in a world where time, age, pain and sorrow are unknown. How will-ingly would I live forever to preach Christ, but I die to be with Him!"

As he concluded, the candle which he was holding in his

hand burned away and went out. Even so was his life to pass before the sun should rise again. He rode to Newburyport to the home of the Rev. Mr. Parsons, the Presbyterian pastor. He felt his asthma coming on again and was able to eat but a little gruel for supper. He went to his chamber and for a while read the Bible and Dr. Watts's Psalms. Then he sat up in bed and prayed—prayed for a blessing on Bethesda and its orphans, prayed for all to whom he had preached on both sides of the Atlantic.

Till three o'clock in the morning he slept fitfully with anxious friends sitting by. The asthma began to choke him. He got out of bed and went to an open window for air. Twice he said "I am dying!" Seated in a chair with his cloak wrapped round him he breathed his last. It was six o'clock on the morning of September 30, 1770.

Amid the weeping of ministers and people, the frail form was laid in the vault of the Old South Presbyterian Church of Newburyport. In November when the news reached England, John Wesley preached the memorial sermon.

Not quite fifty-six, George Whitefield had dedicated himself to his ministry for thirty-four years, travelling thousands of miles over sea and land, bringing a new light into thousands of lives, awakening the English-speaking world to a consciousness of the divine in its first great revival of religion. His voice was stilled. But it was not the end. Whatever of truth, whatever of power, whatever of good to man lay in him became his legacy to the succeeding generations.

# CHAPTER VI

## SATELLITES OF WHITEFIELD

Am I a soldier of the cross,
A follower of the Lamb,
And shall I fear to own His cause
Or blush to speak His name?
CHARLES WESLEY.

WHILE Whitefield like a meteor was flashing across the American horizon, lesser luminaries, reproachfully called the "New Lights," glimmered with reflected radiance. They presumed to borrow from him things incidental to his thought and action, to adopt and capitalize the very errors he later regretted and retracted, and to magnify all to their own glory and justification. And though he drew upon himself some opposition, these satellites were responsible for most of the bitter detraction consequent upon the course of the Great Awakening.

Whitefield's partiality to divine "impulses" within the human frame they construed to their own advantage by proclaiming an indwelling of the Holy Ghost, calling them to preach, filling their mouths, and guiding their steps and providing signs in proof of their inspiration. They took his words—"God seems to show me it is my duty to evangelize and not to fix any particular place"—as authority to invade and disrupt churches far and wide.

A horde of exhorters, many of them uneducated, some

of them of doubtful ordination or none, went out over the country in the name of Whitefield. Quoting his sanction, they denounced inhospitable pastors as sons of Belial leading their flocks "blindfold to hell" and initiated separatist movements within the churches. All their extravagances of behavior, all the untoward manifestations produced among the people who fell under the spell of their ranting were austerely attributed to the pervading Spirit. And who would dare rebel against God Himself speaking through His servants?

Two of the New Lights began their sacerdotal careers with the blessing of Whitefield who was impressed with their manifest devotion and unaware whither it would lead them. They were Jonathan Barber and James Davenport, the self-anointed prophets of Long Island. Barber at Oyster Ponds (now Orient, L. I.) and Davenport at Southold, ten miles away, simultaneously had visions of being "eminent instruments" in the salvation of souls in the great revival they foresaw in the advent of Whitefield, whom they regarded as an "angel of the Lord." They prayed together for guidance. Then one Saturday night in March, 1740, Scriptural quotations came to Barber adjuring him that the set time was come for him to arise for Zion. He fainted. Thereupon he went about proclaiming his experience.

Taking no money or change of clothing, relying wholly upon the Holy Ghost to tell him where to go and what to say, Barber had a strenuous season with Davenport at Southold and stirred up the countryside for twenty miles to Oldmans. There the Holy Ghost ceased operating. He said there was a "cloud upon the tabernacle."

Unshaven, ragged and growing fat in his idleness, Barber lingered for several months till the "call" should be renewed. He got wind of Whitefield's sailing for Rhode Island and beat him to Newport. Whitefield firmly believed that the Holy Ghost brought Barber to him. "We took sweet counsel together," says Whitefield. "My heart rejoiced." Barber joined up. He went with Whitefield on the New England campaign and became the Superintendent of Spiritual Affairs at the Orphan House.

Davenport did not fare so well in his roving ministry, though he was as well recommended. Gilbert Tennent called him a "heavenly man." Whitefield never knew anyone who "kept so close a walk with God." And the Rev. Jonathan Parsons, the Lyme (Connecticut) pulpiteer who later warned his fellow-citizens against lack of discrimination regarding the works of the Holy Ghost, at first found Davenport one "living so near to God that his conversation was always in heaven."

Barber seems to have been a come-up lay exhorter, an intruder within the altar rail. The First Church Society of Southold, dating from 1640 and the earliest English-speaking church in New York, has no mention in its records of any Barber occupying its pulpit. But then, he would not have been at all "regular" and the clerk might have been a stickler for form. Town files disclose his signature as a witness to three deeds, between "yeoman and husbandman" and "husbandman and cordwain," of lands "situate in Oyster Ponds Lower Neck," the habitat of the Barbers. On one of these conveyances the name of Sarah Barber is appended and she may have been to Jonathan what the first Sarah was to Abraham.

On the other hand, Davenport was a man of consecrated lineage and thorough education. His grandfather, the first James, was a noted London minister who came to be one of the founders of New Haven and pastor of its first

church. His father, the Rev. John Davenport, born in
Boston and graduated from Harvard College, was settled
at Stamford, Connecticut, when James the second was
born in 1710. This third generation of preachers was reckoned second "socially" in his class of twenty-three at Yale
in 1732. While in college he suffered a breakdown and was
treated by a Dr. Hubbard for a physical malady that probably underlay his mental aberrations later on in life.

The eastern end of Long Island was settled by Colonists
crossing the Sound from Connecticut long before English-
men presumed to set foot upon the island of Manhattan.
Southold was a place of solid Christian brotherhood, at
least three denominations uniting in common worship under the rooftree of the First Church Society. Their first
pastor was the Rev. John Young whose sacred dust re-
poses in God's Acre nigh the second edifice, built in 1803.
The pastorate of James Davenport dates from 1738 to
1746, though the last six years of it were mostly *in absentia*.

For Jonathan Barber touched off the fuse that de-
tonated an explosion of super-sanctification. James Davenport strode out from his parsonage in his shirtsleeves into
the main thoroughfare one morning and startled Southold.
"Thieves, liars, adulterers and hypocrites!" he cried in ex-
ecration of his peaceful people. It was an amazing day and
yet only a beginning. "Signs" pointed the way to Davenport. He tried his hand at healing,—fasting and praying
for the recovery of an insane woman. On the day he set
for her restoration she died. Taken to heaven in answer
to prayer, he said.

More prayer, and then his eyes lit upon the Scriptural
passage telling how Jonathan and his armor-bearer attacked
the Philistines. Taking unto himself an armor-bearer, he
climbed the hill to Easthampton on his hands and knees,

fulfilling the Word though the snow was deep. Twenty were converted. That clinched the "call" of James Davenport.

He went where the revival fire was blazing hottest and had been preaching in Philadelphia and New Jersey with the Tennents, Samuel Blair and others when Whitefield rejoiced to meet him at New York in October, 1770. The next Spring he landed at Stonington for a conquest of Connecticut. His first sermon struck down a hundred and in the course of eight days he added another hundred gospel scalps, including those of twenty Indians. More success at Westerly, Rhode Island, less at Lyme, Connecticut, and then he struck out on the high road of martyrdom, starting at Saybrook, thundering through New Haven, and finding his Sanhedrin in the State Legislature at Hartford.

The while he was calling sinners to repentance, it seems his special commission was to bring unconverted ministers to an accounting. "He will bless the House of Aaron," his Scriptural direction read, but Aaron's brethren resented being branded "wolves in sheep's clothing" and seeing their flocks drawn off by the strange shepherd. Davenport demanded of every parson his "experience" and, failing to elicit a satisfying reply, invoked the wrath of heaven even upon some of the patriarchs of the pulpit.

In May, 1742, Davenport and his "armor-bearer," Benjamin Pomroy, were hailed with a writ of arrest before the State Assembly, which had just passed an Act curbing the intrusions of itinerant exhorters as fomenting disorders and abuses. Defying this law, Davenport had added to his lashings of the clergy the prophecy that the end of the world was near at hand.

At the close of the first day of his examination, Davenport undertook to harangue the crowd, but the sheriff importuned his departure. Thereupon the prisoner cried out: "Lord, Thou knowest somebody's got hold of my sleeve. Strike them, Lord, strike them!" To this Pomroy added: "Take heed how you do that heaven-daring action!" Partisans rushed the sheriff, but he stood his ground. That night a mob ranged round the house of confinement and it required two hours for the magistrates to disperse it.

Till dawn clashing prayers arose from the excited town of Hartford. Then the militia was ordered out and muskets kept peace to the conclusion of the trial on June 3. The Assembly decided that Davenport's mental faculties had been disturbed by "enthusiastical impressions and impulses" and that, deserving of pity, he should be sent home to Long Island. Committing Connecticut to the Lord's care "in spite of all the malice of earth and hell," Davenport suffered himself to be transported.

By the end of the month Davenport appeared in Boston, declaring that "the Lord sent me," and assailed the unregenerate of the pulpit with redoubled fury. The very ministers who had sponsored Whitefield in Boston united in a drastic reproval of the intruder and the Grand Jury indicted him for "slanderous and reviling speeches against the godly and faithful ministers of this Province, viz.: that the greatest part of said ministers were carnal and unconverted men; that they were leading their people blindfold down to hell; and that they were destroying and murdering souls by the thousands."

Brought to trial, Davenport was adjudged "non compos mentis" and so "not guilty." Having planted the seed of separatism in Massachusetts, Davenport betook himself to New London, Connecticut, for the same purpose. Here he reached the climax of his career. Acting upon "holy intuition," he bade his followers purify themselves by letting him commit their vanities to the flames.

Nigh the shore the faithful heaped their wigs, cloaks, breeches, hoods, gowns, rings, necklaces and condemned books, including those of Increase Mather and Jonathan Parsons the Lyme (Connecticut) revivalist. Then upon a Sabbath morning, while the exorcised people marched round and round singing hallelujahs, Davenport threw on his own velvet breeches and set fire to all this worldliness. One saner than his brethren persuaded them to retrieve their clothes, but as the books went up in smoke Davenport shouted that even so were the authors to fry in hell.

That was the uttermost extremity. In the Summer of 1744, Davenport, having recovered a measure of rationality, published his retraction, begging forgiveness for transgressing "the laws of justice and charity" in judging ministers and provoking separations, and confessing that "impulses and impressions" had led him astray under the influence of "the false Spirit." Those who had been his followers, however, denounced him and his confession and went on with their separatist churches for some years till the excuse for their organization was gradually lost to sight, many of them being absorbed into the Baptist denomination.

Apologists for Davenport traced his behavior to a fevered brain and declared his return to reason resulted from a recovery from this long-standing malady. His progress toward mental health was assisted by the counsel of another revivalist, Eleazer Wheelock, who had himself blundered into extremes of "enthusiasm" and had profited by his own experiences. This Lebanon (Connecticut) divine itinerated through New England, rousing great fervor at Boston, Taunton and Providence.

Large assemblies burst into sobbing and outcries under his preaching and the converted went to the floor as if under sledgehammer blows. Once he raised his voice above the tumult and carried it higher and higher with progressive excitement increasing the confusion. The consequences were appalling to him and, in later retrospect, he feared that there had been many "false conversions." Finally he settled down to the crowning work of his life, the founding of the school for Indians at Hanover, New Hampshire, which afterward became Dartmouth College. In this project he had the sympathy and aid of Whitefield.

The stanchest defender of Davenport at the height of the latter's violence was the Rev. Andrew Croswell of Groton, Connecticut. A sample of Croswell's parallel methods is afforded in what he did in the Church of the Pilgrims at Plymouth whose first pastor was Elder William Brewster. Coming hither in 1742, a year after Gilbert Tennent had made it an estuary of the revival tide, Croswell rent the church asunder.

He threw the fear of God into Plymouth. Taverns were deserted and children no longer played in the streets. The people "gave themselves to reading only the word of God and refrained from their customary vices." In the midst of this awful holiness a storm of opposition arose. Another separatist church was the inevitable result.

Typical of separatist doctrine is that declared by the church founded at Mansfield, Connecticut, by Elisha Paine, an exhorter. Calling themselves "true believers," Paine's followers accepted his dictum that Christ died for certain individuals only and that in conversion God revealed to the redeemed sinner that he was one of the elect. He was one of the most glaring of the New Lights, who included Benjamin Pomroy of Hebron, Davenport's "armor-bearer," and the Rev. John Owen, of Groton, in their constellation.

"Needful Caution in a Critical Day" was the text of a warning issued by the Rev. Jonathan Parsons of Lyme against these diversions from the Whitefield revival. Parsons had done some strong evangelizing of his own, wringing anguished lamentations from people in many places, felling strong men as if under cannon fire, driving young women into hysterics, and eliciting public prayer from little children. In his warning, while urging no cavil against the "operations of the Holy Spirit," he reproved the idea of being saved unto infallibility, saying: "Give no countenance to that absurd notion of depending upon the immediate impulses of the Holy Spirit for every word you say or every action you do." And he admitted that he had almost yielded himself to this "extravagant presumption."

Unquestionably all of these diversions from the main purpose of the revival worked to the disadvantage of Whitefield. Besides the "New Lights" of New England there was also a weak-minded zealot in the South, Hugh Bryan of South Carolina, whose actions spread an unfavorable impression of Whitefield throughout the Colonies. Bryan was so captivated by the evangelist's preaching that he followed on to Savannah and later won high praise in Whitefield's Journal.

On the eve of his sailing for England in January, 1741, Whitefield obliged Bryan by correcting the latter's manuscript which was afterward found to contain a charge that the clergy "broke their canons." Bryan's confession implicated Whitefield who had to give bond for appearance in the case.

The next record of Bryan is in the Spring of 1742 when he set himself up as a prophet, led a small army of fanatics, including some negroes, into the swamps and armed them. He dispatched to the Speaker of the Legislature a twenty-page prophetic declaration which promptly resulted in warrants for arrest being issued. Thereupon Bryan confessed that he had been deluded by the Devil and implored pardon. He had discovered the snares of Satan in the failure of a "sign." It seems he had nearly been drowned while trying to part the waters of a river with a Scriptural rod. This ended his "conversations with the Evil Spirit, the Father of Lies."

Against these deteriorative forces were pitted such strong characters as Gilbert Tennent, Samuel Blair, Jonathan Dickinson and John Rowland who held up the hands of Whitefield after sharing with Jonathan Edwards in the preparation of the New World for the great evangelist. But even they were on the "New Side" as against the "Old Side" in the Presbyterian schism which was finally healed by Tennent in 1758. The "New Siders," identified with the Log College that became Princeton, demanded evidence of regeneration in church members and preachers and their case reached its supreme phase in Tennent's famous sermon an the "Dangers of an Unconverted Ministry."

This Presbyterian faction was responsible for sending to Milford, Connecticut, the Rev. Samuel Finley, afterward President of Princeton, to preach in a church established by Davenport. Finley was arrested as a "vagrant" whose preaching "disquieted the people." Tennent, however, was one of the first to warn the country against "enthusiasm" and Blair, long since venerated in the history of American Presbyterianism, was a close examiner of the soundness of religious demonstrations, especially the bodily motions that accompanied the wailing in his revival meetings.

It was to Gilbert Tennent that Whitefield committed

the task of carrying on the work when he returned to England after the breaking of the ground in 1740. And it was to Tennent that Whitefield owed much of the opposition stirred up against him, particularly through their joint theme of an "unconverted ministry."

Hardly ever have two men accomplishing much the same results been so unlike. Whitefield was the English university gentleman, amiable in manner; his broad, youthful countenance a mirror of strong yet tender emotion; every gesture of his hands, every movement of his impressive frame, clad in the vestments of his Church, graceful yet commanding; his voice with all its modulations the organ of overwhelming eloquence; his mind acutely sensitive and sympathetic, guided by lucid reasoning yet capable of impetuosity and fine passion.

Then Tennent—born in Ireland, educated in a rustic Colonial college, he was a plain-spoken man of rural simplicity; lofty of stature, dignified and grave of demeanor; his undressed hair flowing over the shoulders of a greatcoat bound with a leathern girdle; forcible, indeed bold and awful, in preaching rather than soft and persuasive, deadly in earnest, searching, pungent, dexterous.

Tennent preached in Boston from December, 1740, till March, 1741, and then encompassed New England. The Rev. Thomas Prince insists that he never knew of any crying out, falling down or fainting under the ministry of either Tennent or Whitefield in Boston, but the Rev. George Griswold records such phenomena during Tennent's meetings at Lyme, Connecticut, where perhaps the people had come by the practice under Jonathan Parsons. Tennent wound up with the formation of his own church in Philadelphia in 1744, its one hundred and forty communicants being fruits of the great revival.

In Boston Tennent preached hellfire in the Edwards mode, bruiting the terrors of an offended God, exposing the false hope of the hypocrite, probing the corrupt heart, alarming sinners and lashing "Pharisees" whether of the pulpit or the pew. He wrought "conviction" upon hundreds who were "under concern" for many months afterward and he amassed the final, dam-breaking increment of opposition to Whitefield and the revival.

Calm, rationalizing minds like those of Dr. Charles Chauncy, the Rev. Timothy Cutler, President Holyoke of Harvard and President Clapp of Yale joined in a common stand against the assaults upon the sincerity and righteousness of the ministers of New England and against the inroads of "enthusiasm" among their churches.

First came the pastoral revolt against the effects of the revival as disclosed in the "Testimony" issued by the May 25, 1843, Convention of the Congregational Ministers of Massachusetts against "errors in doctrine and disorders in practice." In July Messrs. Gee, Colman, Prince, Sewall and others friendly to Whitefield published a "Counter-Testimony" upholding the revival and laying its admitted irregularities and extravagances to the wiles of Satan. The original "Testimony" had thirty-eight signatures and the "Counter-Testimony" one hundred and thirty-eight.

Then President Holyoke and the entire Faculty of Harvard College brought out a specific testimony "against the Rev. George Whitefield and his conduct," criticizing his itinerating with an "enthusiastical turn of mind raising the passions" and thus being subversive of "the peace and order of these Churches of Christ."

As to his "enthusiasm," this was defined as acting "according to sudden impulses and impressions upon the mind which he fondly imagines to be from the Spirit of God though he hath no proof." The effect of the literal acceptance of this notion was deplored in that converts of the revival "from the swelling of their breasts and stomachs in the religious agitation thought they were feeling the Spirit in its operations on them."

He was charged with being "an uncharitable, censorious and slanderous man" and his "reproachful reflections" upon Harvard College were cited as evidence of his "rashness and arrogance." In particular his talk of Harvard as in a state of immorality and irreligion was declared a "libellous falsehood" and his characterizing of the clergy as preachers of an "unknown and unfelt Christ" was held a breach of the moral law.

He was branded a "deluder of the people" with regard to his Orphan House in that he gave it no personal supervision but left that duty to the "inspired" Jonathan Barber and in that his accounts of disbursing contributions were not itemized but lumped. (On this point Benjamin Franklin disposed of any suspicion that Whitefield "would apply these collections to his own private emolument," saying: "I, who was intimately acquainted with him, being employed in printing his sermons and journals, am decidedly of opinion that he was in all his conduct a perfectly *honest* man. My testimony ought to have the more weight as we had no religious connection.")

Finally the Harvard critics deprecated Whitefield's setting the example of itinerating and extempore preaching which had let loose the wandering exhorters "thrusting themselves into towns and parishes to the destruction of all peace and order." The pastors of New England were urged "to consider whether it not be high time to make a stand against the mischiefs here suggested."

The Faculty of Yale College endorsed the Harvard

declaration and further accused Whitefield, together with other itinerants, of a "scheme to turn the generality of ministers out of their places and to introduce a new set of such as should be in a peculiar manner attached to you; and this you would effect by prejudicing the minds of people against their ministers and thereby induce them to discard them or separate from them." This charge was based upon the attacks of Whitefield upon "an unconverted ministry."

The strongest indictment of all came from Dr. Chauncy and Timothy Cutler. In his "Seasonable Thoughts on the State of Religion in New England," Dr. Chauncy compiled all the evidence of evangelistic excesses, including the histories of Barber and Davenport, and declared that the censorious mood of the extremists first appeared in Whitefield himself with his harping on unconverted ministers.

Gilbert Tennent, said Dr. Chauncy, imitated Whitefield in spreading this dissentient spirit till in all New England "parents were condemning their children and children their parents, husbands their wives and wives their husbands, ministers their people and people their ministers."

Whitefield's glorying in manifestations in which people drowned him out with their cries and fell down swooning before him drew fire from Dr. Chauncy, who recounted the havoc wrought by emulating itinerants. Among the effects he noted screaming, falling on the ground, writhing in convulsions and stretching out speechless and motionless. And all this fanaticism he attributed to the invoking of "revelation."

Timothy Cutler denounced Whitefield and his friends and followers in these scathing terms:

"It would be an endless attempt to describe that scene

of confusion and disturbance occasioned by him: the division of families, neighbourhoods and towns, the contrariety of husbands and wives, the undutifulness of children and servants, the quarrels among teachers, the disorders of the night, the intermission of labour and business, the neglect of husbandry and of gathering the harvest.

"Our presses are forever teeming with books and our women with bastards, though regeneration and conversion is the whole cry.

"The teachers have, many of them, left their particular cures and strolled about the country. Some have been ordained by them *Evangelizers* and their *Armour-bearers* and *Exhorters;* and in many conventicles and places of rendezvous there has been checkered work indeed, several preaching and several exhorting and praying at the same time, the rest crying or laughing, yelping, sprawling, fainting, and this revel maintained in some places many days and nights together without intermission; and then there were the blessed outpourings of the Spirit!

"When Mr. Whitefield first arrived here the whole town was alarmed. He made his first visit to church on a Friday and conversed first with many of our clergy together, and belied them, me especially, when he had done. Being not invited into our pulpits, the Dissenters were highly pleased and engrossed him; and immediately the bells rung and all hands went to lecture; and this show kept up all the while he was here.

"After him came one Tennent, a monster! impudent and noisy, and told them all they were dam'd, dam'd, dam'd; this charmed them, and in the most dreadful Winter I ever saw people wallowed in the snow night and day for the benefit of his beastly brayings, and many ended their days under these fatigues.

"Both of them [Whitefield and Tennent] carried more money out of these parts than the poor could be thankful for.

"All this turned to the growth of the Church in many places, and its reputation universally; and it suffers no otherwise than as religion in general does, and that is sadly enough."

To all of these accusations Whitefield gave answer, not in a spirit of controversy but with a sincere desire to rectify error and repair injury as a matter of common justice. "Wild fire will necessarily blend itself with the pure fire that comes from God's altar," he said. Admitting "unguarded expressions in the heat of less experienced youth," he ventured that he had "Peter-like cut off too many ears." Still, he insisted that a "pure divine power" had been "transforming people's hearts" despite "some occasions of offence" as he preached up and down the country.

Replying directly to Dr. Chauncy, Whitefield said that he came by invitation or he would never have seen New England, conceded that his judging of unconverted ministers was too inclusive and flatly denied any design to alienate the people from their pastors.

Defending himself against the Harvard charges, he regretted publishing to the world the sins of the colleges but asked if at that time there was not a "declension of religion" in them. He upheld his itinerating as coming under divine command through Scripture and his extempore preaching as not being neglectful of study. (His epitaph credits him with eighteen thousand sermons.) He refused to be held accountable for the "hot men" who came after him and, declaring himself a preacher of the ancient Puritan doctrines, disavowed any intention to meddle with the churches of New England or the tenure of their pastors.

"At the same time I desire to be humbled and ask public pardon for any rash words I have dropped or anything I have written or done amiss," he concluded, with a plea for forgiveness even as he also had already forgiven.

Harvard eventually was won over to the Whitefield of maturer years. In 1768, responding to Whitefield's gift of a new edition of his journals and raising of contributions for books to replace the library burned in Harvard Hall, President Holyoke and the Fellows of Harvard College voted that "the thanks of the Corporation be given to the Rev. Mr. Whitefield for these instances of candour and generosity."

Whitefield's star was not dimmed for long. And the revival to which he gave his life survived the backfires and left a permanent impress upon the religious, educational, social and political life of America. Parish despotism was ended with the evolving of the individual conscience and its self-assertion. The change in lives brought about by conversion became something to be reckoned with as a source of public reformation as well as the peculiar reliance of evangelical faith in the new nation about to be born.

In the twenty years following 1740, probably fifty thousand members were added to the churches of New England alone. This takes on significance when it is remembered that the population of this corner of the country was then about two hundred and fifty thousand to three hundred thousand. Throughout the Colonies hundreds of new churches were established, some of them Congregational, some Presbyterian, some Baptist, some "separatist" that afterward became Baptist, and some known as "societies" that were to be the springs of Methodism. The very word of Whitefield's death converted Benjamin Randall, the sailor who went from deck to pulpit and founded the Free Will Baptist Church.

Princeton University and Dartmouth College can be dated from the revival and they with Harvard and Yale were quickened by a spirit of tolerance and liberty of conscience. Religious convictions permeated the entire body politic and implanted the moral strength that carried the country through the Revolution. The Great Awakening was indeed the leaven of American independence.

## CHAPTER VII

## THE WESLEYAN APOSTLES

A charge to keep I have,
A God to glorify;
A never-dying soul to save,
And fit it for the sky.
                              CHARLES WESLEY.

BORN in the revival of religion it initiated among the English-speaking peoples and dedicated to the perpetuation of this veritable new Reformation through its own manner of functioning ever afterward, Wesleyan Methodism was destined to be a vitalizing yet stabilizing force in the nineteenth-century democracy of Britain and America. Its power was to be felt in the social, industrial and political evolution and its strength was to be found on the side of individual freedom as well as individual responsibility to man and God.

John Wesley drew the spark in experiencing his own conversion on May 24, 1738. Then he knew why he had failed as a preacher to the Indians on his only voyage to America. And then he predicated Methodism upon personal conversion and made it the concern of every Methodist to be a saver of other souls besides his own. The Gospel to Methodists became "a living oracle making very real the relations of the personal soul to the personal God."

Necessarily this exaltation of the individual in the sight

of his God invoked an intense current of emotion. In early
Methodism the depth of feeling caused bodily tremors,
convulsive throes, utter inertness; groans, tearful cries, victorious shouts. Men and women addressed themselves to
God Himself and believed they sensed reply. As Wesley's
ministry progressed, these violent manifestations subsided
though they were to reappear spontaneously on the American frontier in the decade after his death. He preferred
not to condemn them altogether nor yet to regard them as
if essential.

Such emotion marks the transition of a life crisis. With
or without external indication, it is characteristic of all
evangelism, in the individual and in the mass. John Wesley's
own conversion is perhaps the best illustration of what
this means in Methodism.

Wesley had been Methodistic since his association in
November, 1729, with that group which derisive Oxonians
called the "Holy Club," originated by his brother Charles
and enrolling such memorable names as those of George
Whitefield, Robert Kirkham, William Morgan and James
Hervey. But it was not till he met Peter Bohler, the ardent Moravian, in the Winter of 1738, that John Wesley,
though a priest of the Church of England, was "convinced
of unbelief, of want of that faith whereby alone we are
saved."

What Wesley meant was that his faith in God hitherto
had been incomplete in not comprising a sense of pardon
for sin,—the evangelical promise of free justification or
grace through the mediation of Christ. He felt that he
ought to cease preaching, but Bohler told him to preach
faith till he got it "and then because you have it you *will*
preach faith."

Wesley went out and preached that for which his own

heart hungered and thirsted most. His Church denied him its pulpits, but he went down to Fetter Lane. He closed his prayerbook and broke into extempore supplication as the months slipped by. In the midst of his pleading for greater faith it was borne in upon his burdened mind that "he that believeth is passed from death unto life—believe and thou shalt be saved, for God so loved the world—."

Then came his hour. He marked it. It was quarter to nine on the evening of Wednesday, May 24, 1738. The place was the meeting house of the Methodist society in Aldersgate Street where the leader was reading Luther's preface to the Epistle to the Romans describing the change which God works in the heart through faith in Christ. "I felt my heart strangely warmed," Wesley said of his experience. "I felt I did trust in Christ, Christ alone for salvation; an assurance was given me that He had taken away *my* sins, even *mine,* and saved *me* from the law of sin and death!

"I began to pray with all my might for those who had persecuted me. I then testified openly to all here what now I first felt in my heart."

Examining himself in respect to the change wrought in him, Wesley declared himself "a new creature," new in his judgments of himself, of happiness, of holiness; new in his designs "not to indulge the desires of the flesh but to have the life of God again planted in the soul"; new in his desires and inclinations, love, joy and hope, even sorrow and fear, "all pointing heavenward"; new in his conversation and actions, the whole tenor of his life "singly pointing to the glory of God." And he concludes: "I trust that I am reconciled to God through His Son."

Behold a "new man in a new world" fired with a love for God which immediately manifests itself in love for fellowmen and exemplifies itself in the spirit of evangelism. That is Wesley. That is the Methodist. It is the fulfilment of those words spoken to Nicodemus: "Except that ye be born again!"

From that time onward for half a century John Wesley preached the faith that was in him, "the life of God in the souls of men," "a religion of love and joy and peace, having its seat in the inmost soul but ever showing itself by its fruits in every kind of beneficence spreading virtue and happiness all around it." He implanted this .faith in others and they in still others and so the Wesleyan apostles carried it the length and breadth of Britain and across the sea to America.

It was a ceaseless revival and this revival to the Methodists was the "work of God." The only way ever to become a Methodist has been to get converted and the only way to stay a Methodist has been to continue in the evangelical spirit. But, as attested by Wesley's typical experience, the Methodist conversion has implied the moral judgment of the rational self, a mental as well as an emotional quickening. Hence the evolving of the Methodist mind that built the Methodist Church in America.

For Wesley himself never conceived a separate church. He broke with the Moravians, to whom he owed his conversion, because of their antinomianism (religion supplanting the moral law) and their extremes of mysticism, and he broke with George Whitefield, the first incidental maker of Methodists in America, over Calvinism with its particular election of the redeemed to which he opposed his Arminianism, the doctrine of freedom of the will, self-determination and personal choice under a God "willing that all men should be saved as reasonable creatures endued with understanding to discern what is good and

liberty to refuse or accept it." But Wesley to the day
of his death on March 2, 1791, in the eighty-eighth year
of his age and the sixty-fifth of his ministry, remained
within the fold of the Church of England and considered
his Methodist "societies" only a means of bringing greater
faith to communicants of that Church.

It was in these societies, however, on both sides of the
Atlantic, that personal participation and personal responsibility, self-determination and self-discipline inevi-
tably nurtured individualism which was a contributing factor in the struggle for industrial justice and political
liberty. It is true that Methodism, because of the suspected
Toryism of its British clergy, came under a cloud in America during the Revolution, that some of its preachers were
forced to leave the country and that others, amid the general indiscriminate stigmatization, were mobbed, stoned,
tarred and jailed. Still the Methodist militants kept on
evangelizing, one of its notable converts being the future
circuiteer, Ezekiel Cooper, the son of an officer of the
Revolutionary Army, who heard his "call" under the
preaching of Freeborn Garretson to soldiers in Maryland.

So Methodism grew in the hearts of the American people
and emerged from the conflict to give its blessing to their
Constitution. Then in the days of unsettlement, when the
new nation was groping its way, the faith became a steadfast anchorage for thousands of souls. And the Revolution
which won independence also gave to the world the American Methodist Church.

The turning point came in 1784. Methodist "volunteers" and Wesleyan "missionaries" had been ranging the
Colonies since 1766. The outstanding missionary, Francis
Asbury, made Wesley's "General Assistant" in 1772, had
brought the societies through the war and persecution and

now, with the severance of ties with the King and his Church, stood faced with the necessity for the establishment of a new ecclesiastical order. The revival fire was to blaze on an altar of its own.

For all his opposition to the Revolution, most notably expressed in his injudicious "Calm Address to the Colonies," John Wesley had accepted the achievement of independence as the result of "a very uncommon train of providences" and was still the spiritual father of American Methodists. In this year of 1784 their General Conference passed a resolution declaring that "during the life of the Rev. Mr. Wesley, we do recognize ourselves as his sons in the Gospel, ready in matters of Church Government to obey his commands." Three years later the Conference, at his behest, rescinded this acknowledgment because in the intervening time independent authority had been created.

Over the protest of his brother Charles, the hymnologist of the revival, whose conversion under Peter Bohler preceded his own by only three days, John Wesley, on September 2, 1784, at Bristol laid his hands upon Dr. Thomas Coke and sent him a Bishop to consecrate in turn Francis Asbury in America. The second ordination, in the presence of five hundred people in Barratt's Chapel, Kent County, Delaware, in the month of November, completed one of the most astounding episodes in religious history.

John Wesley, who in the beginning had taken the world for his parish, had gone back of the Apostolic Succession to the Primitive Church and transmitted the first call direct to the shepherds of a church that, while newly autonomous, could thus conceive of itself as springing from the fountain source of Christianity. And it did even so.

The immediate motive of Wesley's Promethean audacity

was to provide the American Methodists with an ordained pastorate to administer their sacraments, but the larger significance was the bestowal of a divine commission to evangelize a continent in spite of itself. Forthwith Methodism considered itself on God's business and God's business came to include not only the saving of souls but also the abolition of slavery and the prohibition of liquor, both as hindrances to the advancement of the Kingdom on earth.

This is the true genesis of the ruthlessness of righteousness. Contrary to bitter criticism in the era of the Eighteenth Amendment, American Methodism, per se, has not been political nor has it sought for itself political dominion, but rather, with primal evangelical zeal, it has been supremely conscious of fighting the "battle of the Lord." In 1920 the weapon was the slingshot of David, in 1928 the sword of Gideon. For always the Methodists have been at Armageddon. They were so constituted from the first. Even as it was written: "They fought from heaven."

The holy warfare began in America on that Autumn day in 1766 when Barbara Heck, the "mother of American Methodism," disrupted a card game in her kitchen and compelled Philip Embury to begin preaching in his house on a thoroughfare in New York that had more grogshops than dwellings. Into that original Methodist society came the one-eyed exhorter Captain Thomas Webb in full scarlet regimentals of the British Army. It was his collecting genius and Barbara Heck's inspiration from on high that built on John Street the first Methodist edifice in the New World.

The America of that day, a thinly settled strip from the Appalachians to the Atlantic with Boston, New York and Philadelphia comparatively small centers of population, stood at the crossroads of its destiny. It was the eve of the Revolution and events were moving fast. Everywhere was unsettlement. Moral issues were swallowed up in political. The Puritan Church was raking over the embers of the spiritual glow enkindled by George Whitefield, the Presbyterians and Baptists were standing still, and the Church of England had all but lost its hold. There was indifference to moral sanctions and almost hostility to religion. The time was ripe for Methodism.

The pioneers of the faith in New York,—Barbara Heck, Paul, her husband, Embury, the Switzers, Sauses, Gasners and Schuylers,—were of the evangelistic mold and temper, the children of Protestant exiles persecuted out of the Rhine Palatinate who found refuge in England and then Ireland where Wesleyan itinerants had converted them.

While Embury plunged into spreading salvation from his John Street pulpit, Captain Webb, his erstwhile preaching partner, followed tradition and took Methodism on the road, blazing revival trails across Long Island and then southward through New Jersey and Delaware till in 1767 he roused Philadelphia, where he was instrumental in the founding of St. George's Church, the greatest fortress of Methodism for forty years. This veteran of Louisburg and Quebec, portly of build, martial in bearing though grotesque with his eye patch and shattered arm, was wont to begin his diatribes by flinging his sword down beside his open Bible.

Not long after Methodism had begun sprouting from New York, Robert Strawbridge, an emigré Irish itinerant, hewed out and raised the log edifice in Frederick County, Maryland, that became a stamping ground for Wesleyan revivalism. He ranged not only that State but also Delaware and Virginia and penetrated to Pennsylvania, boldly

anticipating the day of independent Methodism by baptizing his converts and licensing some of them to preach
in his wake.

Another to undertake the redemption of Maryland was
John King, who was probably the first to preach Methodism in Baltimore. An anvil borrowed from a blacksmith
shop and set up on the corner of French and Front streets
was his original pulpit. Again he mounted a table at Baltimore and Calvert Streets and this time the militia, on
"training day parade" and lacking an enemy to practice
upon, turned their rum-roused bravery upon the parson.
The captain intervened and King bellowed on. He was
an uproarious exhorter. It was to him that John Wesley
had to address the admonition to "scream no more at the
peril of your soul."

"God now warns you by me who he has set over you,"
Wesley added. "Speak as earnestly as you can, but do not
*scream*. Speak with all your heart, but with a moderate
voice. It was said of our Lord—'He shall not cry'; the
word properly means he shall not *scream*. Herein be a
follower of me as I am of Christ."

The advice was needed by many of the American zealots—like Benjamin Abbott and Lorenzo Dow whose
rampageous rantings brought their revivaling into the
realm of demonolatry.

Benjamin Abbott played tag with the Devil. The Fiend
chased him and he chased the Fiend. Abbott claimed the
victory and was not contradicted. In fact, his marvellous
recitals of diabolical experience won so many converts in
New Jersey, Maryland and Delaware that his score was
up with the highest. Before his conversion in 1773 at the
age of forty, Abbott had dreamed of a peep into a heaven
of dazzling splendor, where he was told "Not yet, Ben-

jamin," and also of super-furnaced hell stoked by spike-tailed imps who had him by the head and feet and were about to feed him to the flames when he woke up.

It was during his soul struggle at a revival near Salem, N. J., that he matched speed with Satan. He felt the hot breath on his neck as he slammed the door on the Enemy after a race to his home. Then he had a vision of the Christ that ended his doubts, took away his sin and sent him out to preach till that day in 1796 when he went "shouting home to glory."

Abbott's form of evangelizing was a pursuit of the Devil as dwelling within the bodies of sinners. He came to grips with the Adversary and the wrestlings were marked by down-falling, screaming and prostrating. A whole meeting house full of people would topple under the glare of his uncanny eyes and his thunders of damnation.

Asbury met him and frankly was mystified. All this was apart from Methodist doctrine, but there was the evidence manifest and the clarifying application of psychological analysis was not to be available to the world for half a century. Abbott was not only meddling with hypnotism but was himself the victim of auto-hypnosis.

Lorenzo Dow—"Crazy" Dow he was called—was another votary of visions. A Connecticut Yankee, born at Coventry in 1777, he was probably epileptic from childhood and this may account for his convulsions and trances. He dreamed of realistically operative heavens and hells and, after his conversion by a Methodist itinerant in 1796, his febrile brain, distraught from days of weeping, praying and fasting, conjured an encounter with the ghost of John Wesley enjoining him to preach.

Unaccepted by any Conference, once licensed as a lay exhorter only to jump all bounds, Dow, the self-styled

"Cosmopolite," roamed from the Atlantic Coast to the Mississippi Valley and from Canada to the Gulf of Mexico, kicking through the somber traditions of New England pioneering Protestantism in Alabama and Florida, and rowelling his hundreds upon hundreds through turmoils of mental and physical contortion to his peculiar variety of conversion.

Twice he voyaged to England and Ireland where he vainly tried to innovate the camp meeting idea which captivated him on the Kentucky border and of which more will be told in another chapter. After 1804 his wanderings were shared by a wife, Peggy Miller, ingenuously referred to as "my rib," who acquired a wealth of material for her compilation of "The Vicissitudes of Life," the companion piece to "The Dealings of God, Man and the Devil as Exemplified in the Life Experiences of Lorenzo Dow in a Period of Over Half a Century."

Dow would drop into a place as if a cloud had let him fall there and the revival was on. His hair streamed down his back and his beard tipped his gaunt waistline. It seemed like a reincarnation of the Lion of the Tribe of Judah, albeit a hungry lion, with eyes flashing fire and voice roaring damnation.

As time went on, Dow's preaching got to be a continuous jeremiad and those who came under its influence joined in his moanings and groanings. His bodily afflictions became more acute and many a sermon was interrupted while he suffered a fit in the pulpit. His warped mentality ventured into prophecy with a proneness to calamity and once he had remarkable luck. About a year after a prediction by him the Mississippi Valley was rocked in 1812 by the worst earthquake in the history of the country. That was the peak of his work. Loyal Peggy, "plain as a pipestem but a woman of more than ordinary mind," as one who knew her said, trudged along beside Lorenzo whenever his raw-boned nags fell by the wayside till she died in 1820, fourteen years ahead of her eccentric husband.

Abbott and Dow were typical of many itinerant disseminators of individual interpretations of a meaningfulness of religion accepted as Methodistic but actually based upon crude theologizing and irrational tests of spiritual experience.

Among early Methodist evangelists of the solider sort were Robert Williams, Ezekiel Cooper, Freeborn Garretson and Jesse Lee. And they are to be distinguished as revival promoters from such church organization builders as Richard Boardman, Joseph Pilmoor and Thomas Rankin, who were sent over by John Wesley to consolidate the gains made by conversion.

Williams landed in Norfolk, Virginia, in the early Fall of 1769, a volunteer preacher from Ireland. He began his work much as the modern Salvation Army officer sets about it by standing on a street corner and singing a hearty hymn. He got his crowd. He prayed and preached, telling first the Lord and then the people why he was there. Afterward the wife of a sea captain gave him shelter in her home. There Williams prayed her into conversion and also besought the redemption of her husband at sea. It is in Methodist history that the skipper recorded an answer to the prayer that night in the ship's log. Whether this be true or apocryphal or mere coincidence, it happened in a day when to most men miracles were miracles.

Though Williams preached his way to Philadelphia and New York, it was in Virginia that he most advanced the cause of Methodism. Radiating from his famous Brunswick Circuit, the Gospel tidings swept the State in 1775, borne

first by Williams and then by George Shadford and a
phalanx of salvationists under the generalship of Asbury
himself. In that first year of the Revolution eighteen hundred Virginians were converted. After the war, in 1787,
the revival went through again, attaining cyclonic dimen-
sions and drawing more than three thousand to the Methodist altar amid a veritable wildfire of extreme emotional
stress. Bending like feeds in a gale, rich and poor, white
and black, the people experienced a contagion of vocal and
spasmodic tumult that presaged the vortex of overwhelming mass agitation in the frontier camp meetings at the
outset of the new century.

In the course of a decade the revival spread northward
through New England, westward over the Alleghenies
and southward into Baltimore, engulfing Baptists and
Presbyterians but finding its greatest power in the Methodists. It was accepted as wholly religious, the way to understanding of the truth. Men of faith preached it and
drove it forward. The sincerity was there and the self-
sacrifice and courage that proved the exuberant vitality of
a church in the making. It was a spiritual overflow, a
Springtime freshet likely to have muddy and tumultuous
waters, eventually to be cleared as they settled into calmer
channels.

The Field Marshal of the Baltimore revival in 1789 was
Ezekiel Cooper, one of the early stalwarts of American
Methodism. Tall and straight as an Indian, making no pre-
tense to oratorical style, he was a cogent reasoner that
could command a multitude. Born in Caroline County,
Maryland, in 1763, he had been preaching about four years
when he led the singing, praying thousands through the
streets of Baltimore to the Methodist mercy seat during
that memorable summer. At the climax, with the whole

city inflamed by a progression of the same emotional outpourings that characterized the revival in Virginia, Cooper
quoted the cry of the day that "the Methodists at this rate
will get all of the people."

He lived to see the denomination increase from a few
thousand members to a round million in the United States.
Converted by Freeborn Garretson, the itinerant who with
such men as Joseph Hartley and Philip Gatch defied mobs
and preached throughout the Revolution, Cooper in his
career imprinted his name on the Methodism of Philadelphia and New York, and as Presiding Elder of New England brought to fruition the evangelistic work of Jesse
Lee. Upon his death in 1847, Cooper was accounted the
oldest Methodist minister in the world. And he had kept
faith with the words addressed to him by John Wesley in
the last letter written to America by the progenitor of
Methodism:

"Lose no opportunity of declaring to all men that the
Methodists are one people in all the world, that it is their
full determination so to continue."

There were many others who followed the Wesleyan injunction to his apostles, from the fiery James O'Kelley,
whose secession in Virginia led to liberalizing the governance of the church, to Richard ("Dicky") Allen, the ex-
slave in Philadelphia who rose to be the first Bishop of the
African Methodist Episcopal Church. But greatest of all
was Francis Asbury. Consecrated to his calling almost from
the cradle, he came to America as a missionary for Wesley
and grew in spiritual stature with the church that he built
upon evangelistic genius.

Mothered into Methodism, he was converted at the age
of fifteen and when he was twenty-one, in 1768, he was
swinging over circuits in his native England. He came to

America as a "volunteer" in 1771 and discovered the future of his faith. For forty-five years he preached free universal grace to a people contending in the conquest of a wilderness, struggling through a revolution, developing a democracy. His name is linked with the names of every Methodist preacher of his era and with every place to which they penetrated. He was the spear-point of the relentless revival. Every individual who heard him sensed a condemnation of sin and a freedom in personal redemption.

With his consecration as Bishop came the larger aim, the creation of a church that should live by evangelizing till Judgment Day. He strove for a rigorously simple church, even resenting bells, steeples, pews and organs at first, and ever magnifying the poor and humble soul in the sight of the God that had been made its refuge. He fathered the discipline and organization, the press and the Sunday school of Methodism.

But before all else Francis Asbury was a maker of Methodists. He rode with the revival tide which in the last years of his life took him westward and into the camp meeting Canaan of Methodist evangelism.

## CHAPTER VIII

## CAMPFIRES ON THE FRONTIER

The Son of God goes forth to war,
A kingly crown to gain;
His blood-red banner streams afar;
Who follows in His train?
REGINALD HEBER, 1783–1826.

REVIVALISM in America soared to its heights and plumbed its depths when in 1800 it crossed the mountains and followed the sturdy early settlers into the isolation of the border lands of Kentucky, Tennessee and Ohio, the strategic battleground of religion in the westward march of the nation. It was here that cataclysmic holiness attained its uttermost degree in the mass metamorphoses of "twice-born" strong men who willed the winning of the wilderness.

Crucified in the agony of despair, benighted souls by the thousand were led through an emotional and physical paroxysm to an instantaneous release from the conscious bondage of sin. To preacher and penitent this was miraculous. It was the regeneration that the revival has always had for its purpose though in succeeding years the "rebirth" has come to be accomplished without those primal pangs.

It was a primitive folk, however, who lighted the night fires of the first camp meetings along the frontier, a conglomerate population that was peculiarly susceptible to the extremes of religious excitation engendered. A sprinkling of New Englanders of the Puritan strain were insufficient to serve as a balance. Scotch-Irish emigrants to the South predominated. Rugged and independent, brave and adventurous, fervid in emotion and alert to the dangers of Indians and wild beasts, they had filtered through from Virginia and the Carolinas and with their axes and rifles had made their way to the fertile Cumberland country. Mingled with them in the far-flung settlements from the Green River and Kentucky on the north to the Cumberland River and Tennessee on the south was a rabble of a lesser breed, lazy, cruel and criminal, that had swarmed like locusts over the trail.

Uncultured for the most part, but shrewd and resourceful, the solider element, dwelling in rough log homes, made the most of their Bibles and the few books they had brought along. Still, with the rest, they had cut loose from the ties that maintained the tradition of the seaboard communities. Churches were rude, few and far between. Social life was restricted to villages where it expressed itself in political strife, tavern brawling and "court day" orgies. Gambling, drunkenness and immorality were rife and worse wickedness flourished in the unleashed passions of the border,—man's inhumanity to man and man's defiance of things once held sacred. Here were real sinners,— sinners capable of a tangible realization of their guilt. They were tinder for the impending revival conflagration.

It has been written that this revival "came straight from God." Perhaps the chronicler felt that it was in answer to the "Concert of Prayer" in which all evangelical denominations joined throughout the country in 1795. Suppliants everywhere—in New England, the Middle States and the South—Methodists, Baptists and Presbyterians— sensed a response in themselves. President Timothy Dwight

"THE CAMP-MEETING"

of Yale College started a revival in which seventy-five out of two hundred thirty students were converted and "times of refreshment" quickened one hundred fifty New England churches. This current coursed through Western New York and Pennsylvania, onward up the Ohio and Allegheny Valleys and into Kentucky and Tennessee.

The actual bearer of the torch into the borderland, however, came out of the South and drew in behind him the momentum of the Methodist revival forces that had rumbled through Maryland and Virginia under the generalship of Asbury. Once again an evangelist was acclaimed a Boanerges, "son of thunder." It was James McGready, whose heralding of hell first made North Carolina tremble and then brought him a note, written in blood, warning him to leave the State.

McGready had begun preaching in 1788, when in his late twenties, under a Presbyterian license. His Calvinism was of the Edwardean temper and temperature. He would reach out with a mighty swing of his arm and in pantomimic parallel would pluck out a figurative sinner and dangle him over the brimstone brink. Then to those quailing under his invective and imagery he would offer a Wesleyan way of escape leading through conversion to rebirth.

It was said that his glowering visage, compelling eyes, and thunderous voice augmented the terrors of his composite Calvinistic hell and Methodistic regeneration. Elder Barton W. Stone, the pastor of the Cane Ridge (Kentucky) Presbyterian Church who borrowed coals from McGready's sacrificial altar at Red River, said of him:

"His person was not prepossessing, nor his appearance interesting, except his remarkable gravity and small, piercing eyes. His coarse, tremulous voice excited in me the idea of something unearthly. His gestures were *sui generis,*

the perfect reverse of elegance. Everything appeared by
him forgotten but the salvation of souls. Such earnestness,
such zeal, such perfect persuasion . . . I had never before
witnessed."

Back home in Carolina he had aroused fierce opposition.
Accusing him of "running people distracted" and divert-
ing them from their necessary occupations, his enemies had
burned his pulpit and then menaced him with the gory
missive. But he spoke a language that Logan County, Kentucky, understood. And when he took over the pastorate
of Gasper River, Muddy River and Red River in 1796, he
come into his own.

McGready found in Red River a hell on earth that even
the worst inhabitants recognized. "Rogues' Harbor" the
place was called because it was the refuge of murderers,
horse thieves, highwaymen, thugs and bankrupts gathered
from all over the East. "Regulators" applying the lynch
law fought pitched battles with the ruffians till McGready
arrived and a transformation began.

He began by binding his backwoods parishioners to a
solemn covenant to unite in a schedule of special prayer
for pentecost, repentance and redemption. Every Saturday night and Sunday morning and all day on the third
Saturday of every month the common petition progressed
and the common will was welded. Powerfully praying
fathers and mothers in Israel from miles around swelled
the ranks of the suppliants. They interceded for their own
souls and for the sin-sunk souls outside the Bethel. As
the invocation intensified it particularized and the wicked
heard and bolstered the very resistance that proved their
ultimate undoing.

Twice the revival tide rolled up and twice it receded,—
in 1797 and 1798. Then in the Summer of 1799 it burst

over iniquitous Logan County like a deluge. And James McGready was the moving spirit of the roaring wind and rushing waters that swept men, women and children off their feet. He brought down the thunders of damnation and lightnings of self-conviction upon the hundreds and then the thousands of screaming refugees from wrath eternal that swayed, twitched, yanked and stiffened out in the rigor mortis of pseudo-immolation.

Into the maelstrom came John and William McGee, brothers, the one a Methodist exhorter and the other a Presbyterian minister. In the midst of his preaching John was seized with tremors that choked his words and the spectacle evoked a tumult when he finally gasped that God was shaking him. William sank to the floor of the pulpit and many in the house were stricken unconscious.

Thereafter, says Davidson in his History of the Presbyterian Church in Kentucky, William "would sometimes exhort standing . . . or sitting or lying in the dust, his eyes streaming and his heart so full that he could only ejaculate 'Jesus, Jesus!'" In a personal account of their first day with McGready at Red River, John wrote:

"William felt such a power come over him that he quit his seat and sat down on the floor of the pulpit, I suppose not knowing what he did. There was a solemn weeping all over the house. At length I rose up and exhorted them to let the Lord God Omnipotent reign in their hearts and submit to Him and their souls should live. Many broke silence. The woman in the east end of the house [previously mentioned as vocally constant] shouted tremendously. I left the pulpit and went through the audience shouting and exhorting with all possible ecstasy and energy, and the floor was soon covered with the slain."

More brethren of Aaron soon pitched into the onslaught

upon the sons of Belial. With the McGees, the Presbyterian come-outers William Hodge, John Rankin, Robert Marshall, Richard McNemar and John Thompson and the Methodist William Burke, who was raised from penitential dust to pulpit glory, helped to rock the river tabernacles of McGready. Others pushed far afield and seismic salvation spread under their feet. Baptists, like Louis Craig and Elijah, his brother, brought Boone and Brocken Counties of Kentucky into the upheaval and Elder Barton W. Stone, the Presbyterian who later became a leading light of the Disciples of Christ, drew the Red River whirlwind home with him to Cane Ridge in Bourbon County where it spiraled to maximum velocity.

Day and night, month on end into another and yet another year, ever widening in territory, the battle raged. Crops were deserted and the business of towns neglected. Families and whole neighborhoods took to the trail afoot, horseback and in wagons, and from fifty to a hundred miles converged on the sacramental centers. Churches could not hold the thousands who poured in. Thus the Western camp meeting was born of imperious necessity.

Singing woodsmen hewed out of the forest at Gasper River in July, 1800, a gospel ground walled by sombering pines and roofed by the starlit sky. Trees were felled in rows for pews that radiated round not one but half a dozen log pulpits from which the evangelists would all preach at once. In the bordering timber, the covered wagons and improvised tents of the pilgrims circled the salvation site. Cooking fires fringed the encampment and pitch flares stuck in the bark of trees left standing here and there flickered over the vast assemblages of the night.

Barton Stone, drawn hither by the word that had gone out, tells of the "multitudes that came together and continued a number of days and nights encamped on the ground during which time worship was carried on in some part of the encampment."

"The scene was new to me and passing strange," he says. "It baffled description. Many, very many, fell down as men slain in battle and continued for hours together in an apparently breathless and motionless state, sometimes for a few moments reviving and exhibiting symptoms of life by a deep groan or piercing shriek or by a prayer for mercy fervently uttered.

"After lying for hours they obtained deliverance. The gloomy cloud that had covered their faces seemed gradually and visibly to disappear, and hope, in smiles, brightened into joy. They would arise, shouting deliverance, and then would address the surrounding multitude in language truly eloquent and impressive.

"With astonishment did I hear men, women, and children declaring the wonderful works of God and the glorious mysteries of the Gospel. Their appeals were solemn, heart-penetrating, bold and free. Under such circumstances many others would fall down into the same state from which the speakers had just been delivered."

Elder Stone recounts sitting beside some sinners of his acquaintance through their throes observing "the momentary revivings as from death, the humble confession of sins, the fervent prayer, the ultimate deliverance, the solemn thanks to God and the exhortation to companions and people around to repent" with the effect that "several sank down into the same appearance of death."

"After attending to many such cases," he goes on, "my conviction was complete that it was a good work, a work of God. Much did I see then, and much have I seen since, that I consider to be fanaticism, but this should not condemn the work. The Devil has always tried to ape the works of God and bring them into disrepute."

Divine or demoniacal, the "works" increased. Camp meetings sprang up in rapid succession along the whole frontier from the Green River to the Cumberland. They were magnets to the revival and in them it went beyond all bounds.

Preachers and penitents alike were stampeded into a species of mesmerism or hypnotism at the height of the epidemic furor. Involuntary twitchings, known as the "jerks," would rack the body. The head would twist from side to side faster and faster till it spun the rest of the palsied frame. Rending cries burst from the lips of the "jerkers," screams of anguish, shrieks of terror. Some howled and some, down on all fours, even barked like dogs. They leaped as if jabbed. They whirled like dervishes, rolled, wormed, hopped like frogs. And finally they plunged headlong, grovelling on the ground till they collapsed in cataleptic rigidity.

The "jerks" were accepted as concomitant with conversion and people came to camp meeting expecting to see them. Some invaded the enclosure to revile them only to fall into their grip. One man at a meeting of William McGee tried to fortify himself against them with whisky, but the bottle was shaken out of his hands and a sudden snap of his head broke his neck. Hundreds would be stricken at a time and the more they resisted for the sake of dignity or out of "hardness of heart," the surer they seemed destined to suffer. Of the twenty thousand massed at a Cabin Creek (Kentucky) camp meeting more than a thousand went down in one great sweep and squads of men were delegated to lay them in rows away from the milling throng till they should be "delivered" hours later from their condition. The "bearers of the slain" were a regular feature of the camp meeting ever afterward.

It was at Cane Ridge, however, that the momentum of the border camp meeting catapulted to the zenith. Elder Barton Stone, imbued with the inspiration of McGready's three-river shrines in Logan County and reinforced by the impetus of the scores of parallel plants of holiness that mushroomed all over the frontier region, evoked the avalanche at Cane Ridge in August, 1801.

From all parts of Kentucky, Tennessee and Ohio the multitude descended upon the gospel ground. All the camp meetings became one camp meeting. James B. Finley, who with that other famous Methodist circuit rider, Peter Cartwright, was there, estimated the assemblage at twenty-five thousand and declared the noise was like the roar of Niagara.

"The vast sea of human beings seemed to be agitated as if by a storm," he said. "I counted seven ministers, all preaching at one time, some on stumps, others in wagons and one—the Rev. William Burke (Methodist) was standing on a tree which had, in falling, lodged against another. Some of the people were singing, others praying, some crying for mercy in the most piteous accents while others were shouting most vociferously."

Cartwright said that the meeting was protracted night and day for a week, that, though it began under Presbyterian auspices, "ministers of almost all denominations flocked in from far and near" and that of the twenty-five thousand gathered to hear the preaching "between one and two thousand souls were happily and powerfully converted to God." As the "heavenly fire spread" he reported that "at times more than one thousand persons broke into loud shouting all at once and the shouts could be heard for miles."

Elder Stone's personal account discloses the oneness of mind that prevailed in this great emotional togetherness, saying:

"The roads were crowded with wagons, horses and footmen moving to the solemn camp. It was judged by military men on the ground that between twenty and thirty thousand assembled. Four or five preachers spoke at the same time in different parts of the encampment without confusion. The Methodist and Baptist preachers aided in the work, and all appeared cordially united in it. They were of one mind and soul: the salvation of sinners was the one object.

"We all engaged in singing the same songs, all united in prayer, all preached the same things. The numbers converted will be known only in eternity. Many things transpired which were so much like miracles that they had the same effect as miracles on unbelievers.

"This meeting continued six or seven days and nights and would have continued longer but food for the sustenance of such a multitude failed. Many had come from Ohio and other distant points. These returned home and diffused the same spirit in their neighborhoods. Similar results followed."

It is clear that the power of suggestion was rampant, that imitation was inescapable. The drama of Cane Ridge depended upon these elements. Flanked by campfires blazing against the forest gloom, with the exhortations of the preachers rising in impassioned fervor as the night progressed, the serried rows of people rhythmically swayed together in concerted song, sob, and shout. And with the dawn they joined hands by the hundreds in a final "sing-ing ecstasy."

During the day the crowd would shift from one preach-ing stand to another as the word sped that prophecy was here or a miracle was there, that an epidemic of the "jerks" was on or fresh converts were emerging from their fits to tell of their experiences. Now the frenzy would mo-mentarily subside, but a piercing shriek yonder on the other side of the clearing would bring a rush to that spot and soon the shaking, leaping, laughing, weeping, swoon-ing tumult would be resumed. Little children, caught up in the furor, "preached" from the shoulders of their par-ents, repeating the lurid cant of their elders till they lapsed into incoherence and senselessness. It was computed that about one in six fell with the "slain" at Cane Ridge.

After this the camp meeting system of revivalling was well-established. By 1803 the zeal abated but the excite-ment had not wholly died down in 1805 when Lorenzo Dow, the Methodist itinerant, bore witness to the "jerks" under the effect of his preaching in Knoxville, Tennessee. Poor old "Crazy" Dow, for all his eccentricity, was a shrewd observer and was well aware that these gyrations were produced by gospel incendiaries like himself.

"I have seen all denominations of religion exercised with the jerks," he said, "gentleman and lady, black and white, young and old. I have passed a meeting house where I ob-served the undergrowth had been cut for a camp meeting and from fifty to a hundred saplings were left, breast-high, for the people who jerked to hold on by. I observed where they held on they had kicked up the earth as a horse stamping flies.

"I believe it [the jerking exercise] does not affect those naturalists who wished to try to get to philosophize upon it, and rarely those who are most pious, but the lukewarm, lazy professor [of religion] is subject to it. The wicked are more afraid of it than of smallpox or yellow fever and are subject to it; but the persecutors are more subject to it than any and they have sometimes cursed and swore and damned it while jerking."

Among the naïve backwoodsmen the agitations were counted valuable and essential to soul salvation. Even Peter Cartwright at first attributed the "jerks" to the judgment of God though later he realized that conversions obtained by such means were often spurious and that the impressions under them, mistaken for perceptions of truth, might be delusive.

The whole species of *Americana horribilis* probably started with genuine religious feeling. Then the vivid imagery of personal sin and its desert of eternal damnation took possession of the subliminal consciousness and induced a psychic storm. The subsequent contortions and falling into rigidity were pure hysteria. Involuntary imitation was responsible for the spread of the devotional delirium into orgies of nervous excitement. And the suppressed fear of yielding was doubtless the most potent cause for the seizure of resistants.

The preachers, on their side, were carried along with the current. They were exhilarated like actors in a play that is evoking an emotional response from its audience. They could justify to themselves their course as availing against hardness of heart and as producing manifest results. In fact, they did declare that the morals and religion of the new West improved following the revival. But this does not condone the gamut of excesses that was finally checked by the limit of endurance, a fear of bedevilment and some rationalized opposition.

The revival that had come from East to West and run wild now took the reverse direction and, strong and stirring in spirit but bereft of its morbid phenomena, it touched nearly every State in the Union. In New England, for instance, mild and simple measures were employed in emphasizing the immutability of the moral law and the necessity of regeneration. And in the West the camp meeting, now a permanent national institution for religious renewal, settled down to straight preaching of balanced men, the rugged, earnest, honest circuiteers of such stuff as brought out Cartwright, Finley, and Finis Ewing.

The fate of the promoters of the sound and fury is what might be expected with the return to more normal ways of getting religion. McGready of the hypnotic eyes and awful voice spent himself with his effort and died in 1817 at the age of about fifty-seven. The others repudiated their churches and became schismatics. Their teachings had been subversive of ecclesiastical authority, a phase of one type of evangelism that still prevails, in claiming for each convert an inner light which interpreted the Scriptures and directed worship regardless of accepted interpretation and prescribed forms. Separatism was the consequence and more "New Lights."

McNemar was tried for anti-Calvinism and suspended from the Presbyterian Church together with Thompson, Marshall, Stone and John Dunlevy, who joined with him in forming a new presbytery. The sect incorporated the worst features of the late revival, introducing voluntary leaping, dancing, skipping, jerking, rolling and barking, holding prayer matches to decide controversies and making much of visions. Grasping one another by the hand, the devotees would indulge in a general holy shaking till their church edifices rocked with them. This was the "right hand of fellowship" to increase the working of the spirit in accordance with their basic belief that God abiding in the soul of man was magnified by such exercise of the inward feelings.

The New Lights suffered considerable persecution, some of which might be traced to a suspicion that in trying to perpetuate these aspects of the camp meeting they were endangering the morals of the community. It is true that unbridled passions were loosed in the utter lapse of self-control at some of the camp meetings. The human and the spiritual love motives have always been closely akin. And precautions finally had to be taken to protect the chastity of the young. Even so it is recorded that "bastardy increased" in the aftermath of camp meetings.

Their absolute freedom of worship disrupted the schismatics in June, 1804. Marshall and Thompson returned to the Presbyterian fold. McNemar and Dunlevy joined the Shakers, "Mother Ann" Lee's "United Society of Believers in Christ's Second Appearing." And Elder Stone alone remained steadfast, till in 1832 he took the remnant of the New Lights over into the Christian Church organized by Alexander Campbell.

The Shakers had come into Kentucky from Watervliet, near Albany, New York, in 1805 proclaiming that the revival there was the culmination of their millennial hope. Their name was derived from the violent tremblings that overtook them under strong religious emotion. Pledged to lives of celibacy and severe simplicity in dress and conduct, they dwelt in agricultural colonies on a communistic basis of labor. Ann Lee was the "first mother, or spiritual parent, in the line of the female." To this day the sect are known for their frugality, temperance, industry and honesty.

The revival strengthened the Shakers, the Baptists and the Methodists, but the Presbyterians lost ground in the consequent schism. In 1803 there were thirty-one presbyteries, three hundred and twenty-two ministers, forty-eight probationers; in 1804 there were twenty-seven presbyteries, one hundred and thirty ministers and thirty-three probationers. Lacking enough ordained ministers, the Church had to license lay preachers, some of whom insisted upon reservations denying the predestinarian tenets. Three of these men,—Finis Ewing, Samuel King and Samuel McAdow, all powerful revivalists,—finally stepped out and formed the independent Cumberland Presbytery that was more Methodist than Presbyterian.

In the border country the Baptists gained ten thousand members and the Methodists another ten thousand. But the Methodists profited most of all. They took over as their own the sounder, saner type of camp meeting that developed and used it throughout the Union with a resultant increase of forty thousand communicants. Bishop Asbury expected to see five hundred camp meetings in a single year.

The revival that ushered in the nineteenth century was a long time in subsiding and its effects were felt permanently in the establishment of the Sunday school and foreign missions, as well as the camp meeting that kept religion abreast of the migration westward. In New England it accomplished the transition from State aid to the self-support of the Church which took on fresh life and vigor. And it implanted the humanitarian feeling and force that were to energize the movement for the abolition of slavery and spiritualize the material advance of the nation.

CHAPTER IX

SINGING A NEW SONG

Awake, my soul, stretch ev'ry nerve,
And press with vigor on;
A heav'nly race demands thy zeal
And an immortal crown—
And an immortal crown!

PHILIP DODDRIDGE.

TOWARD the rounding out of its first century
as a transcendent force upon this continent, now
rising, now waning only to return with renewed
power, the religious revival was borne more and more on
the wings of song, first the hymns inspired by liberated
spirituality across the sea and then, in the camp meetings
of the frontier, the anthems that burst spontaneously
from the hearts of the American people.

The story of evangelical music is interwoven with all the
annals of the revival and yet it stands by itself as something above and beyond preachers and preaching. For the
hymn was the prayer of the penitent and the hallelujah
of the redeemed. And to others it was the metrical version
of an experience to be shared, the dynamic source of
evangelistic persuasion.

A sense of personal participation and the universal responsiveness of the human race to natural rhythm, the
very core of the group spirit, are inherent in revival singing. Lacking such a background, pulpit eloquence is like

a giant tree without soil in which to take root. It creates receptiveness and it reinforces the appeal. From the beginning the revival made its own music and ever since, adapting itself to changing moods, it has drawn the breath of its life from generations singing themselves into salvation.

Previous to 1736, the Church of England had no hymn book, though the Psalmody, arranged by Tate and Brady, was familiar and so were Jeremy Taylor's "Golden Grove" and George Herbert's "Temple." The dissenting churches, in particular the Puritans of New England, were also employing the Psalmody. But congregational singing had not yet come to life. Still there were hymns already written and waiting to be sung as a new song.

Almost before the Methodist movement was known, Philip Doddridge (1702–1751), the gentle English scholar and minister, gave to the modern Church as the legacy of his short life "Oh Happy Day, When Jesus Washed My Sins Away." Then the trumpet tones of the lofty hymns of Isaac Watts (1674–1748) heralded the Awakening. George Whitefield in his last hours on earth was reading these hymns of the Stoke Newington pastor-poet and they went out in the first Methodist hymnal to vitalize the reborn faith of John Wesley.

It was Watts who wrote "When I survey the wondrous Cross on which the Prince of Glory died," "Joy to the world the Lord is Come," and "Kingdoms and thrones to God belong." And also his were "When I can read my title clear to mansions in the skies," "There is a land of pure delight where saints immortal reign," "O God, our help in ages past" and "Am I a soldier of the Cross?" With these words for nigh on to two centuries sainted men and women have sung faith into their lives.

Watts opened up the gates of sacred song. With him and after him came Augustus Toplady (1740–1788) and his "Rock of Ages"; Samuel Stennett (1727–1795) and his "Majestic sweetness sits enthroned upon my Savior's brow" and "On Jordan's stormy banks I stand"; Thomas Shepherd and his "Must Jesus bear his Cross alone?"; William Cowper (1731–1800) and his "There is a fountain filled with blood"; Timothy Dwight (1752–1817) and his "I love thy Kingdom, Lord," and John Keble (1792–1866) and his "Sun of my soul, Thou Savior dear."

Some of these harpists of Zion were of the Awakening and some were apart from it, taking their inspiration perhaps from quieter streams. Watts himself was an old man when he finally gave his blessing to Whitefield. But their hymns were cloistered till the revival took hold of them and put them on the lips of the multitude. Even then, with all their beauty, there were not enough. The hymn expressive of the pleading and yearning, of the yielding and triumphing, was yet to come. And the Wesleys out of their own regenerative experience gave that hymn to the world.

The Wesleyan hymns kindled and replenished the fervor of the great spiritual revival that was more than Methodist. All the preaching of evangelistic creeds ever since has depended more than anything else upon the obbligato of such song for its effectiveness. These hymns reflected the change of religious atmosphere,—a heightening of emotion, a new note, a new manner of expression. They exalted the atonement; they glowed with the fire of the "free gospel"; they caught the ear of "all that passeth by"; they struck home.

Many of the six thousand five hundred hymns written

by Charles Wesley were revelations of his brother's experience. Both Charles and John tried to translate their adventure in faith into verse and this autobiographical element contributed to the emotional power of their hymns. Their conception of instantaneous release through conversion was individualized. Every singer felt that the call was indeed to "Even Me." And the hymns themselves mirrored the unrest, agony, groping and struggle of the soul; the grace, hope, light and peace held out by faith; the sympathy and guidance toward the goal; the bursting of the bonds and the rejoicing in redemption.

No one sang to himself alone. That first evangel melody was created for hundreds and thousands to join with their voices and their hearts. All became one voice and one heart. As the rhythmic lines swelled in the unison, the spirit touched every one. Belief was instilled. The impulse to consecration was infused. The response was inevitable.

The revival inspired the hymns and then the hymns inspired the revival. Moreover, there is no doubt that the Wesleys came to a clearer understanding of their tenets by embodying them in verse. John had a deep sense of the importance of the hymns, a keen personal joy in hymn singing and a rare skill in applying it to worship. Charles had facility and felicity in composition and was the foremost singer of the new song. Their first hymnal, "Hymns and Sacred Poems," published in 1742, included the earlier hymns of praise by Watts, Doddridge and the others, but in the ascendant were those hymns of experience which launched Methodism into its perpetual revival, established the permanent lines of evangelical hymnody and exercised an influence on the general extension of hymn singing exceeding the bounds of Methodism.

John Wesley began the hymn writing with translations

from the German of the Moravian Brethren, the sponsors of his own conversion. The change wrought in him is disclosed in his different view of God in the hymn translated from Ernest Lange in 1737 and another from Johann Scheffler in 1739. In the first he wrote: "O God, Thou bottomless abyss! Thee to perfection who can know?" And in the second: "O God, of good the unfathomed sea! Who would not give his heart to Thee?"

Other Moravians to find a place in the hymnal through John Wesley were Paul Gerhardt in "Jesus, Thy boundless love to me," Johann Winkler in "Savior of men, Thy searching eye doth all my inmost thoughts descry," Johann Rothe in "Now I have found wherein sure my soul's anchor may remain," Wolfgang Dessler in "Into Thy gracious hands I fall," Gerhard Tersteegen, Bishop Augustus Spangenberg, Christian Richter and Count Nicolaus Ludwig von Zinzendorf, the founder of the Brethren and of their colony at Bethlehem, Pennsylvania.

The hymns from Count Zinzendorf (1700–1760)— "Jesus, Thy blood and righteousness" and "I thirst, Thou wounded Lamb of God, to wash me in thy cleansing blood," as well as one of Gerhardt's—"Extended on a cursèd tree, covered with dust and sweat and blood,"— portended the reason for the split between the Methodists and the Moravians over the latter's sanguinary exultation in an amatory mystical union with Christ. It was then that John Wesley wrote the few hymns which bear his own name. Their evangelistic appeal is revealed in "Ye simple souls that stray from the paths of peace" and "Ho! every one that thirsts draw nigh."

But it was in Charles Wesley that the fullness of power was reached. He climbed the everlasting heights in "Oh, for a thousand tongues to sing my great Redeemer's praise" and "Come, Thou Almighty King." He sang the Messianic anthem in "Hark, the herald angels sing" and "Love divine, all love excelling." He touched the tenderest tie in "Jesus, lover of my soul" and "How sweet the Name of Jesus sounds." And he sounded the clarion call to Christian duty in "A charge to keep I have," "Blow ye the trumpet, blow" and "Soldiers of Christ, arise!"

In later years Bishop Reginald Heber wrote the stirring "From Greenland's icy mountains" and Edward Perronet the triumphant coronation of Christ in "All Hail the power of Jesus' Name!" But they, with all the others, must yield first place to Charles Wesley in the choir of heaven.

The tunes of all these hymns, familiar to this day on both sides of the Atlantic, were from the old English Church of the sixteenth and seventeenth centuries, German chorales and even contemporary popular songs. Apart from the words, the music in itself had strong emotional qualities effective in creating the atmosphere favorable to conversion. But in the mind of the singer who with the years has grown to love certain hymns the phrasing and the melody have always been inseparable. They were probably the story and the music of his own conversion.

The introduction of evangelical hymnody in America was delayed by various causes. There was rooted addiction to the old Psalmody in the Church of England and among the Presbyterians and Congregationalists, though the dissenting faiths did let the song of Watts filter in. Once the Baptists forsook their seventeenth-century scruple against hymn singing, they found less difficulty than the others in taking up the world's new song.

When George Whitefield set out to evangelize America in 1739, the churches had re-established the old Psalmody on a musical basis and those in New England were relying mainly upon the "Bay Psalm Book" without any appreciable turning to Watts. Then, moved by the Great Awakening, many churches became eager for song more in the spirit of the revival and more expressive of their own new-found fervor. The Baptists, at first indifferent, later fell in line with the Congregationalists and Presbyterians who started an immediate and irrepressible demand for an evangelical hymnody.

Whitefield did not fully comply. Though he authorized a reprint of the Wesleyan "Hymns and Sacred Poems" in Philadelphia, he made little use of them, probably because of the Arminianism that permeated them in conflict with his Calvinism. He preferred the moderate strain of Watts's "System of Praise" and made no attempt to develop a hymnody consonant with his preaching till in 1753 he compiled his volume of "Hymns for Social Worship." This had several editions but none after his death in September, 1770. The book was used at a memorial service for him on October 14, 1770, and that is practically the last mention of it.

However, whether preachers countenanced it or not, the people were soon singing the socialized hymn and neglecting the ancient Psalmody. Jonathan Edwards returned to Northampton from a journey afield in 1742 to hear the new note of praise uplifted in his absence. He did not object to the hymns but so grieved lest a tradition pass that his congregation agreed to divide evenly between the psalms and the innovation.

Not only in their churches did the "reborn" sing. They carried the song into the highways and the marketplace. At Gloucester, Massachusetts, in 1744 it is recorded that people going to and from meeting "went singing through the streets and in ferryboats." Dr. Charles Chauncy, the vigorous Bostonian critic of the revival, censured this as "ostentatious" and Gilbert Tennent, the ardent lieutenant of Whitefield, refused to defend it. But Jonathan Edwards was all for it, saying he thought that "an abounding in singing both in and out of meeting was a natural expression of the feelings of the awakened."

From 1760 onward the Methodists outsang them all. The source of their hymnody was naturally across the ocean, but it was not altogether an extension of the Wesleyan mode over new territory. In fact, at first American Methodism refused to take its hymn book from Wesley's hand and never has been particularly anxious to restrict it. The Church leaders here tried to select from its abundance what fitted Americans and to maintain the standards it set. Their followers, however, in revival zeal have persistently overflowed the banks and fairly flooded Methodism with native evangelical hymns.

The independence of song was especially noticeable after the Revolution. Changes were made to take account of the newly won liberty of the nation. For instance, revision was necessary in Watts where David had been less of a fighting King of Israel and more of a patriotic Briton. In 1792 John Stanford, recently come from England, prepared "A Collection of Evangelical Hymns" including selections of the best from the different hymn writers.

Meantime the Baptists had been forging ahead with music. They brought in popular melodies and choruses to go with the emotional character of their preaching. In 1784 appeared their "Divine Hymns or Spiritual Songs," the work of Joshua Smith, a New Hampshire layman, and others who gave currency to a hymn entitled "Christ the Appletree."

Among the Congregationalists and Presbyterians Timothy Dwight's compendium of Watts won great favor and reached its eighth edition in 1821. It was especially designed for revival services. Some preachers were prejudiced against using Watts in this way, but Samuel Worcester of Salem, Massachusetts, went Dwight one better by abandoning the "Christian Psalmody," enlarging the selection of hymns and appending them to the new version of Watts. This book came out in Boston in 1819 and, with subsequent revisions to take in fresh revival music, stood the test of many years.

The spreading of the popular hymn to the uttermost parts of the country, however, was due most of all to the Methodists. Their itinerants would penetrate wherever there was a settlement. Not only in their vibrant town Bethels but also in solitary cabins and in open fields they led in song that impressed the sentiments of their preaching. Often only the preacher had a hymn book and he would have to give out the words a line or two at a time. The people gradually memorized favorite pieces and made them part of their lives.

This free form of worship amassed greater and greater crowds in the clearings of the frontier till in 1800 the camp meeting was born in the great Kentucky revival and with it the camp meeting hymn. This hymn was introduced by the Methodists when they took the lead from the Presbyterians and pushed the revival into Tennessee, Ohio, and onward over the circuit-riding trails into the opening West.

With the tumultuous enthusiasm that developed, the old hymns were too sober to express the heightened feelings of both the preachers and the throngs that gathered day and night under the sky. Spontaneous song broke loose. Rough and irregular couplets or stanzas were put together

out of Scriptural phrases and every-day speech with a
liberal interspersing of hallelujahs and refrains. Lay poets
emerged from the ranks of the converted and improvised,
often in crude doggerel, feelingful and picturesque hymns
telling their wondrous story.

The hymns would be caught up by the throngs and
mighty choruses would roll. Sometimes the singing would
become incoherent and be just a common "singing ecstasy"
that rocked the rows upon rows of worshippers. Again
it would be a rhythmic chant of mourning. And yet again
a thunderous jubilation. Words would seep through and
finally the singers would swing back to them.

Out of the camp meeting rose the indigenously American hymn. Some of its pristine spontaneity has been preserved in the series of camp meeting song books which
began to appear in the first decade of the nineteenth century. But most of these printed songs represented a second
stage in camp meeting hymnody. The spirit was retained
while the crudity and illiteracy and overwrought vehe-
mence simmered away.

The type was individualistic, dealing with the saving
of souls, sometimes in direct appeal to sinners, backsliders
or mourners, sometimes by reciting the terms of salvation, sometimes by narrating personal experience. Of the
tunes the leaders demanded nothing more than contagious-
ness and effectiveness.

A recrudescence of the original camp meeting hymn
resulted from the secession of the Primitive Methodists in
1808, led out by Hugh Bourne who insisted upon "freedom" in revival methods in a camp meeting where the
"spirit" should be unrestrained. In 1809 Bourne published
his "General Collection of Hymns and Spiritual Songs for
Camp Meetings." The stirring melodies included many of

those in a pioneer camp meeting hymn book of rude hearti-
ness circulated by no other than Lorenzo ("Crazy") Dow.
The musical prowess of Bourne's flock is disclosed in a
common saying of the time—"You sing like a Primitive."

The circuiteers, besides being robust preachers, were
energetic singers and inspiring leaders in song. The
churches that rose on the worn trails behind them were
imbued with their spirit. The older Methodism back East
drew a spark from it and other evangelical denominations
participated in the ever-growing influence of music.

The new hymn soon overrode the barrier of language
and was shared by the Dutch and German Reformed and
Lutheran Churches. The Dunkers and Mennonites acquired
their own books containing songs of Watts and of the
revival as well as their own compositions to accompany
their "feet-washing" rites.

When the revival was generally quiescent, during the
period roughly between 1830 and 1857, its song stood
still. The Adventists in the forties adapted Methodist
melodies for their millennial march and the other sporadic
denominational evangelizing about the country relied upon
the old tunes. For the most part it was a time of religious
philosophizing on the better side and of congealing faith
from point of view of the evangelical mind.

From the comparative calm of this era emerged the so-
called "literary hymn," due in considerable part to the
lofty, earnest and serene influence of William Ellery Chan-
ning and his Unitarians. Dr. Oliver Wendell Holmes and
Samuel Longfellow contributed this type of hymn at its
best. John Greenleaf Whittier struck a deeper chord in his
"We may not climb the heavenly steeps to bring the Lord
Christ down" and this was the "devotional hymn" of that
same mid-period. With it belong Ray Palmer's "My faith

looks up to Thee, Thou Lamb of Calvary," Phoebe Cary's "One Sweetly Solemn Thought," Harriet Beecher Stowe's "Still, Still With Thee," and Sarah Flower Adams's "Nearer, My God, To Thee."

The "Onward, Christian Soldiers" of Sabine Baring-Gould sounded a militant note presaging a renewed advance of the revival ranks. And Lydia Baxter's "Take the Name of Jesus With You" was symbolical of the transition into the "Gospel hymn" that ushered in the penitential pentecost of 1857 and became the musical basis for every revival afterwards to this day.

The lilting lyrics and the melting notes of the minor key as well have been borne out of the tents and tabernacles and into the streets, homes and workshops. Some of the songs have been timeless stand-bys and have been lifted out of the transitory paper-covered books of the evangel campaign to find a place in the old church hymnals. Probably no one wrote more Gospel hymns than Fanny J. Crosby (Mrs. Van Alstyne) who will always be remembered for her "Saved By Grace," "Rescue the Perishing," "All the Way My Savior Leads Me," "Near the Cross," "Close to Thee," and "Pass Me Not, O Gentle Savior."

Then there are Charlotte Elliott's "Just as I am without one plea Except Thy blood was shed for me," Louisa W. R. Stead's " 'Tis so sweet to trust in Jesus," George Matheson's "O Love that will not let me go," Richard Lowry's "Shall We Gather at the River?" Will L. Thompson's "Softly and Tenderly Jesus is Calling," Katherine Hankey's "I love to tell the story" and Edward Hopper's "Jesus, Savior, Pilot Me."

The one great song from the 1857 revival was "Stand Up for Jesus," written by the Rev. George Duffield in commemoration of the dying words of the Rev. Dudley A.

Tyng, the youthful leader on the Philadelphia "front." Ousted by his Episcopal vestry because of a sermon against slavery, Tyng had established in a public hall a church for all denominations which he opened to the revival.

In the midst of the work, an unusual accident cost him his life. He had gone from his study to his barn floor where a mule was at work in a treadmill machine shelling corn. As he patted the mule, the sleeve of his gown caught in the cogs which drew in his arm and crushed it. Six days later, after an amputation, Tyng died. In his last hour he sent this message to his fellow-evangelists at Jaynes' Hall: "Tell them—'Let us all stand up for Jesus!'"

The words were repeated at Tyng's funeral and made a dynamic impression upon Duffield. The next Sunday Duffield wove into his sermon the hymn-poem wrought from the farewell challenge of Tyng. It was printed in the "Sabbath Hymn Book" (Congregationalist) in 1858 and in the "Church Psalmist" (Presbyterian) in 1859 and promptly included in Methodist and Baptist hymnals. The hymn was a favorite of soldiers in the Civil War and is a revival reliance of the present day.

The hymns of P. P. Bliss—"Amost Persuaded," "Jesus Loves Even Me," "Hold the Fort," "Watching and Waiting," "Let the Lower Lights be Burning," and "Pull for the Shore, Sailor, Pull for the Shore"—were immortalized by the singing of Ira D. Sankey, the great evangel partner of Dwight L. Moody. Sankey wrote hymns of his own too, both words and music, but more often just supplied the music—as for Elizabeth Clephane's "Ninety and Nine." Sankey in later years told the story of this song.

It was in Scotland. Moody had said: "Sankey will sing." Sankey had already sung almost all he had to offer. Moody, who was preaching about the "Good Shepherd," repeated:

"Sankey will sing." Sankey fished out a clipping of verse he had picked up on a railway journey. He resolved to sing the hymn and make the tune as he went along. It was almost as if he heard a voice telling him what to do.

"I yielded to it, and, taking the little newspaper slip and laying it upon the organ before me, with a silent prayer to God for help, I commenced to sing," he said. "Note by note the music was given to me clear through to the end of the tune.

"After the first verse, I was very glad I had got through, but overwhelmed with fear that the tune for the next verse would be greatly different from the first. But again looking up to the Lord for help in this most trying moment, He gave me again the same tune for all the remaining verses, note for note. The impression made upon the audience was very deep; hundreds were in tears."

Another Sankey hymn is "I'm Praying for You." That is, Sankey wrote the music and sang it till it lasted. S. O'Maley Cluff wrote the words. And then there is Edward Ufford's hymn by which Sankey is perhaps remembered best—"Throw out the Lifeline!" The memory of Sankey's singing is bound up with his playing on the little organ he had—or was it a melodeon? And right here a debt of gratitude must be acknowledged to a great-hearted agnostic lawyer, long since beyond any need for doubting, who took his son one wintry afternoon "just to hear Sankey sing."

Another voice in the land along with Sankey's was that of Knowles Shaw, the "singing evangelist," whose "Bringing in the Sheaves" has found its way into almost every Sunday school hymn book. Then came the more ambitious wielders of the power of song—Charles H. Gabriel and Charles M. Alexander among others—and they set their choruses to singing. Both of them were identified with the evangelism of Dr. Wilbur S. Chapman. Alexander had been with Dr. Reuben A. Torrey who carried on for Moody and Gabriel wrote the music for hymns that shook the rafters of William Sunday's tabernacles—"Since Jesus Came into My Heart," "He Lifted Me," and "Brighten the Corner Where You Are."

The Gospel hymn has come a long way and the number of the survivors is remarkable because the melody has always been of the day and the verse attuned to contemporary emotional coloration. Many of the songs could not endure transplanting from the Victorian vineyard to the soil of twentieth-century sophistication. "Easy" to sing, "catchy" and sentimental, they vanished when the only books to contain them wore out and were not restored.

Those that linger on are deeply deserving. They are like conversions which lasted. They are of whatever good there is in the revival. They perpetuate the very spirit of religion, the human response to love divine and the kinship of the generations hearing and answering the voice of the Psalmist who cried—"O sing unto the Lord a new song: sing unto the Lord, all the earth!"

This was the song that filled the heart of man before he gave it words, the song the shepherds may have heard nigh Bethlehem the night the world was new again. Through the centuries never stilled, it has lived in the everlasting evangel hymn. And yet no poet has more than sensed the measure of its majesty. Only in the artless freedom of the earliest song of all have the power and the glory known no bounds.

Such music was brought to America by a stolen and an oppressed people. In their plantation days of servitude and in the "protracted" and camp meetings after their liberation, the Negroes adapted the Christian Gospel and the revival to their own fathomless religious tradition and their response in song was from a racial stream flowing from the elemental springs of mankind's nativity.

The crooning of "Swing Low, Sweet Chariot," the swinging cadence of "The Old Ark's A-Movering" and "All Over God's Heaven," the pulsing pathos of "Nobody Knows the Trouble I've Seen" and "It's Me Standing in the Need of Prayer," and the exultant peal of "Roll, Jordan, Roll" and "When the Stars Begin to Fall"—all pour out the ingenuous, unimpeded high feeling of a race with a unique natural musical sensitivity, a soul aglow with the first light of creation. The Negro spiritual is the purest revival melody of all time.

# CHAPTER X

## SALVATION RIDES THE CIRCUIT

> Must Jesus bear the cross alone,
> And all the world go free?
> No, there's a cross for every one,
> And there's a cross for me.
> THOMAS SHEPHERD, 1665–1739.

IT is the second Sunday of September, 1832. A multitude of Methodists are gathered in camp meeting at Springfield, Illinois, drawn from homes a hundred miles around by the name of one man. A new presiding elder is coming from Kentucky, a bronzed veteran of the circuits whose voice, now the clangor of an alarm bell, now the chime of a throbbing hymn, has been ringing in the wilderness for a quarter of a century, whose renown was borne over the mountains and through the valleys and across the plains as swiftly as the Gospel message he himself is bringing.

Breakfast fires are smoldering as the motley company of backwoodsmen and their families flock to the preacher's stand for the eight o'clock service. The sun shines down from an azure sky and the day is perfect for the far traveller, but he does not appear. The great horn blows for the eleven o'clock convocation, the hour always set apart for the heavy guns to boom from the pulpit, and still the sole expectation of this vast assemblage is not fulfilled.

Preaching there must be and one from the circuit ranks

PETER CARTWRIGHT

steps into the breach only to falter and stumble as he
senses the disappointment in the air. The restless crowd begins to disperse. Some of the men are hitching up their
teams to depart. Suddenly a shout is raised and trace-
chains clatter with falling whiffletrees. A lone rider forces
his way through the rush to the pulpit. He reaches up
and hands a message to the trembling hand of a preacher.

"Dear brethren," the parson reads to the people, "the
devil has foundered my horse, which will detain me from
reaching your tabernacle till evening. I might have performed the journey on foot, but I could not leave poor
Paul, especially as he has never left Peter. Horses have no
souls to save, and, therefore, it is all the more the duty of
Christians to take care of their bodies. Watch and pray,
and don't let the devil get among you on the sly before
candle-light, when I shall be at my post."

A single resonant voice coming from the midst of the
throng starts a soul-stirring hymn. On the second note a
mighty surge of harmony picks up the tune and again and
again repeats its refrain while the woodland echoes with
hallelujahs. The tide has turned and the camp meeting
spirit is at the flood.

Sunset fades from the sky. Watchfires of the evening
gleam amid the clustering tents. Pine-knots sputter over
the heads of the hosts spreading out from the preaching
stand to the distant darkness. A tall, massive figure strides
into the pulpit and a hush falls over the people. It is the
man for whom they came.

Every eye is riveted on him as he gives out the hymn
and leads with sweeping gestures of his brawny arms. What
a head he has! It seems as large as half a bushel. His un-
ruly, thick, coal-black hair, tossed back from his craggy
brows, tumbles over his ears in long curling ringlets. Eyes

of deep, dark fire twinkle in the pulpit flares which disclose the weather-beaten swarthiness of his face and the redness of lips parted in an all-inclusive friendly smile.

He has begun to preach. He is ridiculing the follies of the sinner and his homely wit is pointing a torrent of eloquent humor. Laughter ripples through the throng and then bursts into explosions of mirth while dour parsons look at their feet and sanctimonious folk roll their eyes aloft. Before half an hour has passed he is teasing smiles from them too. Now a gradual change is discernible.

His countenance has lost its waggish expression. As it grows sterner, his voice becomes earnest, solemn, deep and full of pathos. The effect is immediate. The transition is startling. The thousands who were rollicking with him a moment before are weeping with him for the souls that are lost and they are listening with their own eternity at stake.

Again he changes. From the hell opening beneath their feet the people follow him heavenward in a rapture of faith and hope. The whole congregation starts to its feet. He holds out his hands and pleads—this giant of a man— pleads ever so tenderly. Five hundred press forward and are kneeling at his feet.

And Peter Cartwright comes down from his pulpit and prays with the penitents he has brought back to God.

This was the circuit rider, these were his people, and they were met in one of those places of revival power from which branched new broken trails toward the setting sun. Of all the valiant men of God with whom the revival rode to lone cabin, frontier hamlet and camp-meeting concourse, braving the perils of hostile Indians, marauding wolves, storm and flood, Peter Cartwright was the hardest fighter, the bravest pioneer and the strongest preacher. Yet he was of a pattern with the scores of others whose hardihood and self-sacrifice breathed the spirit that won the West. Peter was eight years old when his family went from the James River in Amherst County, Virginia, where he was born on September 1, 1785, to Kentucky and eventually settled at Red River, the "Rogues' Harbor" of Logan County. There his early years were influenced by such travelling Methodist preachers as John Page, Benjamin Northcut and the eloquent Jacob Lurton. But, till James McGready started the great revival at the close of the century, Sunday in Red River was a day of gambling, horse-racing and revelry. Peter had his own speedy nag and was adept at cards, though he had to keep the pack hidden lest his Methodist mother burn it. He turned his back on both temptations when conversion laid hold of him as a lad of sixteen.

It took regeneration a long time to work its way with him. Revulsion over drinking at a wedding started the ferment. His distress lasted for weeks. The elders prayed with him in vain. Wandering alone in a pasture, wringing his hands in anguish, suddenly it appeared to him that a voice from heaven said: "Peter, look at me!" A thrill of hope tingled in his heart but the sense of guilt remained and secret prayers in a cave for three months failed to lift it. Then came Cane Ridge.

While praying with the weeping multitude, he felt again the fire and heard again the voice. "Divine light flashed all around me," he said, "and a voice seemed to say to me: 'Thy sins are all forgiven thee!' I rose to my feet, opened my eyes and it really seemed as if I were in heaven; the leaves, the trees, and everything, I thought, were praising God." His mother raised the jubilee shout and earth and sky rejoiced as her stalwart son stood with the ranks of the redeemed.

Peter joined the Methodist Church and to gird himself

to preach went to school. Taunted because of his faith, he threw his tormentors into a stream and that was his graduation. Forthwith he got from the Rev. Jesse Walker his license to exhort and in 1802 he organized the Livingston Circuit in the sparsely settled Valley of the Cumberland. It was there that he found his moving text "Behold the Lamb of God!" which carried his appeal for more than half a century.

In the Fall of 1803, Ralph Lotspiech, known as the "weeping prophet," then riding the Red River Circuit, raised Cartwright from a lay exhorter to a full-fledged preacher. The novice was hesitant but he put the question into a prayer bargaining that his sermon must convert at least one or it would be his last. A once-boastful infidel brought to the mercy seat was answer enough for Cartwright. After that scores were converted wherever he went. And he wrestled with sinners not only mentally but physically as he rode hundreds of miles preaching day in and day out.

Once a sinewy blacksmith accosted him as he entered a village and announced a habit of thrashing preachers. Cartwright took him on, mauled him, dragged him in to kneel beside the anvil and prayed him through to a conversion as sound as the chastisement. At a camp meeting on the edge of Tennessee drunken rowdies armed with clubs tried to ride down the congregation. The ringleader burst in ahead of the rest. Cartwright yanked him out of the saddle and in the battle royal that followed led in subduing the raiders. Then he resumed his sermon with redoubled energy.

On one of his circuit rounds he discovered a shrew in a local parsonage. Whenever her reverend husband tried to pray she would drown him out and she greeted any

ministerial guests with volleys of curses. She tried her profane talents on Cartwright. He put her out of doors where
she squared off and declared herself half alligator and half
snapping turtle. While she raged in the yard, Peter sang
and prayed with all his might and her six children were so
frightened they hid under a bed. Finally she came to the
door promising to be good. Six months later she was converted.

At the Mount Zion meeting house an obstinate woman
insisted upon keeping the door open in defiance of rules.
Cartwright remonstrated. She shouted and refused to
budge. He lifted her bodily, set her down outside and
shut the door. Meekness was her portion thereafter. Such
pastoral diplomacy was no respecter of persons. It started
some fireworks at a church in Nashville one night in 1818.

A man came in late. Ignoring the frantic signals of the
regular minister to hold up, the pulpit guest kept right on
preaching. The good old pastor pulled Peter's coattails and
told him the newcomer was General Andrew Jackson. In-
dignant over the interruption, the hard-hitting circuiteer
called out: "Who is General Jackson? If he doesn't get
converted, God will damn his soul as quick as he would
a Guinea Negro!" He was warned that he was in for a
whaling, but instead, when the two met on the street a few
days later, the General told Cartwright he was a man after
his own heart. An army major in Logan County did challenge him to a duel once, but Cartwright chose cornstalks
for weapons and they were beneath military dignity.

On his way over the Alleghenies to the Baltimore Conference with the then venerable "Father" Walker in the
Spring of 1820, Cartwright paused to preach to the moun-
taineers. For once his words had no visible effect. A hill
preacher followed with a native song, patting his feet,

clapping his hands and interspersing a fervent: "Pray, brethren, pray!" The whole company burst into uproarious shouting. And even Peter marvelled.

It was on the return journey that they had to put up at an inn in the Cumberland Mountains where a dance was in progress. Peter sat quietly in a corner till a young woman invited him to be her partner. He took her hand and advanced to mid-floor but instead of stepping off he knelt by her side and began to pray. The colored fiddler fled to the kitchen. The dancers were thunderstruck. Then Peter preached. Before morning he converted fifteen. The next day he organized a church with thirty-two members and the innkeeper as leader.

Sailing to the Pittsburgh Conference of 1828 on the river steamer "Velocipede," Cartwright complained of the swearing, drinking and gambling on board. The captain offered to stop it all if the famous circuiteer would debate religion with him. Peter agreed on condition that the mariner should not wax profane. The battle was going to the Lord when the skipper began to curse. Peter's iron hands clamped tightly on the offending jaws and shook them till the teeth rattled. The remainder of the voyage was peaceful if not pious.

Cartwright had no patience with cushioned comfort in the churches. On the Salt River and Shelbyville Circuits he recounts that when he said "Let us pray!" everyone had to kneel. "There was no standing among members in time of prayer," he says, "and the abominable practice of sitting down was unknown among those early Methodists." Nor were there pews or organs or choirs and if Cartwright could have had his way there never would have been any. His aversion to ornate display in meeting caused a wealthy young matron, recently converted, to spend all of a Saturday night in altering her least offensive dress to be plain enough for her to attend the Sabbath love-feast with due humility.

Still Peter Cartwright had enough poetry in him to pause for romance in 1811. On August 18 of that year he married Frances Gaines, who bore him nine chilren and outlived him. Her meager home moved from circuit to circuit in Kentucky, Tennessee, Ohio, Indiana and Illinois. Only a few days in a month would she see her peripatetic husband. Every time he set out on the trail there was danger that it would cost the life of the bread-winner. And his return would bring the circuiteer's pittance that had to suffice for her growing family.

Peter Cartwright relied upon the Lord to provide, however, and feared none except his God in all the hazard and hardship of his journeys. Often he had to pick his way from point to point of timber, blazing the trees as he passed for those who should come after him. He had to plunge into the icy swollen streams of Spring and many a night he slept in the open with eyes half shut lest a slinking shadow venture within the campfire's rim of flickering light. He never faltered. A mighty faith led him on and gave him to know where he was going and why he was going—even to the end of the last trail.

He was no theologian. The settled pastorate of later days would have stifled him. His was a life of saving souls, the more at a time the better. And that was why he gloried most in the camp meeting and through the years rolled up one after another till the very name of Cartwright would start the covered wagons moving toward the next Gospel ground.

At the outset of his career the Logan tradition followed him with its "jerks" and "fits," its groans and cries, its felling of the "slain." Sinners and saints succumbed. At the first jerk the bonnets and combs of the women would fly and their long hair would crack "like a wagoner's whip." The tremor would take men's legs out from under them. And soon the earth was strewn with quivering forms. Cartwright looked out upon such scenes and they troubled him. Were they the judgment of God? Or were people running wild with something as natural as the stampede of a herd? His innate sense of humor soon came to his rescue.

It was at a camp meeting in 1804. The brothers of two fashionable young women sat beside them with loaded whips to belabor the preacher should the "jerks" come their way. Not feeling well, Cartwright took out a phial of peppermint and swallowed a little. To the brothers that was the black magic that unhinged the limbs of their gentle kin. They accused Cartwright and lifted their whips. With a quizzical smile Peter raised his phial and said: "If I gave your sisters the jerks, I will give them to you!" The youths fled and with them all idea in the mind of Cartwright that the "jerks" were anything from heaven. Thereafter, though he did not lessen the fervor of preaching and singing, prayer and testimony, he did resolutely try to hold a tighter rein.

He needed all the control he could command when the earthquake of February, 1812, shook the West to its knees in fear of the end-coming of the world. With houses rocking, chimneys toppling and fissures cleaving the earth, people rushed into the open, some shouting that the Christ was at hand but most of them piteously clinging to one another and imploring divine mercy before the sky should crack through and reveal the Judgment Throne. Day after day the shocks kept coming. Day after day the awful suspense magnified the consternation.

Cartwright was at Nashville. He was calm. But all around him was seething confusion. He tells of a slave girl running with a bucket and calling back to her pursuing young mistresses: "My Jesus is coming in the cloud of heaven and I can't stop to pray for you now!" Over in Kentucky at Russellville Brother Cook of the Logan legion of the Lord even left his wife behind despite poor Tabitha's pleadings. "O Tabby," he said, "it's Jesus and I can't wait for you!"

Hundreds were converted in the revivals that followed. Cartwright accounts for three camp meetings on the Wabash Circuit alone that reaped a harvest of souls literally shaken out of their sins. The earthquake receded in memory but the succession of camp meetings went on. Among the more notable were the 1822 Roaring River day and night penitential season and the Goose Creek encampment of ten thousand. At one meeting two rivals for the hand of a young woman came armed with dirks for a duel to the death. They met at the mercy seat and fell on each other's necks while the glory shout went up to heaven. Always it was the "victory of the Lord." Out across the West constantly multiplied the number of those who were converted by Cartwright.

But individual sinners were not the sole aim of Peter Cartwright. He threw the whole force of his evangelism against the social evils of his time. To him liquor was an abomination and he rooted it out of the pioneer church. To him slavery was a curse upon his country, an affront to God Himself. Born in Virginia, raised in Kentucky, he reached the full stature of moral and spiritual exaltation on the free soil of Illinois. Twice his fellow-citizens along the Sangamon had sent him to the Legislature as the champion of their convictions when in 1846 they decided to promote him to Congress.

His Whig opponent was another Kentuckian who had been borne westward with the emigrant trains, a tall, rangy lawyer with a wit and depth of feeling in his eloquence that more than matched the preacher's own. They met on the stump and Cartwright, thinking of the eternal soul of his rival, asked him where he was going. "To Congress" was the reply. That is just where he went. Peter Cartwright was defeated by Abraham Lincoln.

That was the last time Cartwright ran for office. He fought slavery from the pulpit instead. In 1852 he crossed the country to the Conference in Boston. It was his first visit to New England and his grave respect for its traditions dulled the sermon he was invited to preach. His Yankee brethren bespoke their disappointment. They had heard of a different Peter. Then he gave them what they wanted. The circuiteer let loose the spirit of the West in old Father Taylor's Bethel that night and Boston Methodists shouted just like their brethren of the frontier.

That was his kind of preaching. It was what went into his more than twenty thousand sermons. It was what brought no less than twenty thousand members into the churches on the dozen circuits he rode in the West. And it was of the burning faith that abode within him till death came at Pleasant Plains, Illinois, on September 25, 1872.

The life of the evangel had spanned an entire era in the history of his country. At seventy he had a circuit of five hundred miles by one hundred and it seemed "small" to him compared with the almost unbounded territory assigned to him in his prime. Towns and States had grown up on his trails. Highways and railroads had caught up with him. And the Western Methodists, beginning with a nucleus of a few hundred in 1801, were advancing toward their second hundred thousand.

Cartwright attributed the Gospel gain to humble preachers like himself without literary and theological schooling in contrast to the "sapient, velvet-mouthed, downy D.D.'s" of later days. James Haw and Benjamin Ogden were the first of the itinerants to penetrate the West. After them came the heroic Tucker who died fighting in defense of women folk against an attack of the Indians on the Great Scioto River and such stalwarts as Jesse Walker of Red River, John Strange the sweet singer of Ohio and Indiana, Robert Manley the camp meeting song leader, Dr. Shadrach Bost ,ick of the Western Reserve who ministered to both bodies and souls, Wilson Lee, Samuel Hamilton, Jacob Hooper, Samuel Thompson and John Dew.

Ranging the virgin Cumberland were those near-Methodists of the independent Presbytery led by Finis Ewing. To them came one night George Willetts, the young mountaineer dressed in home-spun copperas and shod with home-tanned red-leather brogans. The voice that stammered a tearful plea to preach was to ring in mountain cabins and camp-meeting clearings for years to come.

The Methodists had their commanders, men of substantial learning and steady vision, who built solidly on the results of the revival. The first Presiding Elder, William McKendree, was the first Bishop of the border, taking his commission from Asbury in 1808. Then followed Bishops George, Roberts, Janes and Morris as the frontier moved westward till Cartwright's son-in-law, the Rev. William R. D. Trotter, crossed the Mississippi to evangelize Iowa.

There was also one outstanding circuiteer of scholarly attainment, the Rev. James B. Finley, graduate of his Presbyterian fathers' academy and qualified practitioner of medicine. His career parallels Cartwright's and for all their difference in culture they worked much the same way toward similar achievements.

The Rev. Robert W. Finley, the father of James (and also of John, another circuiteer) was a Pennsylvanian molded at Princeton College into a preaching patriot of the Revolution in Georgia and the Carolinas. When he migrated from Virginia to Kentucky in 1788, James was seven years old. In the party that braved the almost continuous fighting with Indians were the Revs. Richard Mc-Nemar, Carey Allen and Robert Marshall, whose Presbyterianism was to melt in the fire of Red River religion and be fused into new creeds. The Rev. Barton Stone, their brother New Light, was the successor of Robert Finley in the pastorate of Cane Ridge. In that unforgettable place the elder Finley founded the first high school of Kentucky.

The Finleys pushed on to Ohio in 1796 and the academy set up at Chillicothe was the alma mater of physicians and judges as well as parsons. Zane had cut his trace through a seventy-mile wall of virgin forest to this veritable Eden and soon the flatboats were sloshing along the Scioto. James Finley's chronicle of his youth is replete with tales of bloody Indian warfare against a background of primeval grandeur. He mentions the first Legislature of Ohio convening beneath a giant sycamore and having for its chief duty the passage of a law for the suppression of drunkenness. And then the young dead-shot hunter of the backwoods tells how he was irresistibly drawn back to Ken-

~ JAMES B. FINLEY ~

tucky, to the Cane Ridge of 1801 where the arrow of the Lord pierced his heart.

Finley's conversion was not with the frenzied mass that swarmed to the forefront of the camp. He did not join in the cries. He did not mingle with the "jerkers." The sounds and sights appalled him. But a deeper conviction was stirring within him and on the ride homeward his sins piled up in array before him. He cut loose from his companions and plunged into the woods to pray alone. There he found his salvation, a salvation the Presbyterians and the New Lights alike failed to confirm. After seven years of constant struggle he was led by his wife into the Methodist fold and this Nimrod of Ohio who knew Latin and Greek as well as the haunts of game turned his moccasined feet to the lifelong trail of the circuiteer.

His head thrust through a hole cut in a blanket to protect him from a torrential storm, he rode one hundred and thirty miles cross-country to Zanesville, the nearest location on his first charge, the four hundred and thirty mile Wills Creek Circuit that took a month to round. He had to sell his boots to bring his family on after him, and, like most of his brush-pulpit brethren, he discovered that the usual stipend of twenty-five dollars a year bound him to a virtual vow of poverty. Once on his route he gave an impoverished widow all he had—thirty-seven cents.

His successive circuits kept him ever on the move into new territory, often to regions suspicious of preachers or hostile to them. One of his congregations was hidden in encircling bushes. He had his camp meetings too, some of them with the pulpit help of Bishops Asbury and McKendree, and could count his converts by the hundred. One was Eliza Hankins, an unsophisticated backwoods girl whose salvation shout after a record trance of thirty-two hours was responsible for a general soul-harvest. Among those affected by her was a blasphemous young man. A spasm of the "jerks" choked his defiance of God. Finley set no special store by such outward manifestations and in the case of the young man frankly said that all depended upon whether he stopped swearing.

Both Finley and Cartwright took the offensive against the credal epidemic set afoot by the New Lights and the border rang with their denunciations of "Arianism," "Socinianism," and "Universalism." The first two doctrines were subversive of the Trinity and by the third all mankind was to be saved. It was a duel of revivals. The New Lights lost out. Another crusade was against the rum demon. Cartwright waged his in "class meeting" cross-examination, but Finley invaded the lines of the enemy.

Not only log-rolling, reaping, husking and barn-raising provided an excuse for alcoholic overindulgence but also the gentler diversion of quilting, the social amenities of weddings and the solemn rites for the dead. Other denominations did not mind, but the "fanatic" Methodists made it a rule of their discipline to restrict liquor to medicinal use.

Finley's overt act was refusing to have a ten-gallon keg of whisky for a "room-mate" and threatening to unchurch its obstinate owner if "anything immoral" transpired at his next-day barn-raising. Then Finley opened fire from the pulpit. An old exhorter advised him to quit and go home if he couldn't "preach the Gospel and let private people's business alone." Finley's reply was a forecast of twentieth-century Methodism.

"I will not go home," he said. "I have a mission from God to break up this stronghold of the devil. By His help I will do it, despite of all distillers and aiders and abettors in the Church!"

He started with one old man, who experimented to ascertain that whisky was the cause and not the cure of his headaches, and he got a thousand on one circuit to sign the pledge. And once he boldly exhorted a crowded barroom, thundering at the bacchanalian brawlers: "Awake, thou that sleepest, and arise from the dead, and Christ shall give thee life!"

If this was a work of supererogation, so also was the unflagging annexation of Gospel territory as fast as it was settled. The tribe of Cartwright and Finley never yielded, never retreated. Every camp meeting brought out fresh recruits for the expanding revival and one of them went East instead of West.

John Colby, born in the flesh on December 9, 1787, on the side of Tripyramid Mountain at Sandwich, New Hampshire, and reborn of the spirit twenty years later at Billymead, now Sutton, Vermont, alternated his soul-saving novitiate with sufficient secular toil to buy and saddle the horse that took him in the Spring of 1810 to the Zanesville (Ohio) zone of hard-riding righteousness.

What originally set him off was a vision of himself standing in the Day of Judgment on an endless plain with not a New England rock or gray birch to hide him from the wrath sublime that convulsed the earth and sky. Every bolt from the third heavens had him for its target. Suddenly the commotion ceased, the Gates of Glory opened and John was caught up into the Kingdom. This was the source of the "call" that took him across Pennsylvania, growing in grace by proselyting Quakers all the way, and onward till he stabled his horse with the steeds of the Ohio circuiteers.

With inspiration swiftly upon him, Colby reined about and by June he was back in Vermont rounding up sinners, saving them like Methodists and baptizing them like Baptists. His favored weapon was the prophecy of death. An occasional fulfillment and many a "You're next" made candidates for the river, regardless of the time of year. On January 19, 1813, he immersed a man and wife at Burke, Vermont, a path having been shovelled through the deep snow to the brink and "a hole cut through the ice for their burial with Christ in baptism." The choir sang "Am I a Soldier of the Cross?"

Fifty went into the water with Colby during his first summer and in the six years of his itinerant evangelism eastward to Eastport, Maine, and southward as far as Providence, Rhode Island, between August 12, 1810, and November 28, 1816, he baptized six hundred and forty persons.

Colby's borrowed spark from the West glowed brightest in his native New Hampshire, in the County of Carroll and the towns of Sandwich, Tamworth, Conway, Ossipee and Effingham. It was a region of towering mountain ranges and deep valleys clad with virgin forest. Widening their clearings, the sturdy pioneers were pulling such gigantic, grotesque stumps as those which still fence the road to the Chickville meeting house in the neighborhood where the old settlers of Ossipee heard Colby preach. A few rods away flows the Beech River into which Colby waded and drove his baptismal stake. And yonder in God's Acre sleep most of that congregation who sang by the waters the resurrection hymn.

These people were of the same rugged rural mold that went westward. They also had their struggle with a wilderness. And the Cartwright kind of preaching that had bent knees from the Scioto River of Ohio to the Sangamon of Illinois and thence across the Mississippi brought the farmers and loggers of New Hampshire weeping to John Colby's mercy seat. It was "Thou art the man!" and "Thou art the woman!" as the burning arrows sped from his pulpit.

The holy fire that impelled Colby to preach twice and three times a day for almost seven years finally consumed him. He died on November 28, 1817. In passing, he handed on his torch to Clarissa Danforth, of Sutton, Vermont, one of the first woman evangelists in America. After her conversion by Colby, this young woman "of extraordinary talents, good parentage and much grace" preached to great throngs throughout Vermont for three years. The high sheriff of her county was among the first of her converts. This was of the tradition. Peter Cartwright always brought down his sheriffs when riding the circuit of salvation.

# CHAPTER XI

## THE MORMON MOSES

On Jordan's stormy banks I stand
And cast a wistful eye
To Canaan's fair and happy land
Where my possessions lie.
SAMUEL STENNETT, 1727–1795.

WHILE the clean frontal flame of the westering revival was steadily lighting the way across the country, other fires, luridly gleaming under a constantly shifting pall of unwholesome smoke, were burning back and forth over the ground behind, blistering souls and blighting minds. Over and over again the same rural regions would be seared by the withering blasts of diverse demonologies burgeoning from the innate superstition of the ignorant, credulous and excitable naïve rustics. Variegated New Lights blazed through and after them hydra-headed sects whelped from conjury with Scriptures.

Every latter-day inspiration gathered followers over night about the exorcist who howled from the ash-heaps that it had been vouchsafed to him direct from heaven and spoke in mystical phrases so close to the Holy Writ that he was accepted with the "Word" he was bearing. His converts would take his name or lend it with themselves to his doctrine. Like noxious weeds, this month the Hoskinites would spring up; the next year the Scrogginarians

JOSEPH SMITH

would flourish. And every cult erupted into a revival that mouthed another crater of rampant religionism or spent itself in the guttering embers of disillusion.

Prophet after prophet descended from their backwoods Sinais with the ghostly-graven tables of thou-shalts and thou-shalt-nots, set up their covenantal arks and led out their newly-chosen peoples toward the Canaans of the unfenced West. Feudal fortresses of their faiths were reared in the wilderness and the High Priest was also Lieutenant General of the Lord. One day he would stand in his rough-hewn temple, tell his people what they should believe and eat and wear, stanch sedition with fresh revelation and invoke divine destruction upon the oppressors of the righteous. Another day he would put aside his ephod and girdle and don the gorgeous uniform of his rank in the Holy Army to lead a sally against the Philistines besieging the log ramparts of this earthly Zion.

And whenever an outraged citizenry, surfeited with the proselyting of their kin, orgies of the synthetic sanctuary and the political meddling of an armed horde of zealots, despoiled the stronghold of the prophet, he would rally the faithful to resume the pilgrimage. Then either fanaticism yielded to weariness and hunger or took renewed impetus from persecution, consolidated the remnant and created new walls to protect the altar and once even carved a new State out of the Promised Land.

Even so it came to pass that upon the martyrdom of Joseph Smith, Jr., and the profane sacking of Nauvoo, his habitation of holiness in Illinois, were founded the creed of Mormonism, the Church of Jesus Christ of Latter-Day Saints, the Statehood of Utah and the Tabernacle on the shore of the Great Salt Lake.

Mormonism sprouted in the revival-singed soil of Seneca

County, Western New York, among an uncouth, unstable people pitifully eager for signs and wonders ever since the lesser fry of imitative doom dealers had imported jerks and trances from Kentucky and Tennessee. It had been planted there by a neurotic nomad, illiterate yet cunning, disposed to visions but a regulator of revelation to suit his own purposes.

Old Joe Smith happened to be at Sharon, Windsor County, Vermont, when young Joe was born, on December 23, 1805, the fourth of nine offspring accruing to a rather shiftless, wandering, visionary father and a mother who was the daughter of Solomon Mack, a soldier of the Revolution and a dreamer of profitable dreams wherein angels pointed the way to buried treasure to a generation glad to pay for such advice. Fantasy if little else draped the cradle of the newborn son.

The family was too much on the move to have many comforts or afford opportunity for more than the most rudimentary education of the children. But when it trekked into the Seneca revival belt it got its fill of intoxicating religion, the only social excitement of those who plowed the first furrows in the wake of the woodsmen. Both Josephs were soon steeped in the communal perturbation of Palmyra that even forgot its victuals in the ecstasy of protracted meetings. The Methodists were fervent and that was probably why young Joseph, at the age of fourteen, united with them. As he grew in body he became fluent in speech and the rural folk called him "slick" and "tonguey" as a prolific volunteer of "testimony."

Under the spell of his first "experience," Joseph Junior took to the woods one bright morning in the Spring of 1820 and while wrestling with the Lord in prayer had the first of his countless visions. Impenetrable darkness foreboding swift and sudden annihilation closed about him. In this very moment the heavens opened and Miracle No. 1 transpired.

"I saw a pillar of light exactly over my head, above the brightness of the sun, which descended gradually until it fell upon me," he said. "It no sooner appeared than I found myself delivered. . . . When the light rested upon me, I saw two personages, standing above me in the air. One of them spake unto me. . . . When I came to myself again, I found myself lying on my back looking up into heaven."

So declaimed the future First President, Prophet, Seer and Revelator of the Latter-Day Saints, the Messenger that was to receive and disclose the only authoritative communications from the Almighty in his day to the heirs of the Mormon salvation. And the hungrily listening primitives of Palmyra treasured this marvel against the day that Joseph the son of Joseph should call upon them to believe more and yet more.

Now Joseph waxed strong in his youth and became a mighty digger of wells. But he wasted none of the sweat of his brow. He soon mastered the mystery of the magic twig and set himself up as an oracle to tell others where to thrust in their shovels. From this he graduated into searching for hidden riches and then into the discovery of sacred relics. "Guided by a light from heaven," he turned up an odd stone which "showed me things beyond the ken of mortal men." And this prophetic rock sent him up the hill which must be Palmyra's glory forever.

It was there, Joseph Smith, Jr., informed the world, that in the Spring of 1830 he unearthed a volume of golden leaves inscribed with strange letters—"Reformed Egyptian" —and with them a pair of spectacles. "Urim and Thummim," by which the finder, though unlettered, could translate their recondite meaning. Behold the Book of Mormon!

This Moses came down the mountain and joined himself unto Aaron and together they compounded a new religion. But how much of it was of the mind of Joseph Smith, the Prophet, and how much the mind of the Rev. Sidney Rigdon, one-time Baptist parson of Warren, Ohio, nominated Counsellor and appointed amanuensis, never will be known. This much is certain: Rigdon, through personal acquaintance with a printer named Lambdin in Pittsburgh, had seen the copy of a story, entitled "Manuscript Found," waiting to be set up in type. The author was Solomon Spaulding, a graduate of Dartmouth College, an ex-clergyman widely read in Biblical literature and especially interested in archæology.

Spaulding migrated to Conneaut, Ohio, in 1809 and there, with the further inspiration of the Indian mounds of that State, wrote the religious romance, "Manuscript Found," in which he undertook to connect the American aborigines with the lost tribes of Israel. He recounted the wanderings of the "Nephites" and the "Lamanites," the names of "Nephi," "Lehi," "Jarom," and "Moroni," constantly recurring, and told how the record thereof had been graven on plates of *brass* which, in 420 A. D., had been sealed up and hidden in the Hill of Cumorah, near Palmyra, New York.

The odd names and quaint phrasing of the work distinctly impressed the neighbors to whom Spaulding read his unfolding narrative and the words "And it came to pass" were repeated so often that the community nicknamed him "Old Came-to-pass." The facts regarding the authorship of the book were attested by the sworn testimony of Spaulding himself, his wife, Martha, his brother,

John, his business partner, Henry Lake, and four others.

Two years before the Book of Mormon appeared, Sidney Rigdon, who had been associated with Alexander Campbell in the formation of the Christian (Campbellite) Church, told friends that a book, soon to be translated from *golden* plates, would bring about a religious revolution. Then came the Palmyra "discovery," and if there was any plagiarizing of Solomon Spaulding's "Manuscript Found," it was done with ceremony in the odor of sanctity. Night after night Joseph Smith, the Prophet, sat behind a curtain, peered through "Urim" and "Thummim," pored over the aureate pages alleged to repose in his care and droned the queer mixture of mellifluous ecclesiastical phraseology and native Yankee idiom which Saint Sidney transcribed for posterity.

It was not dogma—that was developed later in "The Book of Covenants" and "The Pearl of Great Price." It was just a quasi-historical narrative accredited to "Nephi," son of the "Prophet Mormon," accounting for the straying to America of one of the peoples who drew a language from the assortment bestowed upon the builders of the Tower of Babel, followed in the sixth century, B. C., by "Lehi" and his "Lamanites," the errant Israelites of the tribe that was lost. After His resurrection, the story continues, Christ came over and preached to the progeny of the far-scattered chosen seed. Then wars destroyed them and the Lord commanded Mormon to see that these events should be chronicled and the record hidden.

It was finished. The veil of the holy of holies was drawn aside and there sat Joseph with empty hands. The precious graven plates had vanished by levitation, he said. Lest anyone ever doubt their original existence, three men— Oliver Cowdrey, David Whitmer and Martin Harris—

came forward and swore they had seen them and though they afterward deserted the faith they never recanted the oath.

The spouse of Harris threw the first monkey-wrench into the godly gearing. This vixenish skeptic, enraged because Smith inveigled her husband into mortgaging his little farm to pay for printing three thousand copies of the Biblical Annex, purloined and secreted forever one hundred sixteen pages of Rigdon's momentous manuscript. There was no attempt at duplication inasmuch as the inspired translator would not venture trying to remember the missing words.

There was one other female fly in the holy ointment. This was "Servant Emma," the wife of Joseph the Prophet, a strong-minded woman who had her own reservations concerning the new religion. Even revelation failed to govern her. One of them enjoined her to "go easy." Another provided plural wives for Joseph. But Servant Emma was in no wise impressed. She did not need to be. Joseph believed in himself and that was enough for the possessor of Urim and Thummim.

For Urim was light and Thummim was Perfection in the Hebrew tongue and Aaron had worn them upon his heart when he went in before the Lord and it was written of old that when Saul, encamped at Gilboa before the Philistines, inquired of the Lord, the Lord answered him not, neither by dreams, nor by Urim, nor by prophets. Joseph knew his Scripture.

And what he did not know he readily improvised. He was at his best as a nomenclator. "Mormon" was doubtless original, but his son, "Nephi," might have been a corruption of "Nepheg," Hebraic for "offshoot," one of those begotten in Exodus. The "Lamanites" were apparently more Post-Revolution than Ante-Deluvian, but "Lehi" their leader borrowed his name from that place where Samson slew a thousand Philistines with the jawbone of an ass. And then "Urim and Thummim"—can it be that Joseph Smith imagined Aaron wearing spectacles when he "went in before the Lord"?

Such things did not occur to those revival-ridden venerators of the new revelation. Here was the Book. It was ordained of God. Here was the Prophet. He talked with God. And here was a revival which transcended all other revivals. For almost a year Seneca County endured it. Then the enemies it made drove out the Saints who "spake in tongues," chased eerie lights and played with holy fire.

Smith and Rigdon pitched camp at Kirtland, Ohio, erected a "temple" and built a "city" around it. Joseph got out his "peep-stones" and there ensued more apocalyptical unfolding. The magnetic Sidney went to preaching and "spirits" took possession of the devotees. Some prophesied and some "interpreted"; some writhed in fits and some swooned. Converts sank down inert as the elders "laid on hands." Seekers brought devils with them to be cast out and the Prophet unfailingly obliged.

Newell Knight was one of the first victims of Satanic sleight of hand. Smith found him with visage and limbs distorted and suffering much in his mind. "Finally, he was caught up off the floor of the apartment and tossed about most fearfully," the exorciser said. "I succeeded in getting hold of him by the hand, when almost immediately he spoke to me and with great earnestness required of me that I should cast the devil out of him, saying that he knew that he was in him and that he also knew I could cast him out.

"I replied, 'If you know that I can, it shall be done.' And then almost unconsciously I rebuked the devil and commanded him in the Name of Jesus Christ to depart from him, when immediately Newell spoke out and said that he saw the devil leave him and vanish from his sight."

Nine spectators were present but only Newell Knight saw the devil take his flight. Other infestations, celestial or infernal, were certainly atavistic. Young men and women were especially susceptible. An account of their antics is given in a letter written in Ohio in September, 1831, as follows:

"They would exhibit all the apish actions imaginable, making most ridiculous grimaces, creeping upon their hands and feet, rolling upon the frozen ground, going through all the Indian modes of warfare, such as knocking down, scalping, ripping open and tearing out the bowels.

"At other times they would run through the field, get up on stumps, preach to imaginary congregations, enter the water and perform all the ceremony of baptizing. Many would have fits of speaking all the different Indian dialects which none could understand.

"Again at the dead hour of the night, the young men might be seen running over the hills and fields in pursuit, as they said, of the balls of fire and lights which they saw moving through the atmosphere."

As for the "gift of tongues," another contemporary observer says: "Those who speak in tongues are generally the most illiterate among the 'saints,' such as cannot command words quick as they would wish, and instead of waiting for a suitable word to come to their memories, they break forth in the first sound their tongues can articulate no matter what it is.

"Thus some person in the meeting has told an inter-

esting story about Zion, then an excitable brother gets
up to bear his 'testimony,' the speed of speech increasing
with the interest of the subject:

"'Beloved brethren and sisters, I rejoice and my heart
is glad to overflowing—I hope to go to Zion, and to see
you all there and to—to—O, *me sontro von te, sontro
von terre, sontro von te. O, me palassate!*'"

This might be gibberish to the gentiles, but it was
sacred sound to the faithful. It defies analysis. The "von"
could be Germanic, the "te" and the "terre" Latiniform,
and the "sontro" and "palassate" Romanic. But these
were not words at all. They were a fortuitous liaison of
the elements of speech in a concatenation of euphonious
syllables,—the product of a fevered brain. In other instances fragments of Indian dialect have leaked into the
"speaking in tongues," but nothing beyond the previous
contacts of those given to the utterance of sonorous in-
tonations of Mormon sanctity.

The heathen of Ohio did not take kindly to such rites
and their animosity grew apace with the luring of adherents
from their midst. The final increment of their antagonism,
however, was the intrusion of the Prophet into business.
Smith's co-operative store undersold the traders of the
countryside and his bank raked in all the Mormon money.
After seven years of operation, the store failed and the
bank smashed. Neither calamity disturbed the faithful,
but their leaders pulled them out in the night one jump
ahead of the sheriff.

The next tarrying place was Far West, Missouri. Another temple went up and became the seat of a roaring revival that increased the fold to fifteen thousand and
resulted in open warfare in which the enraged Missourians
triumphed with heavier battalions. Smith broke jail and

lined out again toward the Promised Land, leading his harassed people up the Mississippi to the site of his greatest glory and his grave. On the marge of the river in Hancock County, Illinois, in 1838, rose his Nauvoo, a citadel of the faith and an independent parochial principality.

Church organization was perfected, Prophet Joseph surrounding himself with two Counsellors, twelve Apostles, "Seventies," High Priests, Elders, Bishops, Priests, Teachers and Deacons. Missionaries were sent afar and proselytes poured in from New England, the Middle States and even from Europe. Wealth came with numbers and then political prestige till the Mormons managed to teeter the balance of power in Illinois. Extraordinary terms were exacted from the State by which Smith attained to supreme military, civil, commercial and ecclesiastical authority within the domain of holy Nauvoo.

Fated to be hedged in by hatred because of their aggressive evangelism, exotic ritualism and alleged depredations, the Mormons formed a feudal army. Joseph Smith took the further title of Lieutenant Commander of the Nauvoo Legion—second only to the Lord of Hosts, Strong and Mighty in Battle—and when he donned his gold braid and epaulets, sash and plumes, no soldier in all time was ever arrayed like him. He glorified God in the Guard Mount and parades were as regular as prayer-meetings. And his special pride in all this religio-military splendor was a buxom squadron of Amazonian cavalry.

His brow was knit and his teeth were set as he took the salutes of the martial saints passing in review, but his eyes kindled and his face beamed when the Daughters of Zion galloped by. It was about this time that revelation first raised the limit on wives.

Joseph was in his heyday. He was gorged with power.

From ruling Nauvoo he had risen to domineer Illinois and even announced himself a candidate for President of the United States. Then he crossed trails with Peter Cartwright, the mighty Methodist circuiteer, and reached the full meridian of his ambition.

Journeying over to Springfield, "Uncle Joe," as the disbelievers called him, made a proposition to Peter. Conceding that among all the Churches in the world the Methodist, his earliest communion, was the nearest right as far as it went but had stunted itself by not claiming the gifts of tongues, revelation, prophecy and miracles guaranteed by Scripture, he proceeded:

"Now, Peter, if the Methodists would only advance a step or two further, they would take the world. We Latter-Day Saints are Methodists as far as they have gone, only we have advanced further, and if you would come in and go with us, we could sweep not only the Methodist Church but all the others and you would be looked up to as one of the Lord's greatest prophets. You would be honored by countless thousands, and have of the good things of this world all that heart could wish."

Peter was not to be tempted. Instead, revolted by what he designated as the "low cunning of this illiterate, impudent desperado in morals," he warmly contested Joseph's batches of Scriptural citation till the Prophet drew his mantle closer and shifted tactics. He mourned that in all ages the good and the right way had been "evil-spoken of" and he warned that it was "an awful thing to fight against God."

"If you will go with me to Nauvoo," he said, "I will show you many living witnesses that will testify that they were, by the saints, cured of blindness, lameness, dumbness and all the diseases that human flesh is heir to. And I will show you that we have the gift of tongues and can speak in unknown languages and that the saints can drink any deadly poison and it will not hurt them. Moreover, the idle stories you hear about us are nothing but sheer persecution."

Peter responded with what his experience had been with Mormons, how they had tried to break up his camp meetings and how he had been forced to throw them out with a threat of lynching. Uncle Joe's wrath boiled over. Cursing his adversary in the name of God of Mormon, Nephi and Lehi, he thundered:

"I will show you, sir, that I will raise up a government in these United States which will overturn the present government, and I will raise up a new religion that will overturn every other religion in this country!"

Treason was out. The sword of Mormon was unsheathed. War was declared. But Peter Cartwright mildly replied, saying, "Yes, Uncle Joe, but my Bible tells me 'the bloody and deceitful man shall not live out half his days,' and I expect the Lord will send the devil after you some of these days and take you out of the way."

"No, sir," bellowed the repository of Mormon righteousness, "I shall live and prosper while you will die in your sins."

"Well, sir," Cartwright concluded, "if you live and prosper, you must quit your stealing and your abominable whoredoms!"

Joseph Smith rode back to Nauvoo with a new resolution burning in his mind. Mormonism was now entered upon its conquest. Raids drew reprisals. Violence begot violence. Plundering, burning and murdering were laid to the zealots of Nauvoo where Mormonism was a law unto itself and legal redress for gentiles was impossible. The enemy was at the gates when disloyalty within started the First Prophet toward his downfall.

"General" J. C. Bennett put himself at the head of the rebels and in the one issue of his newspaper, *The Expositor,* on June 7, 1844, denounced the Prophet and promised to disclose his "misdeeds and immoralities." Smith destroyed the press and was freed of a riot charge by one of his own magistrates. A warrant for treason was issued at Carthage and the Sixth Cavalry of the Illinois Militia was sent to Nauvoo to serve it.

The Lieutenant Commander led out his Legion. It was civil war. Skirmish lines were already in contact when the Governor of the State with pledges of safe-conduct and a fair trial induced Smith to surrender and go to the Carthage jail. This was on June 26. The next day a mob attacked the prison, dragged out Joseph and his brother Hyrum and shot and killed them.

Death had sealed the lips of the first Mormon Mouthpiece of Heaven, but the revelation did not cease. The smoke of the Carthage firing squad had hardly cleared away when another native of Vermont, Brigham Young, Chief of the Quorum of Apostles, came forth to save the Saints. Born on a farm at Whitingham, Windham County, on June 1, 1801, brought up a Baptist and a painter and glazier, he migrated to Kirtland, Ohio, where a laying-on of hands in 1832 admitted him to the priesthood of Melchizedek. His genius as a Scriptural expositor and convert-winning exhorter kept him changing vestments till the mantle of the Prophet fell on his shoulders.

Within a year Brigham had the Mormon Ark again jolting over the plains toward the Land of Canaan. Leaving the main camp at Council Bluffs, Iowa, in the Spring of 1847, he went on ahead with a vanguard of one hundred forty-three and explored the wilderness. On July 24, 1847, he drove the "center-stake" of faith in the Valley of the Great Salt Lake. "Deseret" he named it, which in the mystic tongue of "Reformed Egyptian" meaneth "Land of the Honey-Bee." And so the long-wandering followers of the Word of Nephi at last entered into their inheritance. The ark came to rest in a Tabernacle in the midst of the city that rose on the shore of the saline sea.

The spirit of Joseph Smith lived on. His successor shaped a State in 1849 and declared himself its Governor in defiance of the National Congress which had profanely presumed to substitute "Utah" for "Deseret" and demote it to a Territory. Then in 1852 he confirmed Joseph's plurality of wedlock with a ukase proclaiming polygamy as the celestial law of marriage. Washington ultimately won, but not until more than a thousand Mormons went to jail, millions of dollars in fines were paid for violation of the Federal statute forbidding more than one wife, and the Church, in 1890, reversed itself by revelation.

Meantime Utah had been populated and was blooming like the Garden of Eden. Brigham Young, with the aid of twenty-one wives, contributed forty-eight descendants and on his own initiative discovered alfalfa to the world. He also introduced woman suffrage as a matter of political expediency. But he kept the helpmeets in their places. That is, all save one, Eliza Ann Webb, his No. 19, who divorced him "because she liked nice things," started to "expose" Mormonism and caused his prosecution for polygamy in 1871. He was not convicted. On August 29, 1877, he gave up the ghost and left an estate of one million six hundred twenty-six thousand, five hundred ten dollars, eight cents.

Under the successors of Brigham Young the Mormon

theocracy has been firmly established by adherence to the belief that the church was founded by messengers sent from heaven, all of them seers and revelators. The modern Mormon explains that "God has come in person and spoken to our prophet," the revelations being obtained through "dreams of sleep or in waking visions of the mind or by voices without visional appearance or by actual manifestations of the Presence before the eye."

Expedient corrections have also been revealed with the passage of years and one of the most recent is the edict of 1925 regarding the undergarments of the saints. Joseph Smith got it direct from the Throne that such clothing should leave only the head, hands and feet exposed and should be fastened to the body with strings. B.V.D.'s made no headway in Utah till the new dispensation permitted shorter lingerie and buttons. And then there was a riot in the Tabernacle.

A meeting of ten thousand churchmen assembled in October, 1927, to sustain the underwear revelation was startled by the entry of one Paul Feil, aged fifty, according to the Associated Press, who marched down the grand aisle waving banners and heralding "a message for Israel."

"I plead guilty to delivering a message of peace from God," Paul told the judge who gave him a suspended sentence of five days in jail for disturbing the very peace he sought to bring. He had taken exception to the order of the Church authorities altering shirts, drawers and union suits "because God is unchanging and could not have permitted this deviation from the established custom."

Paul was a throw-back to the olden times when Elder Kimball wrote in his Journal: "I could distinctly see the evil spirits who foamed and gnashed their teeth upon us —we gazed upon them an hour and a half" and when

Elder Hyde fought a whole host of demons who "nearly choked him to death." His brethren had come a long way from the hill of Palmyra and the day of the first Prophet's excavations. The new religion had come through to permanence, regularity and respectability.

But for this one that was successful, scores of others were buried with the avatars of their faith in the wilds of the early West. Always it was the apostolic incentive that led them forth. Always it was the Messianic complex. And one of those that failed deserves to be remembered with the Moses of the Mormons.

It was Abel Sargent, who went out from Morgantown, Virginia, to the neighborhood of St. Clairsville, Ohio, in 1812 with a brand new revelation through which he said he held converse with the angels and was made the Almighty's medium of communication with the world. He roamed about the country with his twelve apostles, mostly women, pretending to heal the sick and raise the dead.

Abel did not believe in any devil or judgment or hell, but proclaiming the annihilation of the wicked, taught that the regenerated soul was part of God and that when the body died was reabsorbed into God. One of his followers finally claimed too much for him and set him to a feat that ended his career. The disciple insisted that the prophet could fast as long as Christ did,—forty days and forty nights. Abel betook himself to a hilltop while his devotees ringed the base in a circle of constant prayer. They ate but he did not. No food could reach him through their impregnable watch of faith.

Day after day the incantations at the foot of the hill waxed stronger and stronger while Abel on the mount, chanting the antiphonal responses, grew weaker and weaker. On the sixteenth morning his voice ceased altogether. He was breathing his last when the twelve apostles reached his side.

But Abel's flock were not yet satisfied. He had told them that he would resuscitate himself after three days. So they laid his body on a bier in the middle of the camp and hundreds thronged in from miles around to behold the miracle.

The appointed time passed. One of the apostles got a revelation and made an extension to three times three days. Gradually vociferous prayer and song gave way to mourning and in turn grief yielded to disappointment and disillusion. The curious deserted first, and then the adherents themselves. At the last the twelve apostles of Abel had to bury him.

If only there had been a spring of water and clump of berry bushes on the summit of that Ohio hill there might have descended the founder of a new church, the settler of a State, the builder of a tabernacle to stand as a monument to his name and memory.

## CHAPTER XII

## THE SECOND COMING

We are pilgrims looking home,
Sad and weary off we roam,
But we know 'twill all be well, in the morning;
When our anchor's firmly cast,
Every stormy wave has past,
And we gather safe at last, in the morning.
                                        Old Adventist hymn.

GROTESQUE silhouettes smudged the stark white walls of the low-ceilinged tent under the dim and streaking light of half a dozen smoky lamps of brass. Twenty rows of New Hampshire farmers, woodsmen and millhands with their wives and sons and daughters were gazing ever so earnestly over the two vacant settees in front of them toward the slight little figure on the platform of creaking planks laid on sawhorses. At his left a woman was half turned round on a stool behind a diminutive organ. One of his hands was uplifted in a gesture of beckoning; the other rested upon an open Bible, most of its pages bulked to one side the center. He had said he must "prove all things." He had preached through from Genesis to Revelation.

These were the last days. Prophecy had been fulfilled. The Seven Seals would soon be broken. And the Son of Man would come to sit in the morning of the Judgment. "My brother, are you ready? My sister, are you ready? This may be the last night of all. Before dawn you may stand before your God!" The preacher's black hair was stringing down over his burning eyes. His thin face was alight. In a gentle voice he pleaded—"Come kneel and pray with me to the Jesus who is coming!"

Davis the evangelist had given the Adventist invitation in the tent he had pitched by the wayside in the Centre Ossipee of only a few years ago. Where he came from did not matter. It was the word he was bringing. Methodists and Congregationalists sat there before him—and here and there one of his own faith left over from revivals long ago —night after night within the walls of canvas. Not a few would pray with him, all would sing with him, and some would rise with a testimony of Christian belief. But of converts none is remembered. The revival departed much as it came. None questioned whither it went. Its message is still a theme for winter firesides—the persistence of the hope of almost a hundred years.

It was found in the Eighth Chapter of the Book of Daniel in the Holy Writ which said:

"Then I heard one saint speaking, and another saint said unto that certain saint which spake, How long shall be the vision concerning the daily sacrifice, and the transgression of desolation, to give both the sanctuary and the host to be trodden under foot?

"And he said unto me, Unto two thousand and three hundred days; then shall the sanctuary be cleansed.

"And it came to pass, when I, even I Daniel, had seen the vision, and had sought for the meaning, then, behold, there stood before me as the appearance of a man.

"And I heard a man's voice between the banks of Ulai, which called, and said, Gabriel, make this man to understand the vision.

"So he came near where I stood: and when he came, I

was afraid, and fell upon my face: but he said unto me, Understand, O son of man: for at the time of the end shall be the vision."

These were the words that William Miller, farmer, sheriff, soldier, and lay preacher, pondered for two years till he concluded in 1818 that Daniel's two thousand three hundred days were two thousand three hundred years, beginning with Ezra's going up to Jerusalem in 457 B. C., computed that 1843 would be the last of them and decided that the "cleansing of the sanctuary" at the "end" meant the moment when time would be no more and Christ would come in person to judge all who had ever lived the while the world disintegrated beneath their feet.

Unusual was the man who reached so remarkable a conclusion. He was born on a farm at Pittsfield, Massachusetts, on February 15, 1782, the son of Captain William Miller, a soldier of the Revolution, and Paulina Phelps, whose father was the Rev. Elnathan Phelps, a Baptist minister. The Millers settled in Low Hampton, Washington County, New York, in 1786. The heir to military and theological leanings educated himself by reading books bought with wood-chopping money. On June 29, 1803, he married Lucy Smith of Poultney, just over the line in Vermont, and went to farming there. Continuing his habit of reading, he browsed through Voltaire, Paine, Hume, and Ethan Allen and became a Deist.

The philosophical farmer was elected sheriff of Rutland County in 1809 and chosen captain of a company of Vermont volunteers in the War of 1812. He fought in the battle of Plattsburgh, September 11, 1814, and stayed in the Army till the following summer. Then he returned to Low Hampton, was drawn into a Baptist revival in 1816, recanted his Deism, plunged into Jordan and emerged dripping with zeal to search the Scriptures as an antidote to the "Age of Reason." All the evangelists had been preaching that Christ would come. William Miller wanted to know *when*.

No rabbi ever eyed the Sacred Scrolls more closely, no chronologist ever applied himself more diligently than the ruminant William Miller in his quest to close the calendar. He was scrupulously honest about it. He had no recourse to special inspiration, miracles or magic. His research was concentrated upon the one Book. From its literal word he made his discovery. It satisfied him. It grew upon him till it ruled his mind to the exclusion of everything else. For what signified any material thought or thing with the end of the world in sight?

The Millennium was at hand and no one knew it but William Miller. He could not keep the tidings to himself. Here was the whole human race to be saved and only twenty-five years remained. He began with his neighbors at Low Hampton and soon yearned to tell all he could before the trumpet of Gabriel should blow. In 1831 he proclaimed the Second Advent to a startled meeting of thirteen sizable families at Dresden, New York, and in the week's revival that followed only two persons failed to be converted. In 1833 he was licensed a Baptist preacher but, beyond adherence to immersion, he did not stay Baptist long enough to be ordained. That same year he nailed his thesis by the issuance of a pamphlet entitled "Evidence from Scripture and History of the Second Coming of Christ About the Year 1843 and of His Personal Reign for One Thousand Years."

He set his feet on the open road and behind him began the march of the Millerites toward the Millennium. His travels took him through New England, New York, New

Jersey, Philadelphia, Washington and Canada. The very ground burned beneath him.

Creeds and confessions were consumed by the new faith of fire. No revival had ever offered so much before. None had been so definite, so peremptory. Methodists and Baptists, Presbyterians and Congregationalists were among those who deserted altars that seemed to lose their foundations. "Hardened sinners" who had been adamant to all manner of pleading till now yielded to the awful fear of the Judgment. Thousands upon thousands trembled before the imminence of the Great Day and then rejoiced in the glorious Expectation.

To the hard and fast in the old denominations it was a subversive separatist scheme of a fanatic; to Miller it was the inclusive divine plan to save them all. The first distinctly Millerite Church was probably the one formed by the sixty converts of his revival in Lowell, Massachusetts. Thence he went to Weston where one parson swung over to him for "shaking the supremacy of various forms of error rife in the community." The Second Advent forthwith was conclusively corrective.

From October, 1839, to April, 1841, Miller figured that he travelled four thousand five hundred sixty miles, preached six hundred twenty-seven "lectures" (he did not call them "sermons") of one and a half hours each and achieved five thousand conversions. While he ranged the Atlantic Seaboard, exhorters rose from the ranks of his converts and roved Westward with the message to Indiana, Ohio and Illinois. Some ministers forsook their pulpits to spread the word that had been impressed upon them. And every believer was an ardent missionary, fortified with argument and convinced of the need to "save" everyone he met before it was "too late."

But the progress was not peaceful. The Millerites themselves were in a constant ferment. The cleavage cut across
communities, churches, families. The hour was nearing
when this one would be rescued, that one would be damned
forever. Outside the pale the disbelievers scoffed and jeered.
Rumbling mobs besieged the holy places where the final
warning was being sounded. An egg sped through an open
window of a hall in Boston and spattered the rostrum.
Miller paused long enough for a however and a comma and
resumed the story of how the sheep and goats would be
divided, raising his voice above the hooting of the hellions.
He was told to leave the city. Volleys of stones shattered
every pane of glass in the building where he spoke at Newburyport but with his people Miller prayed for the "perishing ones" who threw them.

Many doors were closed to the "End-of-the-World
Man," as Miller came to be nicknamed. For two weeks no
home would shelter him and his preaching partner, Joshua
Vaughn Himes, in New York City and they had to sleep
on the bare floor of Apollo Hall on Broadway which they
hired at their own expense. Cot beds were supplied after
the converts began to be counted by the hundred.

The last of June, 1842, Miller borrowed from the
Methodists and initiated at East Kingston, New Hampshire,
the Adventist camp-meeting in this country. It was a
hazardous experiment, for the "Cainites," as the Millerites
dubbed their foes, had a larger opportunity for riotous
mischief and even pitched battle out in the open. The defenders, however, had no objection to fighting for their
cause till the last hour struck. They showed the hard-
hitting quality of their devotion on the camp ground at
Chicopee Falls, Massachusetts, that summer.

The Millerites were led in the fray by Hiram Munger,

an ex-millhand, born in Monson, Massachusetts, September 27, 1806, who had originally got religion from the Methodists and had learned how to deal heroically with ruffians at their camp-meetings. He was still a praying, shouting, singing Methodist when the Millerites came to Chicopee Falls and occupied the Wesleyan Gospel quadrangle. Left behind as caretaker, he joined the rush to the altar of Joshua Himes and switched to the hosts that were standing by for the Second Coming.

Munger squared off with the leader of the rowdies and boxed him to a standstill. The Cainites thereupon retreated. But they returned during another week, tore down the tent of the revivalists and got into their wagons and made the holy night hideous with obscene song. Munger hurled them one by one out of the coach to his aides below who tied them up and prayed for them. It was too much for the enemy, who departed and let the world roll on to its destruction.

Millerite conversions made Munger right at home. They were often primordially Methodistic. Down fell the sinners under the conviction laid upon them. Ten lay prostrate on a kitchen floor through a night till the bell rang in the morning. A young woman heaved over backwards in a cottage revival and shook the dwelling as her head cracked upon a doorsill. Four days and nights she was stretched out stiff and lifeless. Then she arose and upbraided those who were watching for their failure to appreciate God's slaying of the body to subdue its sinful pride. She admitted being conscious all the time, only waiting for the divine will to have its way with her.

At a camp meeting in Palmer, Mass., Brother King S. Hastings prayed for one solid hour and scores were knocked to the ground. A girl reeled momentarily to her feet and pointed a finger at a mocker. He dropped as if shot. Moans in the woods led Munger and Hastings to the side of a "suffering" sister. They diagnosed her trouble promptly, applied prayer and liberated her from her woes.

Himes was camp meeting entrepreneur par excellence in heralding the crack of doom. No circus of his day stretched more canvas. At Concord, New Hampshire, his center pole was fifty-five feet high and under the big top of his tabernacle four thousand at a time heard the harbinger of approaching earthly dissolution. This same tent was raised for seven tremendous days at Newark, New Jersey, and then at Philadelphia where, Himes said, "the wicked and the backsliders quaked and the word of the Lord was glorified." He pulled up stakes and travelled westward, making stands at Rochester, soon afterward to be the scene of the "rappings" of the famous Fox sisters, at Buffalo and Cincinnati. All the way the alarm was sounded and converts made converts in what was to be the last revival.

It was in the Chardon Street Chapel of Himes in Boston that the Message got its start in the Athens of America and gave rise to boisterous antics which the Millerites themselves discountenanced. Himes, a Methodist evangelist from Wickford, Rhode Island, met Miller at Exeter, New Hampshire, on November 11, 1839, delivered his Boston chapel to the prophesier and became his chief disciple. He edited the "Signs of the Times," the first Adventist paper, and published more tracts and pamphlets than any other of his faith. But in his preaching in the transformed Chapel of Chardon Street he had sore trials to contend with.

There was overmuch assistance from the testifying laity. One of these was John Starkweather, wished on Himes as Associate Exhorter. John had a reputation for superior sanctity and was insistent upon signs of grace working in the converts. For him they had to shake and shout and fall in fits. This he denominated the "sealing power." A youth, touched by the Starkweatherian impress, tried commanding a railroad train to stand still but the wheels kept on moving. A young woman essayed walking on the water but the faithful would not let her take the rôle of Peter. All of this Himes declared unseemly in the days before the End. And Starkweather split the congregation and hoisted his own strange banner of salvation.

To Starkweather's lone altar, reared against the Day as he conceived it, came one Silas Lamson, known as the "White Quaker," because of his white attire from hat and shoes to umbrella, frequent inmate of asylums, who delighted in being jailed for disturbing any kind of holy concourse. Lamson promptly found a welcome. All one day he ranted and on into the second till his voice gave out entirely. Then Abby Folsom, his counterpart in Eden, spelled him till he could resume his chameleonic filibuster. While they alternated in variegated oratory, others tried to break in with words they fain would utter and one Lemuel Tompkins created a diversion by whirling like a dervish and grunting like a pig.

Pushing through the crowds upon the sidewalk, the owner of the building strode into the midst of the turmoil and beheld a sight to make the angels weep. Tompkins was wooshing and snozzling as he spun a winding circuit. Sister Abby was reciting at the top of her shrill voice from a tattered scrap-book. The "White Quaker" was booming excerpts from the "Flying Roll," his autobiography extraordinary. Starkweather was howling in the pulpit. And half a hundred of his votaries were enjoying mesmeric ecstasies. The landlord was bewildered, his sense of decency

affronted. The tenants were ejected and Brother Starkweather decamped to parts unknown.

No other such prodigy disquieted the proclaiming of the
Kingdom drawing nigh. Still the Elders looked to wonders
when they joined themselves with Miller. The stars that
fell in the sky above New York City on the night of
November 13, 1833, were a sign of the fulfillment to
S. S. Brewer who became the laureate of the prophecy. He
was of the Methodist tradition and his verses, inexhaustible,
poured from a soul that was full of vision. One of the
seventeen stanzas of his "Jerusalem" unfolds the flower of
his verse:

> Jerusalem, Jerusalem,
> Foretold by prophets long,
> The new creation's diadem,
> The bride of sacred song.
> Jehova is thine architect,
> The mighty God above;
> There with our great Melchizedek
> The saints ere long will rove.

Another Methodist come-outer was R. E. Ladd, a baker
of Springfield, Massachusetts. He peddled bread and Millerite religion from door to door. Vermont contributed
three notables to the hortatory band—Elon Galusha, the
eagle-eyed Shaftsbury lawyer whom the Baptists expelled
for lending his eloquence to Miller; Elder Charles P. Dow,
who unlike his kinsman, Lorenzo ("Crazy") Dow, the
early Methodist itinerant, deplored excitement and importuned serenity as befitting the assurance of the saved,
and D. T. Taylor, a schoolmaster whose preaching survived every date for destruction and produced four thousand sermons in twenty-eight years.

There were women warners too. Miss M. S. Higgins of

Maine went after sinners as a "public duty" and reinforced her evangelizing with the gift of song. She married Elder D. R. Mansfield and together they organized
twenty churches in Indiana. Miss Elzira Armstrong of
Westfield, New York, considered herself one of the last
brides when in 1841 she was yoked with Elder O. R. Fas-
sett, but they lived and preached far beyond the prophecy.
And Mrs. Lucy M. Hersey dismissed her pupils in Worcester, Massachusetts, when the Lord called her to admonish
sinners that the duration of mercy was almost over.

These are but a few of the scores of lesser revivalists
who helped Miller make most of this country aware of one
year in all history whether to accept it as the last or to
scorn the prophet and his prediction. With the exception
of the Eastern Shore of Maryland, to this day a fertile
revival region, the South was impervious despite the
solemn pleadings of George Storrs, the Lebanon, New
Hampshire, Yankee. The West, already familiar with
strong evangelizing and always eager for more, fervidly
prepared to meet the Lord under the tutelage of such exhorters as Dr. Nathaniel Field, the Indiana physician-
preacher.

Out on the high road, shoulder to shoulder with Miller
as 1842 was dying and the fateful 1843 was being ushered
in were the giants of the prophetic hour—Himes, with a
beard like Aaron's, Munger, the chin-whiskered com-
batant of the Cainites, and Luther Boutelle, whose benign
countenance, creased from smiling, bespoke his gentle persistence.

Boutelle was a native of Townsend, Massachusetts, the
son of a pious Congregationalist deacon who named
Luther's brothers Calvin and Ebenezer. Miller converted

him. He felt the inevitable "call." And he started for Grafton, Vermont, with only a penny in his pocket. Providence and his own talent for persuasion got him a horse and buggy.

A storm snowed in his meeting house but again there was intervention. A long team of oxen dragging a sled made a good path for miles right up to the door of the church. Boutelle played on the heart-strings of those Vermonters and when he asked them to go forward with him into the Kingdom, every pew was a mercy seat. Some of them went forth as preachers with the revival watchword —"Behold He cometh!" Boutelle was just beginning. All New England heard him.

Down in profane Park Row of New York City, where the presses of the heathen rolled out daily grists of ridicule Himes took up the challenge. For twenty-four days his "Midnight Cry" ran editions of ten thousand out into the sinful streets and into the mails to spread afar the word of warning, the refutation of reviling. For the sunsets now were numbered. Thus spake William Miller. And he had the Scripture with which to prove it.

Miller spurred rapidly from place to place. Now he was in New Hampshire asking who was on the Lord's side, now in Massachusetts; now he was in New Haven, Connecticut, taking leave till all should meet to part no more and again in Utica, New York. It was the first religious farewell tour. Thousands hung upon his words and when he left all who could fell upon his neck and embraced him. In one city the rum sellers emptied out their wares and turned their bar-rooms into sanctuaries. All the while the Opposition, blind to prophecy but far from voiceless, kept pace in rival pulpits and denominational papers.

But Miller and his preaching cohorts, his tireless pamphleteers and argumentative adherents answered shot for shot in the holy warfare.

Epochs started rolling toward a succession of finalities. Miller conditioned all predictions with an "IF" he had calculated things correctly. He gave to Gabriel a generous leeway for the sounding of the reveille. The trumpet could blow any time between March 21, 1843 and March 21, 1844. But his followers pressed for dates more definite. There must be a Day. Their vigil must have a goal.

After the tranquil passing of March 21, 1843, the first venture in the last year to trig the wheels of time was on April 14, hallowed by two Biblical anniversaries, the Passover and the Crucifixion. Solicitude was only deepened when the Millerites found they had to wait a little longer. All through the summer farms, shops and offices were neglected while galvanic camp meetings, East, West and North, corralled lost sheep for the millennial pasture.

Houses of the Coming Lord in large cities and in the smallest hamlets maintained day after day a continuous threnody for the unsaved. And from streams and ponds innumerable emerged those who had been prepared to face the Judgment. Up in Boston a huge tabernacle seating five thousand was hastily thrown together—it did not have to last long—in Howard Street upon the site of a future temple devoted to scantily-attired burlesque and vulgar vaudeville. The text of the dedication sermon, preached by the ex-Presbyterian Silas Hawley, Jr., reflected the mood of the Millerites. It was from Ezekiel, Chapter XXI, Verse 27: "I will overturn, overturn, overturn it; and it shall be no more, until he come whose right it is; and I will give it him."

Toward the Fall the South awoke to the danger of

greeting eternity unrepentant and urgent calls for preachers poured in from the Carolinas, Georgia, Virginia, Tennessee and Missouri, where the "Midnight Cry," now a weekly, and the "Signs of the Times" had been circulating. Pleas came from England too, for every ship had been taking the printed word across the ocean. The predictions were translated into French and German and the warning even penetrated Asia.

A complete library of the Second Coming appeared in seven volumes with diagrams and chronological charts embellishing the lectures of Miller and the sermons of his computating collaborator, the ex-Methodist Elder Josiah Litch of New England. A new hymnology sang of the resurrected dead, the Judgment and the ten-century reign of Christ in such collections as "Millennial Musings," "The Advent Harp," "Jubilee Hymns," "The Christian Lyre" and "The Second Advent Minstrel."

The year of 1843 waned. It had been fruitful for Miller but it was the wrong one. He discovered that he had mixed the Jewish and Roman calendars. There could be no doubt about 1844. In February, after saying good-bye to New York and Philadelphia, he tried to convince Washington that there would be no election. It was his last stand before the world should come to an end on the twenty-first of March.

Revivals by the hundred throughout the "dying" nation pointed toward the finish. They were all one in awful solemnity and tremendous expectation. At the doors the last-minute sinners in a frenzy of affrighted excitement wailed for their redemption while the skeptics volleyed their derision. The sun rose upon the twenty-second of March. There was a hiatus of disappointment. Miller from his farm in Low Hampton wrote to Himes on March 25 of uncertainty whether to warn the people any more and on May 2 addressed an epistle to believers saying: "I confess my error and acknowledge my disappointment; yet I still believe the day of the Lord is near, even at the door, and I exhort you to be watchful." On May 31 "Father" Miller mounted the rostrum in the tabernacle at Boston and repeated his confession to the Annual Conference. The revival fire burned low.

Then one Elder S. S. Snow made a discovery. This was the "tarrying time" and the "true midnight cry" would be heard on the tenth day of the seventh Jewish month, which would be on October 22. Elder George Storrs on September 24 declared that that day would witness Christ in the clouds of heaven. On October 11, Miller accepted the date and on October 16 the "Advent Herald" gave away its "last" edition. The revival resumed and this time the Millerites despoiled themselves of every earthly thing in anticipation of harps and wings and haloes.

At a camp meeting in Wallingford, Connecticut, great piles of money—every cent the faithful had—were placed upon tables in front of the preaching stand. Anyone could have it that wanted it but the people were so sure they would never need it again it remained untouched. A girl amazed the throng by speaking in "several unknown tongues" for four and a half hours. She had always been bashful before. It was concluded that this was a positive sign. After this the baptisms multiplied and many came out of the water shouting.

In Newington, Connecticut, scoffers pelted Elder King Hastings with apples, dismantled his wagon and scattered it over the camp ground. This was persecution, another sign.

Elder Luther Boutelle journeyed to Boston where he

found a company who had vowed not to separate till the
Lord did come. He advised them to go about their work.
But everywhere the Millerites ceased all secular business
for the final ten days. Elder Sylvester Bliss, the cool-headed
ex-Congregationalist from Connecticut, the biographer of
Miller, wrote that it was a period "of great calmness of
mind and pleasurable expectation on the part of those who
regarded the point of time with interest." The devout, he
added, "gave themselves to the preparation for the event
as they would for death were they on a bed of sickness
expecting soon to close their eyes on earthly scenes forever."

That may have been the way the philosophical con-
templated the Advent, but not the rest of the forty thousand who scanned the sky at the zero hour.

The Philadelphian Millerites donned flowing white
muslin ascension robes and repaired to two big tents outside the city. Western zealots are reported to have climbed
trees and windmills. Night-gown roof parties were held
in New England. The Boston tabernacle housed scenes
more dramatic and more startling than ever were enacted
upon the stage of the theater that later was erected there.
In the sheerest of spotless garments the ecstatic throng sang
the requiem of the world.

In the rural regions crops were left unharvested. A few
devoted souls in the town of Tuftonboro, New Hampshire,
gave away all they possessed and stood empty-handed on a
hill looking out over Lake Winnepesaukee for the heavens
to be rent. The next winter they were fed by neighbors
who had been "unbelievers."

Through the night of termination the faithful forty
thousand waited. With the dawn the hope of many faltered. And to all it was apparent that definiteness had

spelled its own defeat. Miller simply said human chronology was defective and comforted the wavering with the assurance that after all "He yet would come." And so the remnant held together, patiently enduring the country-wide taunts of "When are you going up?" and "What will you take for your ascension robes now?"

In the hour of disillusion new leaders, not like the honestly mistaken William Miller, sprouted like so much poisonous fungus. Some set new dates and one, Joseph Turner of Maine, announced that Christ had come spiritually as a bridegroom, that the wise virgins (his followers) had gone in with Him to the marriage feast and that the door was shut behind them.

Turner, a man of infectious mesmeric power, persuaded a considerable number to adopt his theory in New England and New York. Elder Snow, who was responsible for the October 22 fiasco, pre-empted Turner's notion and set himself up as "Elijah the Prophet," damning all who would not believe him. Turner's sect practised feet-washing and kissing as enjoined by Scripture and professed to be immortal within the Kingdom that had come.

Out of Maine came two more "shut-door" apostles, man and wife, Elder James White and his bride, Ellen Harmon of Gorham. James was but an acolyte. Ellen was the prophet. A rock flung at her head in her childhood had flattened her nose and given her a penchant for visions. Sometimes she gazed in upon heaven; more often she peeped upon rebels or rivals in divers acts of secret sinning. Three diminuendo cries of "Glory!" brought on her trances from which she drew revelations ranging from keeping Saturday as the Sabbath to establishing a vegetarian diet and prescribing lined pants for her female adorers. She kept James busy writing down and publish-

ing her various visions till one of them informed him he
soon would die and he obliged. Ellen lived on to domineer
her sect even to the day of her death in 1915 at the age
of eighty-eight. In her prime she founded and lost a
Battle Creek sanitarium that made corn palatable as a
breakfast food and she amassed and dissipated a moderate
fortune.

But neither Ellen nor James White—none of the ilk of
Turner—can be counted with the direct line of the in-
heritors of Miller, who profited by his experience and
evolved a simple, straightforward faith that would stand
the test of limitless time.

Father Miller wrote his candid "Apology and Defense"
and his followers accepted the principles they shared with
him when they took the name of Adventists and organized
their church in 1845. The Biblical prophecies were held
intact; the attempt to fix a day of fulfillment was regarded
as an inevitable error; and the entire future was declared
the "tarrying time" with the coming of the Lord always
imminent. The urgency of immediate repentance was preserved as the evangelizing force of Adventism. For the
dead were believed to be sleeping till the Judgment morn
when they would rise and with the living learn their fate
forever more.

Once more the presses turned, the itinerants went forth
and the Adventist revival became as incessant as the Methodist—indeed surpassing it in later days because every
Adventist pastor was his own evangel and concluded
every service with an invitation to the penitent. Father
Miller preached until he died in 1849 at the age of sixty-
seven. Elder Joshua Himes, the Jonathan to David, was
among the missionaries to Europe and the founder of three
hundred pastorates in America during his ministry of forty

years. And Elder Luther Boutelle lived on into the nineties planting Adventist camp meetings all over the East.

The greatest permanent Gospel ground that Elder Boutelle helped to establish was dedicated in 1863 on the shores of Alton Bay on Lake Winnespesaukee in New Hampshire. It has been the faith's most strategic spot. Every year New Englanders are still being converted on the wooded plateau and led down the slope to be dipped in the waters which the Indians of old called the "Smile of the Great Spirit."

CHAPTER XIII

GARNERING BY IMMERSION

Savior! Thy dying love
Thou gavest me;
Nor should I aught withhold,
Dear Lord, from Thee.
In love my soul would bow,
My heart fulfill its vow,
Some offering bring Thee now,
Something for Thee.
                              Baptismal Hymn.

THROUGHOUT their long history the Baptists have been overflowing with their message. John Bunyan languished a dozen years in Bedford Jail for persisting in preaching the faith that drove Roger Williams out of the Colony on Massachusetts Bay, where the Pilgrims landed for "freedom to worship God," and into the arms of fortunately friendly Indians on the Narragansett shore. "What cheer?" a feathered chieftain shouted from the rocky marge where some day Providence should stand and come to know a laundry by his very words. And the zealous exile might have answered in a voice the wooded hills re-echoed—"Repent and be baptized!"

But the Reverend Roger did not dip his own flock or his aboriginal brethren till eight years later when, returning from a voyage to England in 1644, he brought over the Scriptural interpretation prescribing consecration by

immersion. Ever after, from icy stream to marble bap-
tistery, in this way the faith was signified by all Baptists,
Particular or General, Primitive or Free-Will, Seventh-
Day or Separatist. And others followed them into the
water. The Methodists permitted it. The Adventists,
Campbellites and Pentcostalites required it. But it was the
Baptists who led the way through Jordan.

Roger Williams was a Particular Baptist, of the hyper-
Calvinist branch that had been almost overwhelmed by
the Arminian General Baptists when Jonathan Edwards
and George Whitefield, neither of them Baptists, achieved
a triumph for Calvinism in the Great Awakening. From
this revival the Particulars had a resurgence of strength,
centering in their Philadelphia Association, formed in
1752, that swept southward into the Carolinas and northward into New England and won over the Separatist
churches set up by the satellites of Whitefield.

Though they benefited by the revivaling of others, the
Baptists themselves, with the exception of the ardent Free-
Will family, looked askance at all human efforts to re-
generate man as presumptuous and inconsistent with the
supreme sovereignty of the God of Calvin. It was reasoned for almost a century that the salvation of sinners
was determined by divine electing grace, that mortal
efforts were needless and useless and that the true power
and glory of the Baptist Church lay in "being still."

Towards 1830 the calm waters began to be rippled.
Baptist pastors started going beyond their pulpits. Then
the evangelists emerged from among them and the flood
tide rolled in and wet the feet of the Canutes of the Baptist communion. Jacob Knapp and Jabez Swan let it loose
and kept it flowing for fifty years. Knapp converted
one hundred thousand souls. Swan waded in and baptized

ten thousand with his own hands. They were followed and assisted by such gifted and courageous men as Emerson Andrews, George Benedict, J. H. Chamberlain, A. C. Kingsley, Lewis Raymond and A. B. Earle. But Knapp and Swan were the first to override the "arch-heresy of lethargy" and evangelize the immersionist creed.

The two great garnerers went at it about the same time and ran a holy race for souls. For the most part they ranged different routes but on several occasions they proved real yoke-fellows in preaching from the same pulpit. Both were plain-speaking individualists with rough-and-ready Yankee characteristics that made them appear eccentric. James Gordon Bennett's New York "Herald" struck them off in this contrast:

"Knapp was a short little fat fellow, and the Devil would bury him in his own fat upon his old gridiron, but Swan was a tall bony fellow, and the Devil could not get him up on the gridiron. Swan has more sense than Knapp and more nonsense, more brimstone, more nitric acid."

The same newspaper, in 1842, gave this picture of Swan completing a day's work at his Stonington (Connecticut) revival:

"Swan baptized near thirty souls, body and breeches; some of them thirty years old in humanity and a hundred years old in iniquity; all washed inside and out—inside by the blood of Christ and outside by the briny waves of Stonington."

Mr. Bennett's journal made much copy out of Knapp's revivals in the Tabernacle Baptist Church of New York City in 1840 and the accounts bordered upon burlesque and caricature. One might as well attempt to ridicule that first Baptist whose voice cried out in the wilderness. Jacob Knapp could not be stopped. His sledge-hammer preaching caused him to be likened to Thor. He thundered with clenched fists. Yet he once said in a sermon: "I never struck a man; I'd never strike a mosquito if he wouldn't sing before he'd bite."

Born an Episcopalian in Otsego County, New York, on December 7, 1799, Knapp was impressed in early youth by the immersionist way of baptism. Repudiating the sprinkling of infants, including that which he had received, he took his plunge as a true Baptist. In 1822 he was licensed to preach and he spent the next three years working his course through the Literary and Theological Institution at Hamilton, New York. After eight years divided between two settled pastorates, in Springfield and Watertown, New York, he jumped bounds and took the first genuine all-Baptist revival on tour in the Autumn of 1833.

His converts wore paths from the mercy seat to baptismal waters in Ithaca, Schenectady and Rochester, New York City, Brooklyn and Boston. In 1840 the Connecticut River was attesting the results of his revival at Hartford. He descended upon New Haven and made seventy Yale students over into Baptists. Then in December, 1841, his second shower fell on Boston and it was saturated with sulphur. The hot rain poured upon the Unitarian vineyard and scorched the Universalist refuge from the now century-old Edwardean Hell. These two denominations were warm under the collar and stiff-necks in the Baptist camp, infuriated by being evangelized at all, pitched into Jacob Knapp.

Menaced by mobs without and pietist cabals within, Jacob stood his ground. Drunkards and gamblers were equal sinners with the holier-than-thous. To all alike he hurled his challenge to be dipped or be damned. And some of the persecutors were cooled off beneath the surface of the flowing fountain.

Jacob pushed out from Boston and new Baptists were raised from the tides of Salem and Marblehead, from the quiet stream in Concord where the patriots had fired "the shot heard round the world," and from the broad Merrimac turning the mill-wheels of Lowell. He gave Boston reason not to forget him and two years later when Jabez Swan followed in his footsteps he inherited the enmity to Knapp. The press took up the cause of the foes of the Baptist evangelists.

One newspaper printed a cartoon of Elder Swan and Deacon Nathaniel Colver, one of his right-hand men in the revival held in Charlestown. A swan with the head of a man was being shepherded by Brother Colver astride Balaam's ass squatting on its haunches under captions of "GO AHEAD!" The revivalist received and read from his pulpit a letter dated "Hell's Corners" and signed by "Otis Clapp, Prime Agent of the Bottomless Pit." While he was preaching upstairs, the Church Committee, which had let his converts accumulate for three weeks by withholding sanction for their baptism, met in the vestry and sought to oust their pastor, shut the house and stamp out the revival.

Like Knapp, Swan was accused of "getting ahead of God." His answer was that the first Disciples were sent on in advance "two by two" by their Lord. That accounted for Knapp and Swan. The Church by-laws were abolished, baptizing began and the fruits thereof were a hundred and twenty-five.

The two Baptist sons of thunder stood together in the old Green Street Church at Albany in 1843 and put their shoulders against the march of the Millerites toward the Millennium. It was a huge edifice for those days, having been intended for a theater and "wrested by the prayer of a sainted woman from the clutches of Satan," and it needed to be to hold the fort against the rampage of the rival religion.

On all sides the Millerite meetings were being thronged by multitudes of the devout from the different denominations, quickening the momentum of their conversions by the mounting fear of the Last Judgment and the expanding exultation of the saved contemplating the immediate appearance of the Christ. But the Baptist bethel maintained a deep solemnity, a profound calm, and held a sundering world to its orbit.

Steadily the Baptist revival progressed. Its leaders for the once ceased to be preachers of doom and damnation and became teachers of the way to live and die in an immovable faith. Long into the nights the people would linger in the sanctuary, bent on outpraying the Millerite agitation and finding their own peace. The baptistery tank was filled. Knapp and Swan waded in together and before they finished three hundred had broken the surface of the waters in their arms.

Other churches opened their doors to the revival till fourteen meetings were in simultaneous operation. Lewis Raymond came and joined the evangel captains. The newspapers spread the tidings all over half a dozen counties. Three thousand men and women were converted. And on the final day this army of the saved marched through the streets of Albany behind Knapp and Swan to the Albany railway station where hymns and hallelujahs were raised in a great farewell.

Jacob Knapp swung westward and was an evangelist till

he died in 1874 at Rockford, Illinois. Jabez Swan, his co-disciple, clung to New York and New England and fastened the Baptist tradition forever to the rocks of his native Eastern Connecticut shore.

It was in defense of that coast that Jabez Swan felt the first responsibility of a man's estate. Born at Stonington on February 23, 1800, the son of Joshua Swan, an industrious yeoman, and Esther Smith, the daughter of Simeon Smith, a Baptist Deacon of Groton, Jabez showed the stuff of his ancestry when on August 9 and 10, 1814, he served as powder-monkey to the Yankee artillerists who repelled an attack of the British from the sea. While the seventy-four-gun ship Ramilies, the forty-four-gun Pactolus, the Terror and the Dispatch bombarded the Point, barges loaded with troops attempted a landing only to be riddled by the gunners of Stonington. Fourteen-year-old Jabez smelled battle. And he showed the valor that was to burn as brightly in the pulpit as it did behind the cannon.

His earliest recollection was a cottage revival that crowded his own home and filled it with the lamentations of the lost and the glorifications of the saved. In his young manhood, after his father had moved to Lyme, he experienced his own conversion with the help of an all-night thunder storm that lashed heaven and earth. He found his "new world" when the skies cleared in the morning. And then a dream of thrice felling the devil in a wrestling match convinced him that he must be a preacher on the Jordan.

Licensed on May 12, 1822, he struggled with small supply charges for three years, meantime marrying Laura Griffin, of East Haddam, to share his poverty and ambition. In 1825 he rode horseback to Hamilton, New York, where he worked his way through to graduation from the

Theological Institution in 1827. His wife toiled as a seam-
stress. He labored in fields near by three hours a day for
thirty-seven and one half cents and preached Sundays for a
dollar a month in a schoolhouse at Lebanon.

On one wintry ride to his meeting, his eyelids froze
and his horse wallowed in impassable snowdrifts and he
missed both the inspiration of the service and the much-
needed dollar. Study came hard to him but he mastered
more than at least one of his professors intended by breaking away from the strict Calvinistic "limited atonement"
and concluding what he daringly preached in his ordination sermon—that Christ died for all.

Later, as an evangelist, he stripped the doctrine of
"election" of all chances of balking immediate repentance
for full salvation. But he insisted that baptism by immersion was the only door to the visible church and that the
unbaptized be excluded from communion. The "hopers"
—who believed but had not yet been into the water—he
consigned to the "Devil's Common," a dangerously arid
middle ground.

In the five years of his first pastorate at Stonington, he
ventured a revival that netted twenty at the river. In his
next charge, at Norwich, New York, where he was also
paid two hundred fifty dollars a year, he was drawn into a
four-day "protracted meeting" at Pitcher where for the
first time he saw an "anxious seat" used. Baptist penitents
behaved like Methodists, wailing, shouting and gesticulating. But at the end they trod the Jordan brink and Swan
helped baptize the hundred that stepped out.

In another revival at Oxford he recalls a man hurdling
over the heads of the people in the pews to reach the penitential bench. Swan's eight years at Norwich were a continuous round of revivals throughout Chenango County.

The miracle of conversion repeated itself in a hundred different ways and once pulled the preacher himself into the mystic maelstrom.

One night at Norwich he was called down from the pulpit to parley with a young lady in great distress about her soul. He named the Lord as a remedy but she recoiled "like a person bitten by a mad dog on seeing water." "Oh, don't name that name to me," she cried. "That is the very name I have despised and ridiculed." After the whole congregation had prayed for her, she had to be carried home. Swan was sent for.

"She was in a rocking chair, with her hands clasped upon her breast, and gnashing her teeth as though she would take them out of her head, and was past speaking," says Swan. "As I stood before her, I gained a view of the finally lost in hell. All my strength seemed to leave me; I trembled from head to foot."

It seems varied spiritual reinforcements had been summoned, for "a good Methodist brother," also present, put his arms about Swan and said: "Don't give up; we had such a devil as this at a camp meeting and we prayed him out. It is a dumb devil, but God will cast him out."

A sigh from the prison-house rewarded a long season of prayer, but it was forty-eight hours before the girl regained her feet and voice. Then she went to meeting and put up a prayer of redemption that exceeded all the prayers Swan had ever heard. He set her down as a brand plucked from the burning. The river did the rest. She was one of the three hundred three Swan baptized in Norwich alone. Swan built a church and filled it at Preston and put in four "dewy" years, constantly evangelizing the while, at Oxford. Then, done with pastorates, he set out upon his career as an itinerant revival engineer.

Owego, New York, witnessed Swan's first independent effort. There was power in that revival. It began with a deacon delving for deeper grace, weeping in the sanctuary till his brethren joined with him. He fell to the floor and appeared to be dying. Raised by prayer, he was apparently quite blind. At length his sight returned and he clapped his hands, shouting "Glory to God!" It might have been in a Methodist camp meeting. But it wasn't. And Swan was glad Baptists could get struck with the same sort of lightning.

From Owego, he went to New York City and among the hundred converts baptized at George Benedict's church was a hard-sinning Fulton Market butcher who afterwards became a deacon. A tour up-State followed with hard work and little guerdon. Six weeks in one place yielded twenty dollars; six weeks in another were requited with twenty-two dollars and a pair of shirts. He fared better at Providence, Rhode Island, in later years, where he began saving souls in Perry Davis's famous Pain Killer factory, then in the basement of the Davis home. All the unconverted among the mixers of Pain Killer got religion. Davis himself hired a hall seating four thousand and, at the close of ten weeks of baptizing in the river where Roger Williams had immersed his brethren, he paid Swan five hundred dollars. The evangelist applied the money toward paying for his new church in New London.

In June, 1842, Swan started in his old home town of Stonington the series of Connecticut revivals in which he made his name a memory. "Old hopers" and new converts walked with him into Jordan. A child who prayed a drunken father into conversion was baptized with him. The church could not hold the throngs and the Congregationalists threw open their edifice and shared the twenty-mile radius of salvation.

Success at Stonington brought a call from Mystic where Swan thrust in the evangelical sickle on Sunday, August 14, 1842. Though large auditories assembled, a week passed without a conversion. Swan introduced sunrise prayer meetings and they proved to be of moving solemnity. The first fruit was Sister Fish, an "old hoper," and as she came exultant up out of the liquid, Brother Swan proclaimed in a loud voice that there yet was room. The command was like the voice of the Almighty to the halting believers on the shore dwelling on the "Devil's Common."

Three fine old salts gave answer. Captain Jeremiah Wilbur stepped forward, peeled his coat and offered himself as a candidate. Captain Jesse Crarey and Captain George Wolf trimmed sail and stood alongside. This was no time for a formal consultation. The parsons and the brethren on the beach shouted unanimous assent and rejoiced as the skippers followed the Lord in the initial ordinance.

Back to the church for more preaching, down to the water for more baptizing thrice that Sabbath the elder led the people. Daily baptisms continued for twenty-six successive days. Secular work ceased in Mystic and Groton. Schools were closed and the haunts of trade deserted. Farmers with their families drove in from the countryside. Resounding hymns and booming prayers awoke the whole town with every dawn as the sunrise chorus lifted up its voice in the open air in front of the church. And day and night rose and fell the sound of praise and supplication.

On Sunday, September 11, with the dipping of nineteen in the Mystic River, three hundred twenty-four had been baptized. Swan marshalled them in a hollow square on the Conference House lot in the midst of a great concourse of people and in an address buckled on their Gospel armor against backsliding. This redoubled the revival and produced phenomena not seen since the New Lights had blazed through a hundred years before. Every night men had to be carried home. They insisted that they were happy in ecstatic visions of heaven and that they were willing to "sit and sing themselves away to everlasting bliss."

Swan himself was prostrated in the pulpit—his strength leaving him while he was preaching on the "glorified state." He thought his time had come and standing, as it seemed, on the top of Pisgah's mount, he looked over into the Promised Land and actually began to take leave of earthly friends. Prayers drowned out the rumble of Elijah's chariot wheels, however, and Jabez returned to the body with more work to do before the spirit should leave it.

Gravel Street, leading from the foot of Pequot Hill to the riverside, was thronged on the last day of the revival when seventy-two entered the water in relays while Swan and three other elders synchronized their efforts in a "union baptism." Every rising evoked a fourfold "Amen!" and a verse of a gladsome hymn from the "cloud of witnesses" fringing the shore. Last of all was a Congregational deacon. Swan got the consent of the Baptists and shouted "Come on, Deacon!" As the good man came up from the water he simply said: "Now I'm satisfied."

The baptizing evangelist proceeded to New London where in ten weeks, with all the churches joining in, he harvested a thousand converts, three hundred of them for the Baptist granary. On several occasions the saved couldn't wait for the dawn of another day but followed Jabez the Baptist out of the meeting house at midnight and marched singing through the streets of the city to the river.

There was no sleep for either the sinful or the righteous on those nights. The processions passed up Main Street on the rejoicing return journeys, through Church and Union Streets to the First Baptist Church and thence to the dooryard of Deacon Isaac Harris where, after prayer and benediction, the paraders dispersed. These were not New London's first midnight marches. A century before this James Davenport had led his Separatist New Lights over the selfsame route shouting hallelujahs and chanting "Come to Christ! Come to Christ!"

The record of the Stonington, Mystic and New London revivals was completed thirty years afterward with the observation that most of the conversions lasted. Jabez Swan returned to settled pastorates along this coast and held them to a ripe old age. But to the end he never missed an opportunity to advance a revival and to stand in the water and seal its results in the only way he knew, the way of the man of the wilderness who first descended into Jordan.

These were the great days of the Baptists. They aligned themselves against slavery and intemperance, expanded their missions and educational institutions—including Brown University at Providence—and exerted a considerable influence upon the religious life of the country.

Paralleling the Baptist extension was the growth of a "come-outer" body, the Disciples of Christ or so-called "Campbellite Baptists" originated by Thomas Campbell and his son, Alexander. The Campbells, Irish "Seceder Presbyterians," emigrated to Western Pennsylvania in the first decade of the nineteenth century and founded a "Christian Association" which was refused admittance to the Pittsburgh Synod. The Association was transformed into a church advocating the abolition of human creeds and confessions of faith and the union of all Christians under the specific injunctions of the New Testament.

Rejecting infant baptism and accepting immersion, the Campbellites for a time teamed with the Baptists. Then they pulled out and advanced independently in an aggressive, not to say belligerent, revival of their own, invading all denominations, proselyting freely and multiplying rapidly till they took their place as a substantial church among the others.

While the immersionist adherents were having their "awakening," the Methodists were still evangelizing and keeping their altar fires aglow. Like the Baptists, they lost members to the Adventists at the height of the Millerite excitement but after this subsided in 1844-45, they steadily gained ground despite the division of North and South on the question of slavery, the partisans repairing to their churches to sanctify their convictions.

Outstanding among the Methodist evangelists of the first half of the century was John Inskip, son of an English emigrant, who prayed out the devil and prayed in his salvation in a Pennsylvania corn field and set out a-preaching with two of his converts as allies, Billy Elliott and McColley the ex-pugilist.

Among those converted at that first Vineland camp meeting, in which the whole enclosure became a kneeling-place for "mourners," was the son of Bishop Matthew Simpson, a pioneer in Methodist higher education. Born in Harrison County, Ohio, in 1811, Simpson was one of

the early circuiteers, a friend of John Strange the evangel
singer of the backwoods, and a camp meeting magnet. A
professor of natural science, he was chosen President of
Indiana Asbury College in 1839, but afterward went back
to the pulpit. His friendship with Abraham Lincoln is
conspicuous in Methodist annals. It was Simpson who
spoke the last words at the grave of the martyred President.

This period also produced the Rev. James Caughey who
was a deep influence in the life of General William Booth
of the Salvation Army of later days. Other revivalist
denominations than the Baptist and Methodist were the
United Brethren in Christ, whose guiding stars were their
founder, Philip Otterbein, and Martin Boehme the Men-
nonite, and Jacob Albright's Evangelical Association which
specialized in German-Americans.

At the turn of the mid-century the combined effect
of all the revivals, whether with the baptism of water
or the baptism of fire, showed a net gain for religious
America. Whereas in 1800 it was estimated that only one
out of every fifteen persons was connected with an
evangelical church, in 1850 the reckoning of the saved
was put at one in seven.

Starting with his father's blacksmith shop as a bethel and
the anvil as a desk to pound upon in 1833, Inskip aver-
aged a convert a day for almost fifty years, ranging all
over the country and even touring the world. In September, 1852, he tackled New York, a Sodom "wicked with
theaters, balls, drinking and gambling saloons conspiring
to lead the unwary into paths of error and crime." But
his Madison Avenue conversions fell far short of those
in New England and the West. He revisited Manhattan in

1864 after serving as a chaplain with the Union Army and infused a militant spirit that brought hundreds to the mercy seat.

Inskip inaugurated the national camp meeting movement of the Methodists at Vineland, New Jersey, on July 17, 1867, giving out the opening hymn—"There Is A Fountain Filled With Blood"—which was sung with such spirit and power that it was adopted as the battle-song of the now organized Methodist source of greatest inspiration. He presided over forty-eight of the fifty-two Vineland camp meetings held during his lifetime.

In the Spring of 1871, Inskip preached across the country as a "field evangelist," dropping in on the Mormons at Salt Lake City and reaping his biggest harvest in California. A lawyer, a judge and a doctor knelt together at his mercy seat. One woman forgave the slayer of her husband and another the murderer of her son. In one service twenty parsons were prostrate on the ground with the penitents. Then it was said that a "haze of golden glory" encircled the heads of the bowed worshippers, a symbol of the "baptism of the Holy Ghost with fire."

CHAPTER XIV

## MID-CENTURY STIRRINGS

Just as I am, without one plea,
But that Thy blood was shed for me,
And that Thou bidd'st me come to Thee,
O Lamb of God, I come! I come!
                    CHARLOTTE ELLIOTT, 1789–1871.

EVERY revival, the evangelists have told America, which has had more striving for redemption than any other part of earth, every revival has been conceived by God who inspired and directed His instruments in turning back toward Heaven the steps of His wayward children. The well-beaten paths to the Throne of Grace criss-crossing one another on this continent for two hundred years after the Pilgrims sang away the Indians at Plymouth Rock were first trod by solid squads of evangel chieftains either united by doctrine or marching under a common denominational banner. Great names were on the lips of the converts down the line but none stood out alone, none was a movement in himself.

With Whitefield were Edwards, Tennent and Davenport, all bound to militant Calvinism. Asbury had his Cooper, his Williams and his unforgettable Lorenzo Dow and before anything else they were stanchly Methodist. Out on the border McGready was only a ranker with Stone of Cane Ridge and Ewing of the Cumberland. Cartwright and Finley were outriders of the Wesleyan circuiteers. Knapp and Swan concentrated upon immersing Baptists. Miller had Himes, Munger, Litch and Boutelle to shape the Adventist survival. And even Joseph Smith never would have produced the Book of Mormon without Sidney Rigdon, and his saints owe the rest to Brigham Young.

The one-man revival of national significance was born in the doldrums between regional and sectarian group evangelizing in the second quarter of the nineteenth century. That is, permitting the premise of divine authorship, an individual would set it going and carry it through. Countless preachers have pulled a call out of the ether, or, more accurately from the subconscious margin of their minds, and launched soul-saving campaigns of their own, but they have left their imprint on the small areas and short periods which circumscribed their efforts. Only a few broke through the barriers of distance and time to emblazon their records on the roll of the Golden Age of Evangelism that ended with the last bearers of the Moody tradition.

Charles Grandison Finney, the Presbyterian logician, nurtured at the bar and matured in the pulpit, was the greatest revivalist on his own till Dwight L. Moody bulked on the evangelical horizon. Coursing alongside of Finney were Asahel Nettleton, the calm Congregationalist, John Newland Maffitt, the cross-eyed, bow-legged Beau Brummel Methodist incongruity from Ireland, and the cautious and solemn Daniel Baker, another Presbyterian, who ranged the South and the Southwest specializing in colleges. Besides them there were the eccentric Jedediah Burchard, the gloomy Edward Payson and the spirited Dr. Lyman Beecher. Finney, however, outshone them all in

~ "SAVED IN THE LORD'S OWN TIME AND PLACE" ~

*(Finney Wrestling in Prayer)*

ground covered, duration of activity, intensity of message and net results for the Gospel granary.

Born in Warren, Litchfield County, Connecticut, on August 29, 1792, of parents not particularly religious, Finney was brought up in Ontario County, New York, near Sacketts Harbor, the "burnt district" of revival rampaging where both Mormonism and Millerism budded. At the age of twenty he had taught school to finance himself through the study of law in a country office at Adams, Jefferson County, New York. It was here that he had his first contact with hyper-Calvinism in the sermons of the Princetonian Rev. George W. Gale, whose preaching "rather perplexed than edified" him.

Gale cited Scripture as authority for many of the main principles of the common law and the neophyte barrister took the parson up on it, checked the Bible against Blackstone till he developed a personal logic of the Holy Writ that divided him from Gale and laid the foundation for the uncompromising forensic evangelist of the near future. Finney's own conversion in 1820 was not under the pressure of a revival, but was a combination of rationalizing and lone emotional struggling.

Convinced of the "reality and fullness of the atonement of Christ," he resolved that all required was for him to give up his sins and accept the Christ. Confronting himself with the question of "when," he said, "Yes, I will accept today or die in the attempt!" He entered the woods and vowed he would not come out till he had given his heart to God. So the Lord and his angels looked down upon a bearded man clad in a black frock coat kneeling on the pine-needles amid the brush, wrestling in prayer.

His inward soul hung back. There seemed to be a

"binding" upon it. His vow was bending. He was almost too weak to stay upon his knees. He thought he heard someone approaching and opened his eyes and glanced over his shoulder. A consciousness of his obdurate pride flashed upon him, an overwhelming sense of wickedness in being ashamed to have anyone see him in prayer, and he cried out to the treetops: "I will not leave this place if all the men on earth and all the devils in hell surround me!" The sin appeared awful, infinite. "It broke me down before the Lord," he said.

That let him out of the woods. Returning to his law office, he shut himself up in an unheated, unlighted back room to pray down the grace and the glory.

"It seemed as if I met the Lord Jesus Christ face to face," he said. "It did not occur to me then, nor did it for sometime afterwards, that it was wholly a mental state. On the contrary, it seemed to me that I saw Him as I would see any other man. He said nothing, but looked at me in such a manner as to break me right down at His feet . . . and I fell down at His feet and poured out my soul to Him.

"I wept aloud, . . . made such confessions as I could with my choked utterance, . . . bathed His feet with my tears, . . . yet I had no distinct impression that I touched Him. As soon as my mind became calm enough to break off from the interview, I returned to the front office . . . and was about to take a seat by the fire when I received a mighty baptism of the Holy Ghost . . . that seemed to go through my body and soul like a wave of electricity.

"Indeed, it seemed to come in waves of liquid love; it seemed like the very breath of God; it seemed to fan me like immense wings."

This impression, which came without expectation, lasted

till late in the evening when a member of the church choir
—Finney was leader of the choir—found him weeping
and asked what "ailed" him and if he was "in pain." After
a while Finney mustered enough equanimity to reply: "No,
but so happy that I cannot live." Still later he said: "My
sense of guilt was gone; my sins were gone; I do not
think I felt any more guilt than if I had never sinned."
Finney was elected and now the only question was the
election of every soul he could reach. He began with his
father and mother and could not wait for a formal course
in theology before putting his scythe to the holy harvest.

In the face of clerical opposition he was ordained at
Evans Mills on July 1, 1824. He preached an extempore
ordination sermon that created "an awful solemnity." It
was at Evans Mills that a young woman, a member of the
church for eight years, discovered through Finney that she
had "never known the true God." The effect was that she
had to be carried home where she lay in dumb anguish for
sixteen hours. Finney was encouraged. Conviction of sin
and alarm for the safety of souls loosened the knees of the
countryside.

The lawyer in him that had reasoned out the need for
his personal salvation was dominated by the preacher who
had emerged from the subsequent storm of feeling like
that which prostrated Saul of Tarsus on the road to Da-
mascus. "You are not in hell yet!" he shouted to those who
first yielded to his words. Hell to him was as definite a
place as a railroad station and the arrival of a sinful soul
as sure as that of a train. But when he had made everyone positive of his destination, he would say: "Now let me
lead you to Christ!" Practically none was unwilling.

The sentiment was infectious. At Antwerp, near Evans
Mills, while an aged German woman was tearfully testify-

ing another mother in Israel pushed through the throng to embrace her and cry "God bless you, my sister, God bless you!" The whole congregation thereupon fell upon one another's necks and wept.

Gouverneur, a stronghold of the Universalists, Finney's special aversion from the outset, was taken next. In the presence of the hard-headed settlers from New England, Finney debated the Universalist leader, vanquished him with Calvinistic ammunition and converted him. The revival was a huge success. At De Kalb he found that the Methodists and Presbyterians had been fighting over a revival, decided both were wrong, put on his own and carried the day. He annexed Rome to the Kingdom and converted five hundred in Utica. The count of the converts in his first campaign was more than three thousand. He liked numbers. Unlike his rural-faring predecessors, he made up his mind to besiege the large towns and cities. Under him the American revival took a new direction and objective.

Finney was better as an orator than as a composer of sermons that would endure in cold print and sometimes he descended into a studied vulgarity, excusing himself on the ground that he must talk in terms the common people would understand, their own every-day habits of communication. At the same time his religion imposed a rigid asceticism, prohibiting the use of tobacco, coffee and tea. Liquor, of course, was anathema to him. He gave the churches no peace, accusing them of somnolence and inertia and regarded his revival as a wakening, quickening force.

"It seems to be part of God's system that Christians are always asleep except in revivals, and very often then," he said. "The natural and habitual state of the Church has always been that of sleep."

His was the real Gospel, also, in contradistinction to the "unphilosophical doctrines" of the pietists of the past whom he charged with delaying the conversion of the world. "For centuries but little of the real Gospel has been preached," he declared, "and those great doctrines, in which the fathers, the reformers and the whole Church have been almost unanimous, have been leading down colonies to hell." Naturally, the clergy did not like to have their ecclesiastical stock in trade unshelved and labelled spurious. But the shock was sufficient to warm the pews under the too comfortably settled parishioners. Finney never failed to rouse. His genius for persuasion did the rest.

Though he struggled with the Edwardean theory of the sovereignty of God, he repudiated the concept of total human depravity and vigorously maintained the freedom of the will to make a choice of destiny. That put him in conflict with the strict tenet of "election" from which he never wholly escaped. In a controversy with a Universalist —an advocate of the ultimate saving of all mankind— he explained that the atonement of Christ "did not consist in the literal payment of the debt of sinners but simply rendered the salvation of all men possible." But he was merciless to rebels against his modified Calvinism and his wrath fell heaviest upon the Universalists who were particularly active from 1830 to 1860, the palmy days of Finney.

It was hell or heaven with him and everywhere he went throughout the East he demanded and got immediate decisions. To do this he initiated the modern evangelistic method, compelling the penitent to signify his stand and clearing the way for him to the anxious seat. It was the first salvation trail, yet to be paved with sawdust. Deaf to remonstrances, he plied a "faithless generation" with dramatic, sensational preaching and had sinners prayed for by name. Unfortunately this gave self-righteous back-biters a chance to tell the Lord in public what sort of neighbors they did not like and why.

Ruthlessly he appealed to fear. Comforting a sinner was cushioning him in hell. In his sermon on the text "The Wages of Sin is Death" he painted luminous billboards lining the bottomless pit on all sides with the words:

"You will get your wages," he trumpeted, "just what you have earned, your due; nothing more, nothing less. And as the smoke of your torment, like a thick cloud, ascends forever and ever, you will see written upon its curling folds in great staring letters of light this awful word—wages, *wages*, WAGES!"

Shades of Edwards! And foregleam of the searchlights throwing a legend glorifying chewing gum upon the clouds above tall-towered Manhattan! Perhaps, when Aimee Semple McPherson learns of Finney's feat she will beam "Wages" one thousand candle-power strong against a wall of sulphurous mist steaming round the stage of Angelus Temple while her choir, robed in flaming vestments, wails the word into her microphones.

Finney did not need any property man or electrician. As he uttered this pronouncement, he stretched his tall form to full height and stood transfixed, gazing along his trigger finger at the glittering cloud he had conjured, his clarion voice at crescendo penetrating the hearts of his hearers. Hell might also have heard.

The devil was very real to Finney too. He warned a man

driving him over the road to Stephentown to a revival
there that Satan might possess the nag and incite it to bolt.
"Strange to tell," he said, "before we got there the horse
ran away twice and came near killing us. The owner expressed the greatest astonishment and said he had never
known such a thing before."

The evangelist was fond of the fate of Sodom and
Gomorrah. To Antwerp, where there had been no preaching till he came, he said: "Up! Get you out of this place,
for the Lord will destroy this city." In fifteen minutes
peradventures were ascending in prayers for Antwerp, the
congregation "falling from their seats in every direction
and crying for mercy." In fact, Finney observed, "If I
had had a sword in each hand I could not have cut them
off their seats as fast as they fell."

At Gouverneur his reverend assistant told the young men
that God would break their stiff necks within a week
either by converting them or sending them to hell. All
were on the safe side in time. A youth swooned during
Finney's first sermon at Rome and the leading men of
the town held an inquest at the hotel the next morning.
Many of them had to be carried home on shutters before
Finney concluded the session.

Like Abraham, Finney "communed with the Lord,"
though not always so successfully. A young woman who
had wilted under his hypnotic eye and tongue had the
temerity to become a Universalist. He was "astounded that
I could not break through with my faith and get hold of
God with reference to her case." Even worse was a magistrate, elected to the Legislature, who refused conversion
till he had completed his term and carried out pledges to
political friends which were incompatible with his first
becoming a Christian. These were unique exceptions. Fin-

ney's prowess was bruited ahead of him. Cities were all
steamed up before he arrived with his revival. The safety
valve usually blew off before his departure. After Utica,
Auburn capitulated and Troy fell.

The Spring of 1829 found him in Wilmington, Delaware. Thence he essayed Philadelphia where for a year and
a half he was met with the city's customary placidity.
Reading and Lancaster were stepping-stones to New York.
Anson G. Phelps hired a vacant church for him in Vande-
water Street for three months and then bought a disused
Universalist edifice at Broadway and Prince Street.

It was in New York that Finney put on the best "act"
of his career. A woman had been sitting down front eye-
ing him with cool insolence night after night. He prepared a sermon just for her in which he portrayed the devil
as a destroying archer. He drew a figurative bow and let
fly an imaginary arrow at the woman's heart. She rolled
senseless in the aisle. Jonathan Edwards's "bow of God's
wrath" had been bent again!

Rochester, Buffalo and Providence were assaulted. Then
Finney turned toward Boston. Opposition had now reached
a fever heat. Lyman Beecher called him "unintelligent"
and denounced his methods. Addressing the evangelist he
said:

"Finney, I know your plan and you know I do; you
mean to carry a streak of fire to Boston. But if you attempt
it, as the Lord liveth, I'll meet you at the State line and
call out all the artillerymen and fight every inch of the way
to Boston and then I'll fight you there."

Finney stole a weapon from the Bostonian arsenal. He
put on dignity. The militia would have been powerless.
Received with cool courtesy, he produced some good re-

sults but, as Boston phrased it, "slipped on more ice than he broke."

Lyman Beecher, who was pastor of the Bowdoin Street Church while his brother, Edward, held forth at Park and Tremont Streets in the edifice later made famous by Dr. J. L. Withrow as standing on "Brimstone Corner," tartly remarked after one of Finney's exhortations: "You need not be afraid to give up all to Christ, your property and all, for He will give it back to you."

Having now a wife and three children, Finney settled down for a time as pastor of the Second Free Church in New York. While here he saved "The Evangelist" from extinction because of its anti-slavery agitation by writing a series of articles on revivals for the periodical. In 1835 he redeemed himself on this point by taking a theological chair at Oberlin College in Ohio with Abolitionist students expelled from Lane Seminary as a nucleus of his class. He later took the presidency of Oberlin on the condition that none be barred because of race or color and through great vicissitudes, during which the fortunes of at least two patrons were wrecked, he firmly established the college.

In the Fall of 1843 he took to the revival road again and captured Boston. The city gave up to "endless punishment" and the necessity of "entire sanctification" without a single backfire. Possibly the Old Guard clergy were grateful for something to offset the Millerite invasion or they may have remembered the Unitarian joy in Finney's provoked attacks upon Puritan orthodoxy at his previous revival. The Marlborough Hotel was converted into a chapel which witnessed the high water mark of Finney's evangelical career in this country.

England accorded him a welcome and success. Then in the Winter of 1855–56, he answered a Macedonian cry from the lawyers of Rochester, New York, and in a revival noted for its rationality in contrast to the recent rantings of Jedediah Burchard, he brought the higher type of thinking men and women into church membership. Finney's native common sense had supplanted terror with reasoned retribution, the austerity of heaven with divine love. Evangelism entered modernity with him.

Oberlin was under his masterful guidance till 1866. Death came on August 16, 1875, after only three hours' illness from a heart attack. He was survived by his third wife. All three women held up the hands of the greatest evangelist of his generation. His epitaph might well read —"soldier of the Cross, friend of freedom, great and growing soul."

Asahel Nettleton, till his death in 1844 the closest contemporary of Finney, was also of the Edwardean mold though he was adamant against sensationalism and mobbing men to the mercy seat. Instead of excitement he sought to inculcate meditation; instead of crowd contagion he individualized salvation. His converts thought and felt their way back to God in calm reflection alone with Him. But he recognized the necessity of bringing men to the point where they would shake off their inhibitions and start toward the light he set before them. With no attempt to rouse unbalancing passions, he did preach powerfully to search, reach and move the deepest sensibilities. The atmosphere of his revivals was one of breathless stillness and most profound solemnity.

Asahel (meaning "Made-by-God" in the Hebrew) was a genuine New Englander in birth, education, manner and, when he got it, in Congregationalist faith. He was born on a farm at North Killingworth, Connecticut, on April 21, 1783, and was a sturdy young husbandman of eighteen when he leaned upon his hoe, considered his sins and pondered his eternal destiny. He was reviewing the pleasures of a ball on the morning after. "We must all die and go to the Judgment," he thought, "and with what feelings shall we then reflect upon these scenes?" He was overcome with the sense of his lost condition; the struggle lasted for ten months. Then—as with many another— "old things passed away and all things became new."

At the age of twenty-two, he entered Yale where he was one of President Dwight's right-hand men in the revival that tried young souls in 1807–08. His ambition was to be a foreign missionary but he found enough heathen at home to occupy all of his days. Licensed to preach on May 28, 1811, he was ordained an evangelist in the Summer of 1818 and during a decade engaged in forty revivals. Among his converts was Emerson Andrews, the Mansfield (Massachusetts) Baptist evangelist who wrought forty thousand conversions from three hundred revivals in thirty-eight years.

Nettleton's major work was in Connecticut and Rhode Island where he endeavored to overcome the lingering fanaticism incited by Davenport. Once, at Salisbury, Connecticut, he took hold of a shrieking, groaning community, restored peace and carried his revival through to a calm success.

He had his numbers too. More than two thousand were converted by him at Saratoga Springs in 1819. And he was unafraid of the big centers of population. Brooklyn heard him and so did the large towns of Massachusetts, New Jersey, Virginia and North Carolina. He never had time to marry and he was always poor. The last half of his life was marred by his prostrating illness of 1822 and his declining years, from 1833 to the end, were spent in teaching theology at the East Windsor (Connecticut) Seminary.

To Nettleton the revival was the direct intervention of God. On one occasion he overheard a churchman remarking—"Mr. Nettleton has come and now we shall have a revival of religion." The words pierced him to the heart. Weeping, he took his leave. "I can't stay here," he said. "The people are in the wrong state of mind." They repented, however, and he returned to the "harvest field."

He could be dramatic. His sermon on "Lazarus and Dives," delivered at the culmination of a revival, was his best in this vein. He took the people to the glories of heaven with Lazarus and to the tortures of hell with Dives. He summoned Dives back from perdition. Wrapped in a sheet of flame the rich sensualist followed the preacher's finger down the aisle, the people shrinking away from him. Now the tormented soul ascends the pulpit. "Listen to one risen from hell," the evangelist says and then in despairing tones he impersonates his Dives warning the world. Nettleton was wielding the two-edged sword. But always he sheathed it. The peroration was addressed to the personal conscience. It was an appeal to pause and think and pray—alone with God.

Countering Nettleton's studied avoidance of sensationalist extremes and eclipsing Finney's grandest passion in the perturbation of the wicked, John Newland Maffitt, the Methodist meteor, burst upon this country in the year of 1822. Melodramatic in the highest degree, tropes and metaphors adorning his unimpeded flow of scintillating oratory, he was a master of human impulse in the mass and literally ran away with his audiences.

Here was a character in the revival pulpit that has never

been paralleled. His personality in itself was amazing. Born in Dublin in 1794, bred to his father's trade of fashionable tailoring, in early life he was a devotee of the "painted and powdered beauties of the stage." He brought his love of personal finery to these shores in 1819 and certainly needed it to cover his physical imperfections. Padding concealed the disproportion of his shoulders and the bow of his legs, and elegance in raiment combined with tonsorial attention to offset his crossed eyes and harelip. Men grudgingly voted him "passably good looking" but women, after he began preaching, followed him from church to church in adoring crowds.

His vanity knew no bounds. At the height of his fame—in Philadelphia, New York and Cincinnati—he would drive to his barber and having undergone an exquisite operation upon his bell-shaped head, he would ride to church bareheaded with his hat in his hand lest the elaborate arrangement of his coal-black hair be disturbed.

He left in Dublin the beautiful corset-maker's clerk who was the bride of his unhappy first marriage. Evidently she died, for during his "metropolitan itinerancy" in this country he married one of the thousands of his feminine admirers, a well-to-do Miss Pierce of Brooklyn who proved to be another thorn.

He had tried unsuccessfully to preach in Ireland—perhaps the Irish were too aware of the blandishments of blarney—but the moment he braved the Gospel field with one of his brilliant oratorical displays at a camp meeting in Connecticut he was taken by his soft, delicate white hand. In 1822 he received a travelling connection with the New England Methodist Conference and preached to immense audiences in various parts of the country till 1832 when he "located" and his star slowly faded out.

While he was riding high in his orbit he was a sort of pyrotechnical exhalation. He was strong on dramatic entrances. At the crowded Salem Street Church in Philadelphia he had himself passed into the edifice through a window amid a tumult of cheering. It worked so well that he tried it again at the Willet Street Church in New York City, where a ladder was run up against the rear wall, Maffitt ascending it and crawling in at an aperture above the pulpit. Wild enthusiasm greeted him. At Cincinnati he abruptly strode down from the pulpit and into the midst of the people, and opening his hymn book, said —"I will now sing a hymn in which the congregation will please not join." Hardly had his last tremulous note died away when mourners piled over one another to kneel round his platform.

One New York sermon ended in an impassioned appeal for a charity fund. Women threw rings, bracelets, brooches and necklaces into the collection plates. Men tossed in rolls of bills. In another sermon at Cincinnati he dwelt upon the beauties of paradise till his hearers spontaneously burst into a united shout of "Glory!" Then he wrought a simile of eternity—a little bird taking a mouthful of the earth and flying off with it once every thousand years. "This task, though requiring millions upon millions of ages and but dimly shadowing the awful word, eternity, would at last come to an end," he said, "but the punishment of the lost shall endure forever!"

Many good Methodists were doubtful that Maffitt had ever really experienced religion, but, judging from his writings—"Tears of Contrition, or Sketches of My Life," he had at least approached the Throne, albeit through the instinct of rather selfish fear. Many were the unkind things said of him and they cut to the quick. In 1841 he was Chaplain to the National House of Representatives. Here for the last time his eloquence was appreciated. He died suddenly of cardiac trouble in May, 1850, declaring almost with his last breath that his enemies had broken his heart.

The last of the larger stars revolving around Finney was Daniel Baker, whose light was steadier and cooler than that of all the others. The life of this Princetonian Presbyterian began in Georgia in 1791 and ended in 1857. His evangelizing began in 1813 at Hampden-Sidney College and went on the road after a conquest of Princeton in 1816, taking him across the country from the City of Washington to Texas.

All the way—in Harrisonburg, Virginia; Savannah, Georgia; Frankfort, Kentucky; Tuscaloosa, Alabama; and Holly Springs, Missouri; and over the States of Louisiana, Florida, Missouri, Arkansas, Ohio and the Carolinas—he held to a singleness of purpose. He declared himself a man of one book, the Bible, and of one idea and object, the salvation of men. He converted twenty thousand.

As a revivalist he was a diplomat, always placing himself subordinate to the settled pastors and thus making friends everywhere. And he was brief. His sermon limit was half an hour. He had a compendious repertory of simple, forceful discourses that never wore out. They were delivered in a sonorous voice that was audible to its lowest range and capable of vibrant earnestness and pathos.

His was an intensely serious, devout mission. No criticism of evangelism in his day could have applied to him. But Finney and Maffitt drew enough fire for one generation. About the worst said of the new revival school was uttered in 1828 by the Rev. Seth Williston, pastor of the

First Presbyterian Church of Durham, New York. Like Dr. Lyman Beecher of Boston, he was aiming at Finney.

"When ministers of the Gospel and Christian brethren, instead of observing the rule given by their divine Master for each to tell the other his faults in private, do, in a public manner, denounce each other as cold and stupid and dead and enemies to revivals; and when prayer and intercession for others is made instrumental of publicly blackening their characters, it is a device of Satan," he said.

Taking a shot at Finney's practice at Albany, New York, of having men and women paired in praying, Williston continued:

"It is thought by some that revivals of religion cannot be carried on with power unless females take a more prominent place than they have done and employ their gifts in exhortations and prayer in meetings composed of both sexes. But if this practice be not according to Scriptural rule, it will not benefit the cause."

On this he quoted Saint Paul as saying: "Let your women keep silence in the churches. Let the woman learn in silence with all subjection. But I suffer not a woman to teach, nor to usurp authority over the man, but to be in silence."

Assailing unscriptural means of alarming the impenitent, Williston said: "Let us never invent threatenings of our own to excite their fears. Should it be said that a new era in revivals has commenced and that greater severity is now found to produce a powerful effect in arousing stupid professors and stupid ministers, it may be said in reply—If a new era has commenced, yet another Bible has not been given, the old rules are still to be followed: 'Rebuke not an elder, but entreat him as a father.' And there are some methods practised that may be termed *mechanical,* which, I fear, are not so safe as they are expeditious."

Williston was indeed a prophet. The revival had entered a new epoch and only time could unfold the inventive genius of man in furthering its mechanical progress with which ever afterward its original and underlying spirituality has had to contend.

# CHAPTER XV

## POST-PANIC REPENTANCE

Stand up, stand up for Jesus,
Ye soldiers of the cross;
Lift high His royal banner,
It must not suffer loss:
From victory unto victory
His army shall He lead
Till every foe is vanquished
And Christ is Lord indeed.
GEORGE DUFFIELD, JR.
Written in Philadelphia, 1858.

NEW motive as well as new method distinguished the advance of the American revival of religion into the second half of the nineteenth century. Economic incitation, whether spontaneous or designed, appeared alongside though not superseding the preachment of future torment as a compelling factor behind the natural human impulse to escape the immemorial plight of mankind. Hell was materialized on earth. It was experienced. Men traced the consequential course of their own lives toward it till they stood on the brink of utter despair. Broken bankers and breadline derelicts were one in being actually "lost" while the soul was still in the body.

Neglect of religion was the accepted cause of disaster; return to religion was the way out of the enveloping darkness. Faith became first palliative, then propitiative and finally restorative. And the discovery that it "paid to serve the Lord" was the origin of the talking point for the eventual super-salesmanship of salvation which triumphed under William A. Sunday. Eternal hell was only enhanced. It remained as something so much worse than temporal misery and for another seventy years gave the revivalist a double advantage over the world, the flesh and the devil.

None can question the personal and public good in religious redemption from moral and material failure. The street-preaching Salvation Army and Volunteers of America have salvaged the down-and-outer with drumbeat and trumpet call of "the Blood and the Fire." No soldier will ever forget the followers of the Booths who put religion into doughnuts in France and knelt by the stretchers pressing to parched lips the cup in the Name of Him Whose brothers were lying there.

But there is another side of the utility of religion. Its value has been recognized and deliberately used by masters of this world's affairs and possessions to keep the "have-nots" mindful of their eternal welfare rather than that of their condition here on earth. Sometimes they have profited merely incidentally by the humbling effects of a revival; sometimes they have actually instigated a revival for the express purpose of maintaining the economic status quo.

John Wanamaker, the merchant of pious memory, was perhaps unaware of the significance that might be attached to his words when he said of the Moody revival in Philadelphia: "I give this testimony as a *business man* standing in the witness box and bearing witness to the truth. Hundreds of men converted, *out of work* and wandering about the streets, have been kept in the way

they chose when they embraced the religion of Jesus
Christ."

It was the way of safety for the constituted social and
economic system. It gave a mansion yonder for those who
had no place to lay their heads here and the bread of
eternal life to make up for the lack of a square meal.

Mill bosses in Connecticut gladly stopped their water-
wheels while Jabez Swan exhorted their lint-dusted girls
at the looms. Charles G. Finney melted a whole roomful
into tears when he eyed down a young woman trying to
mend a broken thread at New York Mills, near Utica.
William A. Sunday has always carried his message from
the tabernacle to the worker in the shop. The steel men
of Pittsburgh welcomed him to the mills where union or-
ganizers get no admittance. He talked perhaps of the wages
of sin and surely not of those which enter into collective
bargaining to feed, clothe and shelter the children of labor.

Yet these evangelists were supremely concerned with
the saving of souls no matter where they found them. The
making of better employees was merely collateral and then
only in the mind of an observant employer. Slave traders
in ante-bellum days always put a premium on Christian
chattels. And now "free" labor is doubtless more grateful
for what it receives, less likely to grumble and more sub-
missive when it is sufficiently preoccupied with religion.
The accomplishment of this desideratum is worth a going
price in the modern industrial South.

This is on the word of one of today's leading evangelists
of the South, himself the son of an evangelist famous on
both sides of the Atlantic: some Southern cotton mill
managements pay half the cost and supply the location for
revivals that keep their workers in constant concern for
their souls. It is good business. It maintains industrial peace

regardless of wages, hours or any such mundane and transitory considerations. And the lesser order of under-Aarons who perform these rites are to be relied upon as loyal to the standards set by the masters of the mills.

Plant and capital have been moved down from New England, leaving unions and protective legislation behind. Gastonia, the very name redolent of Boston genealogy, in North Carolina has forty-two mills within a mile of the court house. Mill villages have risen in both Carolinas, Georgia and Virginia. In every one are the inevitable Methodist and Baptist churches whose pastors are "dependable," industrially speaking. And the traditional susceptibility of the people to the revival makes their territory a stamping ground for a continuous succession of travelling exhorters in tent, tabernacle and camp meeting enclosure. Verily religion there is a refuge and one should not be uncharitable toward those who so thoughtfully help to provide it!

The first widespread revival in response to economic stimulus, however, was neither premeditated nor constrained. The name of no great evangelist can be attached to it, nor the designation of any denomination. For once in religious history a people of themselves, upon their own initiative, suddenly joined hands and invoked their God. They did not need prophet or prophecy. Their common conscience told them why they had to pray and their common predicament dictated what to pray for. It was the wave of repentance that swept this country after the panic of 1857.

A financial crash reverberated through the money centers of the world on October 14, 1857. Wall Street caved in and great speculative fortunes tumbling down dislodged the pillars of sound business itself. An era of reckless prosperity vanished in a forenoon. Public confidence was prostrate. Industry stood still. Ruin confronted leaders in finance and business and immediate desperate poverty was the lot of the wage-earner.

Down in the heart of America's mart of marts a solitary man began praying. For days Jeremiah Lanphier broadcast an invitation but knelt alone every noon in the upper room of the Old North Dutch Church in Fulton Street. "Lord, what wilt Thou have me to do?" was the burden of his prayer. One man joined him, then six, then twenty, then a hundred and finally the meeting-house could not hold the throng of suppliants. Other churches, halls and theaters in New York and Brooklyn were packed daily. The universal petition may well have been "O God, save my soul and restore my credit!" or "O God, save my soul and get me a job!" But in the end it was "I put myself in Thy hands; show me the way out; I will follow Thee!" An item from a newspaper tells the story: "In the busiest hour of the day, it is in the busiest street of the city, noisy with machinery of all kinds, even puffs of smoke coming up from under the ground. Take a seat and watch the worshippers collect. Porters, handcartmen, policemen, ministers and business men, of all ages, gather here for one hour to ignore and get out of the maelstrom-whirl. They feel as if their souls needed care as well as their bodies. Here is sympathy, companionship, with no stress on creeds."

And they all sang straight from the heart. It was Lanphier that started them singing till their hymns rang in the streets of the city. One noonday his pulpit was banked in flowers, the gift of a drunkard who had been redeemed from his weakness. Down on the docks stevedores paused for prayer and aboard two hundred ships seafaring men knelt upon the decks. Even the prisons were touched by the pervading spirit.

On a snowy Monday morning the most sacred season in the history of Henry Ward Beecher's Plymouth Church began in Brooklyn. At the outset only twenty-eight persons assembled. For two weeks Beecher himself refused to come, saying he did not believe in "got-up" revivals and that if the real spirit of revival was in his church the revival would follow. His object was to put the responsibility upon the people. They fulfilled the requirement and a crowded auditory compelled his presence. His sermons were ever new, vivid and aggressive and at the end of every one he invariably invited any present to offer their prayers.

Along with Robert M. Hatfield, another to welcome and advance the spiritual outpouring in New York was the Rev. Theodore L. Cuyler, pastor of the Market Street Church where Lanphier had been a choir singer before he became a "missioner" in Fulton Street. Cuyler conducted the first noon-day meeting in Burton's old theater in Chambers Street. He was also leader in services at a warehouse at the lower end of Broadway. In the six months that followed he estimated that no less than ten thousand people reconsecrated their faith. Cuyler's later ministry took him to the Lafayette Avenue Presbyterian Church in Brooklyn where in 1866 the Rev. Francis E. Clark founded his first Society of Christian Endeavor.

The flame spread all over New York City and then leaped to Philadelphia. There, led by George H. Stuart and the youthful Dudley Tyng whose dying words inspired George Duffield's "Stand Up for Jesus," the hymn of the 1857 revival, Jaynes Hall on Chestnut Street was thronged by three thousand a day for several months.

One critical journal averred that "though six thousand

attend the twenty daily prayer-meetings in New York Satan still has a majority as fourteen thousand go nightly to the theater still." This statement was controverted by the leaders in prayer, but it might have been true, with no credit to the devil, because in times of public worry the theater always has taken what cash could be spared for the sake of relief from the pressure of circumstance.

The voluntary revival sprang up all over the country. Free of charge the telegraph companies at given hours carried thousands of prayerful messages—possibly a policy to which can be traced the indexed forms wired for standard fees now at Christmas and Easter. Newspapers ran off extra editions heralding the progress of the movement as it gathered headway in Boston, Providence, Albany, Buffalo, Pittsburgh, St. Louis, Washington, Cincinnati, Cleveland, Chicago and Omaha. In Cleveland one thousand joined the churches and in St. Louis it was reported that "the awakening far outran the churches." In most of the cities all business was suspended during the hour of the prayer-meetings.

A merchant in Chicago while conferring with a country customer looked at his watch and remarked—"It is almost twelve o'clock, almost time for prayer-meeting." The astonished client went with him and was converted. Dwight L. Moody, then selling shoes in Chicago, wrote home to his mother—"I go to meeting every night. Oh, how I enjoy it! It seems as if God were here Himself. O mother, pray for me! Pray that this work may go on till every knee is bowed."

From Kansas it was reported that the concert of prayer there had resulted in the conversion of many young men who were preparing for the ministry. A mother in Saratoga rejoiced in the conversion of two sons. Accessions

cheered churches in New Jersey, Pennsylvania, Michigan,
Rhode Island and South Carolina. A man in New Orleans
wrote that he hired a convert of the Fulton Street (New
York) meetings who later became a member of Congress
and that another convert succeeded in business in San
Francisco. The economic motive was bringing economic
fruits. Yet the revival should not be misjudged. It was
essentially a deep, rational movement, based upon prayer
rather than preaching, that restored the spiritual balance
of thousands of American people.

The New York Times said editorially of the revival:
"It is most impressive to think that over this great land
tens and fifties of thousands of men and women are putting to themselves at this time, in a simple, serious way,
the greatest question that can ever come before the human
mind." The Journal of Commerce put in its word: "Such
scenes are quite unprecedented. On former occasions we
have had great clerical demonstrations, but this religious
movement is characterized by features which give it the
impress of a divine origin and to ascribe it to human
agency is little short of blasphemy." The New York Tribune devoted a whole eight-page number to reports of
the revival meetings. Newspapers everywhere lent their
columns to chronicle the events of the revival and to support it editorially.

The conversions in the 1857 revival were estimated anywhere from three hundred thousand to one million. No
exact count could have been kept. It did not matter. The
real significance was individual, between man and his God,
and there was none to gain glory by numbering the
"saved." Clear-thinking analysts, like the Rev. A. J. Patterson, a Universalist pastor of Portsmouth, New Hampshire, whose church participated in the revival, conceded

that "a religious awakening always follows in the track of a business depression." Declaring that this was "convincing evidence of the reality of religion," he continued:

"When men lose their fortunes and their hopes, when they see how insecure are things material and earthly, when their poor, disappointed hearts are bleeding and desolate, then they turn to religion for strength and consolation. The Gospel which in prosperity they neglected now claims their earnest attention in their hour of greatest need.

"This dollar, which before the eye of greed had expanded until it overarched the earth and hid the sky, had turned back from its glittering disk the rays of heavenly light which started from God to enlighten and warm our hearts. Men who sneer at the awakening because it is the result of financial difficulties can know but little of the philosophy of human nature. It is natural for us in seasons of trial to turn to God for help."

In all this acknowledgment of deserved retribution and turning to the Lord firmly believed to have sent it, there was but one attempt to take advantage of a penitent people by working up a regular preaching revival. And, of all places, this happened in Boston.

The revival took possession of every pulpit in Boston save one and the national momentum of the penitential impulse was borne in upon the city. It was in a fervent Boston assembly that a stranger got up, saying he was from Omaha and that on his journey East he had found towns and cities bowed in supplication all the way. He gave the revival the phrase that has stuck to it ever since—"a continuous prayer-meeting for two thousand miles."

Boston thawed; Boston melted; Boston caught fire. Park and Tremont Streets earned the name of Brimstone

Corner from the sermons in the church that still stands there.

Then from that one pulpit which stood aloof from the plethora of prayer and preaching came the greatest rebuke ever administered to the religious revival. It must take its place as the worthiest and most sincere and intelligent opposition expressed in all the evangelizing of America up to the present day. It was delivered by the Rev. Theodore Parker, brilliant and courageous preacher, pioneer in the freedom of religion and advocate of the liberation of the slaves when it was dangerous even in New England to be an Abolitionist.

Speaking in Boston Music Hall, not for from the Park Street Church and the historic Common, on Sunday, April 4, 1858, on the theme of "A False and True Revival of Religion," Theodore Parker said:

"It is Boston, March, 1858, Saturday afternoon, in a meeting-house. I find men and women met together for prayer and conference—honest-looking men and respectable—I meet them every day in the street.

"Most exciting speeches are made, exciting stories are told, exciting hymns are sung, fanatical prayers are put up. Half the assembly seem a little beside themselves, out of their understanding,—more out of their conscience, still more out of their affections.

"One says, 'The Lord is in Chicago; a great revival of religion is going on there.' Another says, 'Oh, the Lord is in Boston; He is pouring out His spirit here.'

"Appeals are made to fear.—'Come to Christ! There is an eternal hell for you if you do not come; an eternal heaven if you will. Come to Christ! Choose now,—you may never have another opportunity. This night thy soul shall be required of thee.' Prayers are made for in-

dividual men, now designated by description then by
name.

"One obnoxious minister [Parker himself] is singled
out, and set up as a mark to be prayed at, and the petitioners riddle that target as they will. One minister asks
God to convert him, and, if He cannot do that, to remove
him out of the way and let his influence die with him.

"Another asks God to go into his study this very afternoon and confound him, so that he will not be able to
finish his sermon—which had been writ five days before;
or else meet him the next day in his pulpit, and confound
him, so that he should not be able to speak.

"Another prays that God will put a hook into that man's
jaws, so that he cannot preach. Yet another, with the
spirit of commerce in him, asks God to dissuade the people from listening to this offender, and induce them to
leave that house and come up and fill this.

"I ask a grave, decent-looking, educated minister, 'What
is all this?' The answer is, 'Why, it is an act of religion. The
Lord is in Boston; he inspires us miraculously. He has
made us all of one heart, and of one mind. He hears our
prayers; He will answer our prayers.

"It is a revival of religion; it is a great revival; it goes
all over the United States; even some Unitarian ministers
begin to thaw, at least, to soften. The Lord is in this house
to save the people. 'Glory to God in the highest, peace on
earth and good will to men! . . .'

"God is variable, ill-natured, revengeful; he will go into
a minister's pulpit and put a hook into his jaws so that
he cannot preach. That is the God of Park Street Theology! . . .

"When I hear of a revival of religion I always ask, what
do they mean to revive? What feeling, what thinking,

what doing, what being? Is it a religion that shall kill a boy; that shall stone a man to death for picking up sticks Saturday afternoon; that shall butcher a nation; crucify a prophet; talk gibberish; torture a woman for her opinion and that opinion a true one?

"Or is it a religion which will make me a better man, husband, brother, father, friend; a better minister, mechanic, president, street-sweeper, king—no matter what —a better man in any form?

"Just now there is a revival of religion, so called, going on in the land. The newspapers are full of it. Crowds of men and women throng the meeting-houses. They cannot get preaching enough. The poorer the article the more they want of it.

"Speeches and sermons of the most extravagant character are made. Fanatical prayers are put up. Wonderful conversions are told of. The innermost secrets of men's and women's hearts are laid bare to the eye of the gossip and the pen of the newspaper reporter.

"The whole is said to be a miraculous outpouring of the Holy Ghost, the direct interposition of God. You look a little more closely and you will find the whole thing has been carefully got up, with the utmost pains. Look at the motive.

"You remember the efforts made last year—the prayer meetings, conference meetings, the preaching and the talk in the newspapers. Not much came of it. Now circumstances are different.

"The commercial crisis last Autumn broke great fortunes to fragments, ground little ones to powder, turned men out of business by thousands. Then, some religious men, of all denominations, full of Christian charity, set themselves to looking after the poor. The work was well done—never better. Then to prevent the unexpected increase of crime, by an increased attention to justice and charity. That too, was well done—greatly to Boston's honor.

"But other men would improve the opportunity to make church members and enforce belief in the ecclesiastic theology; so they set the revival machinery in motion. Men like to follow the multitude.

"The means of getting up a revival are as well known as the means for getting up a Mechanics Fair, a country muster, a cattle show, or a political convention. They have only to advertise in the newspapers and say, 'The Rev. Mr. Great-Talk is to be here today. He is exceedingly interesting and has already converted men by the scores or by the hundreds.' Then they hang out their placards at the corners of the streets.

"It is a business operation. It reminds me of the placards of the rival clothing dealers in North Street; and Park Street Church is the Oak Hall of ecclesiastic business in slop clothing. There is nothing more miraculous in the one case than in the other.

"Last year, it did not succeed very well, for business was good and men with full pockets were not to be scared with talk about hell. Now, the commercial crisis makes it easy to act on men's fears. The panic in State Street which ruined the warehouses fills the meeting-houses today. If the black death raged in New Orleans, the yellow fever in Cincinnati, the plague in Philadelphia, the cholera in New York, the smallpox in Boston, the revival would be immensely greater than now.

"Now we are always to expect some extravagance in the action of a force so strong as this. Some good will be done by this movement. Let us do justice. There are wicked men who are only to be roused by fear. Some will be converted. The dread of hell is stronger than fear of the gallows. Some will be scared out of their ugly vice and crime. . . . But it is only the men who commit the unpopular, small vices that are converted. Such as do the heavy wickedness, those men are never converted until they are too old for any sin except hypocrisy.

"Then there are weak men, who are not wicked, but who can be easily drawn into vice—gambling, drunkenness, licentiousness—some of them will be checked in their course, and become sober men, outwardly decorous.

"Then there are unsettled men and women, who want a master to put his invasive, aggressive will on them, and say they shall or they shall not. They will find a master. It is true, they will shrink and shrivel and dry up. But they want a master and, finding one, they will grow no more and be tormented no more. Ceasing to think, they will cease to doubt; and when they have made a solitude, they will call it the peace of Christ.

"But the evil very far surpasses the good. Many men, well-born, well-educated, will turn off in disgust from real religion. They will become more selfish, more worldly, proud, heartless, hostile to every effort for human progress, —with no faith in God, none in man, none in immortality, none in conscience,—their lives devoted to the lower law. Many of them will be church members, for the actual atheist of today is cunninger than ever before, and entrenches himself within the church. There is no fortress like a pew against the ecclesiastic artillery.

"Such a revival will make more men of this stamp. They are the greatest obstacles to the community's progress. It is not drunkards, it is not thieves, it is not common brawlers who hinder most the development of mankind.

It is the sleek, comfortable men, outwardly decorous, but inwardly as rotten as a grave.

"Then, others, who were brought into the churches full of zeal, full of resolution, they will be cursed by the theology they accept, and will be stunted in their mental, moral and religious growth. For with the idea of God, that He is an ugly devil, of men, that he is a sinful worm, and of religion, that it is an unnatural belief in what reason, conscience, heart and soul cry out against, what true, manly piety can there be? Fear takes the place of religion. . . .

"Piety is not delirium. It does not expose to the world the innermost sanctuary of man's consciousness, and make common talk out of what is too sacred for any eye but God's. . . .

"The effect on the morality of the people is not less bad. Honest industry, forgiveness, benevolence,—these are virtues not thought of in a revival. I do not hear any prayer for temperance, any prayer for education, any prayer for the emancipation of slaves, for the elevation of women, for honesty, for industry, for brotherly love; any prayers against envy, suspicion, bigotry, superstition, spiritual pride, malice, and all uncharitableness.

"The newspapers tell us fifty thousands are converted in a week. That is a great story, but it may be true. The revival may spread all over the land. It will make church members,—not good husbands, good wives, daughters, uncles, aunts; not good shoemakers, farmers, lawyers, mechanics, merchants, laborers. . . .

"Suppose you could convert all the merchants, all the mechanics, all the laborers of Boston, and admit them to the churches that are getting up this revival, you do not add one ounce to the virtue of the city, not one cent's worth of charity to the whole town. You weaken its intelligence, its enterprise; you deaden the piety and morality of the people. . . .

"The churches need a revival. No institution in America is more corrupt than her churches. No thirty thousand men and women are so bigoted and narrow as the thirty thousand ministers. . . .

"A real revival of religion—it was never more needed. Why are men and women so excited now? Why do they go to the meeting-houses, and listen to doctrines that insult the common sense of mankind? They are not satisfied with their religious condition. They feel their want. . . . This movement shows how strong is the religious faculty in man.

"In the name of Democracy, politicians use the deep, patriotic feeling of the people to destroy the best institutions of America and the world. In the name of God, ministers use this mightiest religious feeling to impose on us things yet more disastrous.

"Let you and me remember that religion is wholeness, not mutilation; that it is life, and not death; that it is a service with every limb of this body, every faculty of this spirit; that we are not to take the world on halves with God, or on sevenths, giving Him only the lesser fraction, and taking the larger ourselves; it is to spread over and consecrate the whole life, and make it divine."

This was the voice of a Parker of Lexington where Nathaniel of old defied the British battalion and said to his handful of Minute Men—"If they mean to have war, let it begin here!" The preacher was no less of a soldier. His brave stand did not go unheeded. All that was genuine in the revival that began in 1857 heartened the nation and gave it the spiritual strength to survive, both North and South, the struggle through disunion to reunion in the sixties.

And the ideal that Parker exalted, the true revival of religion, came nearest to realization a decade after his death in 1860 when Dwight L. Moody began justifying to his generation the faith that made lives whole.

## CHAPTER XVI

## ERA OF THE STRAIGHT GOSPEL

There were ninety and nine that safely lay
In the shelter of the fold,
But one was out on the hills away,
Far off from the gates of gold—
Away on the mountains wild and bare,
Away from the tender Shepherd's care,
Away from the tender Shepherd's care.

Words by ELIZABETH CLEPHANE.
Music by IRA SANKEY.

SINGING softly blended with the sweet tones of distant pipes of an organ whose music strayed on after the three hundred voices died away. The man who a little while ago had been telling of his innermost life, making it poignantly akin to the experience of every life, who had been praying with the very thoughts that welled up in the minds of his hearers, who had led them in the hymn that left their hearts a-tremble, this man was now speaking in the dim light with the fainter and fainter strains of the organ following to his last syllable. "Let us now go out and gather on the hill under the stars," he was saying, "and there let us answer the call of the spirit within us."

And so they filed after him, these three hundred collegians, chosen of their fellows for what they were doing, and soon they were met beneath the night sky of Northfield, there upon Round Top, the hill that Dwight Lyman

Moody loved and chose for his final place of rest. For a moment there was silence, a silence in which the three hundred were struggling either to speak or to keep themselves from speaking.

One youth began haltingly. Then the words of self-revelation, yearning for guidance and governance, groping for a fullness of faith to carry him through, rushed from his lips. An impact of suddenly lucid understanding struck the others. Vicariously each had been uttering what had been in him to say. One of them in later years confessed gratitude to the young man who had spoken so eloquently for him and convinced him that his mind was freed without the need of his baring his soul also. He went down the hill, packed his bag and departed. But the rest stayed on till all found peace and a benediction.

It was the Northfield Conference, the legacy and memorial of Moody, America's greatest evangelist who had prayed personally with seven hundred and fifty thousand men and women and preached to a hundred million and helped more than a million to find the way to their God. The schools, Mount Hermon and Northfield, in his ancestral Western Massachusetts village, are his visible monument. Into them he poured thousands of dollars. With his other projects—like the Bible Institute and a church in Chicago—they shared in the one million two hundred and fifty thousand dollars earned in royalties by the hymnal of Moody and Ira D. Sankey. At the end of his life this man, who had renounced a youthful ambition to amass a fortune, left just five hundred dollars, and that by mistake. He had assisted a neighbor in distress and the man had drawn up a mortgage for that five hundred dollars which Moody knew nothing about.

To Northfield Moody also gave himself, his organizing

~ DWIGHT L. MOODY ~

genius, his simple, direct religion. His greatest joy in the last years of his life was in presiding over the student conferences through which he believed the best of his work and its highest aims would be perpetuated.

His religion and his ideal in the preaching of it for more than forty years were bluntly put in his parting words to a group of ministers in the great Convention Hall at Kansas City upon the conclusion of his last revival in November, 1899. Leaning on the organ at the close of the service he said:

"Will you ministers allow me to say a word to you?"

"Yes, yes; say what you want," they replied.

"Well, I'm not a prophet, but I have a guess to make that I think will prove a true prophecy. You hear so much nowadays about the preacher of the Twentieth Century. Do you know what sort of man he will be? He will be the sort of preacher who opens his Bible and preaches out of that. Oh, I'm sick and tired of this essay preaching! I'm nauseated with this 'silver-tongued orator' preaching! I like to hear preachers, and not windmills."

Perhaps Reuben A. Torrey and J. Wilbur Chapman approached this standard, but it was Moody himself who at the culmination of his evangelizing career had brought it to greatest exemplification. He had no time or patience for formal theology or for quarrels with doctrines and creeds. He just opened the Book to the Gospels and took what he found as he found it, the testimony of the Disciples of Jesus. It was the era of the straight Gospel in the preaching of Moody and the singing of Ira D. Sankey and the intelligent, withal emotional, response of the thousands on thousands who heard them.

One text alone discloses the lifelong impulse of Moody—"The Son of Man is come to save that which is lost."

And the heart-searching song of Sankey—"But one was out on the hills away—away from the tender Shepherd's care"—echoed the grand motif on the preaching of Moody. Three words more gave God his grip on Moody and Moody his grip on the souls of his generation. They were Christ's "Come unto Me." It was of them that Sankey sang "Almost Persuaded."

Persistence, fortitude and indefatigable energy were bred in the marrow and nurtured in the background of New England frugality of this one-minded man Moody. Born at Northfield on February 5, 1837, of the stock that settled the Connecticut Valley, he became inured in his boyhood to poverty, toil and hardship in putting his sturdy young shoulders into the struggle of a widowed mother to keep her home together. One of his first tasks was driving cattle to and from pasture for a penny a week. A few terms of country school had to suffice for his education. When he was seventeen he ceased hoeing other men's corn and started a career of his own in which he might have made a success as a seller of shoes instead of a saver of souls.

At first he was convinced that everybody who passed by the store where he clerked on Court Street in Boston had feet that needed to be shod; not many years later he was even more firmly convinced that every person he met had a soul to be saved and that he was the one to save it. Just as he had stood out on the sidewalk and buttonholed customers for shoes, he spent the rest of his life laying hold of all that came in his way and pressing salvation upon them.

To Moody the essence of religious conversion was the consequent determination to convert others. The turning point in his life was simple, swift and direct. He was

wrapping up a package of shoes. His Sunday school teacher
at the Mount Vernon Street Congregational Church, Edward Kimball, dropped in on him and in a few earnest
words urged him to give his allegiance to Jesus Christ.
Moody paused, the string taut in his fingers. "I will," he
replied—and for forty-five years from that day in 1856
to his death on December 22, 1899, he never swerved
from that pledge of fidelity.

He joined the church and tried to speak in prayer-
meeting. The deacons were not impressed. Moody accepted
their verdict, saying, "Well, I can't preach but I can bring
people to hear somebody else preach." He hired and filled
four pews. Then he wanted to teach in Sunday school,
only to be balked by an excess of teachers over pupils. He
went out and recruited his own class. The evangelical compulsion was growing upon him when in that same year
his adventurous spirit took him to Chicago, the new, raw,
rough Chicago just rising at the continental cross-currents.

The nation-wide revival of 1857 was the first that
Moody encountered. It infused in him the zeal that flamed
into the mastering passion of his life and it gave the first
definite direction toward the career for which he was
heading. He was now a wholesaler of shoes. He became a
wholesaler in salvation. As he had gone after business and
got it even so he went out after eternal souls and pulled
them in. It was not yet a revival, however. He started as
an organizer of Sunday schools for which he corralled
members by the hundreds.

Six days with shoes did he labor and on the seventh
with the hoodlums and ragamuffins of tough North Chicago, known then as "Little Hell." On Saturday nights
the stocky figure of the Gospeler loomed in the doorways
of saloons, bolted in and out of tenements, up and down

stairs in dark hallways. Bushy whiskers fringed his iron jaw. Steadily burning eyes were fixed upon those whom he sought. His strong hand was laid upon shoulders as his persuasive voice spoke the brief, abrupt question and command. He never let go of a quarry. One skittish child he chased half a mile and finally traced to an impoverished home behind a rum-shop.

Among his first pupils, afterward respectable gentlemen with names their mothers gave them, were such picturesque characters as Red Eye, Black Stovepipe, Smikes and Darby the Cobbler. They were of the ultimate one thousand five hundred who outgrew North Market Hall and came to worship in a Church that Moody built for them. And they were the "dividends" of the North Market Sabbath School Association, incorporated for ten thousand dollars vested in forty thousand shares at twenty-five cents apiece. It was the Lord's business. Moody had to choose between it and shoes. He was earning seven thousand dollars a year and had hoped to accumulate one hundred thousand dollars. All his talent, all his ambition swung over-night from piling up dollars to increasing the population of heaven.

In 1861 Abraham Lincoln on his way to Washington visited the Sunday school of Moody that in a few weeks was to send fifty soldiers into the Union Army and its leader to pray with the wounded and dying, on the battlefields. "Crazy" Moody, Chicago was calling him. But he didn't mind. Within a decade he was extolling this "madness" in great revivals.

"In my opinion no one is fit for God's service until he is willing to be considered mad by the world," he declared. "They said Paul was mad. I wish we had many more who were bitten with the same kind of madness. As some one has said: 'If we are mad, we have a good Keeper on the way and a good Asylum at the end of the road.' "

Moody was among the stretchers under fire at Pittsburg Landing, Shiloh and Chattanooga and was with the first to enter Richmond. He did more than pray soldiers into heaven; he mustered his regiments into the Army of the Lord for this world too. He was absent from the front at various times,—long enough to marry Emma Revell in 1862, build the Illinois Street Church in Chicago and push both his Sunday school and the newly founded Young Men's Christian Association. In 1867 he raised the money for one Y. M. C. A. hall, named for John V. Farwell, which burned within four months, and, before the ashes were cool, for another and bigger building that took its place. Here the Moody revival took its root, with the same sort of preaching, singing, and "inquiry room" that characterized his way of landing people on the "solid rock" of Gospel religion.

He had discovered that he could preach. At a Sunday school convention where scheduled speakers were lacking he took the rostrum and the diffidence imposed upon him by the deacons of Boston vanished in a torrent of molten words. Sixty conversions ensued on the spot. The gift was his for life and he learned how to use it with all the tremendous physical and spiritual force stored in his powerful frame. Never would he preach to empty pews and never did he have to. From Farwell Hall in the late sixties to the Kansas City Convention Hall in the last of the nineties hundreds of thousands came because it was Moody.

He did not wait for people to come, however, nor did he confine his demands for "surrender" to the thronged

tabernacle when emotions were all ablaze. No moment of
the day or night was anybody within reach of his summons able to escape it. On the street, aboard railway trains
and steamers, in homes, hotels—even in saloons, he would
tackle any stranger with his brusque and startling inquiry
—"Are you a Christian?" It is not recorded how many
times he was told it was none of his business. But it is
certain that he invariably answered that it was exactly
the business he was in. Once a man in Chicago promptly
rejoined "Then you are D. L. Moody!" And another man
who rebuffed him sought him out later with penitential
tears.

The point was that Moody could not stop in his chosen
work. Of all things in the world he abhorred laziness was
the worst. "If we are children of God we ought not to
have a lazy drop of blood in our veins," he said in a revival outburst. "If a man tells me he has been saved, and
does not desire to work for the honor of God, I doubt his
salvation. *I have more hope for the salvation of drunkards
and thieves and harlots than of a lazy man!*" He was for-
giving toward almost everything except procrastination.
On the eve of the Chicago fire, on October 8, 1871, he addressed the largest assembly he had ever faced on "What
then shall I do with Jesus which is called Christ?" He
closed his entry by urging a decision the following Sunday. "What a mistake!" he said afterward. "I have never
dared to give an audience a week to think of their salvation since. If they were lost they might rise up in
judgment against me."

In that fire Farwell Hall, Moody's church and his home
were destroyed. His wife saved only the portrait of him
that now hangs in the Northfield homestead. He clung to
his Bible and amid the ruins opened up the Book and read

to the people that with him they were not impoverished
because they were joint heirs with Christ. That was for
eternity. In two months and fifteen days, with the help
of John Wanamaker and George H. Stuart of Philadelphia and funds raised in New York, Moody had a barn-like
tabernacle erected, dedicated and in day and night service.
He took his choir out from it into the streets and kept up
a high pressure evangelism while the city rose anew from
its ashes.

Moody could not sing. He had an agreeable speaking
voice which conveyed the emotional color of his every
vibrant phrase, a voice of rare timbre that reached whole
auditories of fifteen thousand. But he could not carry a
tune. He knew it. And he also knew the value of music in
giving effect to his preaching. He had choirs in his day of as
many as eight hundred singers but all put together never
could equal Ira David Sankey in the power of musical
appeal to the people.

The two men met at the international convention of the
Y. M. C. A. at Indianapolis in 1870. Moody had led the
Chicago Association since 1865 and Sankey, a delegate
from Newcastle, Pennsylvania, where he was Collector of
Internal Revenue, was anxious to see the evangelist whose
name had already travelled far. Moody was trying to lead
a prayer meeting at six o'clock in the morning of the last
day of the session. The singing had lagged and sputtered
out when Sankey arrived and in his strong, sweet baritone
started "There is a Fountain Filled With Blood." The
meeting was electrified. When it was over Moody sought
the singer.

"Where are you from? Are you married? What is your
business?"—Moody rapidly put his curt questions to Sankey. As to the occupation he summarily disposed of it,

saying, "You'll have to give that up. You are the man I have been looking for. I want you to come to Chicago and help me in my work." Sankey capitulated and the life-long partnership was struck. From a packing box on the street that afternoon Sankey sang "Am I a Soldier of the Cross?" and "Shall We Gather at the River?" and Moody preached to workmen on their way home to supper. A few weeks later Sankey arrived in Chicago with his odd little portable organ, led the Moody family in a hymn before breakfast and that night captivated the crowd that jammed Farwell Hall. "You see I was right in asking you to come," said Moody.

On the night the Chicago fire broke out, Sankey was leading in singing "Today the Savior Calls" as the first engines clanged and shrieked past Farwell Hall. He had to quit on the third verse but ten weeks later in the new Tabernacle he was singing again the songs of salvation— "Saved by Grace" and "Safe in the Arms of Jesus." Other offers were made to Sankey but he stuck to Moody on the upgrade to the great days which linked their names forever.

This other half of America's first evangelistic team was a Methodist Sunday school superintendent and choir leader. His singing had filled his home-town church in Newcastle which he had joined upon his conversion at the age of sixteen. His father was president of a bank, a member of the Pennsylvania Legislature for thirteen years and privileged to prefix the title of "Honorable."

The Sankeys moved to Newcastle in 1857 from Edinburgh, on the Mahoning River in Western Pennsylvania, where Ira David was born on August 28, 1840. In 1861 he went singing off to war with the first to go from Newcastle. Married in 1863 to Fanny V. Edwards, whose father was also an "Honorable," he began collecting revenue for the Government after the war the while his singing made a name for him in his own State as well as Ohio. His devotion to the Y. M. C. A. movement brought him to Indianapolis and Moody in 1870. During their first two years together they were little known beyond the region round Chicago for what they were doing. Then they discovered England for the glory of God and England discovered them for America.

The sagacious Moody made two exploratory voyages, in 1867 and in June, 1872, but even on these he wasted no time. At Bristol, sacred to the memory of Wesley and Whitefield, he converted fifteen, among them John K. MacKenzie, who founded the first British medical school in China. His initial attempt in London was frosty. The people sat stolidly when he asked Christians to rise. But in the "inquiry room" after the meeting, his Gospel workshop where personal contact supplemented his preaching, there was not space to hold the praying people. He had broken the ice.

Now he was ready for Sankey and crossed the Atlantic to fetch him. They landed at Liverpool on June 17, 1873, the anniversary of the battle of Bunker Hill, and opened fire in a two-year campaign throughout the British Isles. In two hundred and eighty-five meetings two million five hundred thousand heard them. They never seemed to rest. One winter Moody spoke and Sankey sang four times daily in a swift succession of ninety towns in ninety-nine days. One was called Mercurius, the other Orpheus.

The British Kingdom did not fall all at once at their feet. Ribald mobs hooted the twang of Moody, parochial clergy resented his putting the Bible into common vernacular, and the press was scornful of the "crack-brained

Yankee evangelists," "abbots of unreason," and "pernicious humbugs." On the other side of the ocean The New York Times, on June 22, 1875, declared itself "creditably informed" that P. T. Barnum had sent Moody and Sankey to England as a "matter of speculation." The Times was misinformed but if the enterprise had been Barnum's it would have yielded the greatest percentage of profit he ever got. The original "investment" was four hundred fifty dollars that was due Moody when he sailed on his mission.

The common people of England and Ireland and Scotland turned the tide. Henry Drummond joined hands with Moody at Edinburgh and Charles Spurgeon in London. The largest halls could not contain the reverent throngs that besieged them. Sankey's cabinet organ, which the Scottish folk had dubbed his "kist o' whistles," became a heavenly instrument as it trailed his voice singing "Jesus of Nazareth Passeth By." The newspapers ceased joking. Music hall quips were hissed down. Publishers could not keep up with the demand for Bibles. The first Sankey Gospel hymn book was thrown together, and though the copies were sold for a penny apiece and the royalty was small, it put thirty-five thousand dollars into the hands of Moody and Sankey on the eve of their sailing home to America where their fame had preceded them and the hour was come for the country's revival of revivals.

Moody had cables from half a dozen American cities beseeching his presence, before he embarked. He brought back the thirty-five thousand dollars hymn book money with him, the English people having refused to let him "pay for the privilege of preaching" to them, and he applied it to the rebuilding of his church in Chicago. He reached these shores the man of the moment. He paused to take counsel.

Up in Northfield, where he bought the farm which became his home ever after, he sat down with Major D. W. Whittle, whom he met in the war, Philip Paul Bliss and George C. Stebbins, the hymn-writers, and Sankey. They had finished the hymnal and the plan for Moody and Sankey to go out to their countrymen when Theodore Cuyler, of Brooklyn,—the Cuyler of the 1857 revival—came personally and persuaded them to begin in his city.

At the Brooklyn Skating Rink in October, 1874, the Moody momentum began rolling with five thousand thrice daily filling the building. On to Philadelphia it moved and there in ten weeks at the old Pennsylvania railroad depot, bought by John Wanamaker for a store and lent by him for the revival, the attendance mounted to nine hundred thousand, every meeting drawing thirteen thousand. The singers numbered six hundred and the ushers three hundred. At Barnum's Hippodrome in New York City in February, 1876, the choir was augmented to twelve hundred and it took five hundred ushers to marshal the total of one million five hundred thousand who day and night for ten weeks stood in long lines on Madison Avenue for a chance to get in. The next Fall a tabernacle in Chicago built for the same purpose held ten thousand at every meeting for three months. Then Boston erected and jammed another with six thousand thrice a day for six months for Moody and Sankey.

Twenty years they traversed the ground over and over, widened the territory and gathered together increasing multitudes of people. Baltimore, St. Louis, Denver, San Francisco, every large city on the continent from Canada to the Mexican border—North, South, East and West they carried their Gospel in word and in song. Everywhere it was asked—"Have you heard Moody preach?" and

"Have you heard Sankey sing?" And what did this full-bearded, broad-shouldered, rough-hewn, two hundred eighty-pound tireless little giant preach and how did this tall, bland gentleman with the sidewhiskers of an old-time floorwalker sing?

They are on the platform together, Moody dressed with severe plainness, no watch-chain, no cuff links, heavy but hard of flesh and solid; Sankey attired in the Sunday morning mode of a leading village churchman, meticulously neat, just a bit unctuous. Save for the light in his far-searching eyes, the countenance of Moody is immobile; his hand is tightly grasping the railing as an engineer grips his throttle just as his train is starting; his mind is concentrated upon the ten thousand human beings in front of him and they are drawn irresistibly toward him. Sankey's forty-four-inch chest arches back from the organ at his knees; he serenely poises his fingers over the keys and looks out across the open hymn book expansively smiling.

"Sankey will sing." The General has delivered an order. In the vast silence ripple the notes of the melodeon. It's "Throw Out the Life-Line." Sankey's face is transformed, glorified, transfigured as the rich, full notes of sweetness and power roll out "across the dark wave" and tug at the heart of the "brother whom someone must save."

"Now you sing." It is another command. The brusque soldier of salvation long ago made up his mind to be obeyed. He gets what he wants. Sankey is still on the ocean wave. Ten thousand voices follow him into "Pull for the Shore, Sailor, Pull for the Shore." Another hymn—this time it's on the battlefront of the soul—"Hold the Fort for I Am Coming." Ten thousand hearts are throbbing with the chorus. Moody booms "Let us pray!" He tells

God the need of His people; he asks His presence, His help, His forgiveness. And then "Amen!"

Moody's Bible is in his hand. He reads it like truth just that moment vouchsafed to the world. He takes his text, closes the Book and repeats it and plunges headlong into his preaching. Perhaps he is with Jacob or Jonah, on the Mount of Olives or at the foot of Calvary. All the while he clings to that Bible and in his rough voice and homely way makes it dramatically real. He channels his thought. Sin is death. Only one way leads out. The love of God is pleading through His Son. "Him, mark you," Moody is saying, "Him—not a dogma, not a creed, not a myth but a person!"

Grammar is slighted with "done" for "did" and "come" for "came." Illiteracy leaks through with " 'tain't no use" and "git right up." But the impetus of eloquence rushes over such slips. "Culture is all right in its place," Moody once said, "but to talk about culture before a man is born of God is the height of madness." This rebirth is his religion and it is in every sermon somehow, somewhere.

Naaman dipping seven times in Jordan, the blind man bathing his eyes in the pool of Siloam—Moody draws the lesson of obedience. The prodigal son, the penitent thief on the cross beside Christ's—Moody throws open the gates of heaven. A short prayer, benediction and the meeting is over, over for all the ten thousand except a few score who press forward to kneel with Moody and Sankey in the inquiry room, clinching conversions.

So Moody preached and so Sankey sang, the one commanding and the other faithfully standing by him. They stood together in tremendous scenes. There was the night devoted to drunkards in Philadelphia when sodden wretches crawled up from the gutters; there was the night in New York when Dom Pedro, Emperor of Brazil, stood up and earnestly, simply assented after Moody had spotted him and said: "Even a great Emperor cannot save his soul unless he bows himself at Christ's feet and accepts Him!"

Then in Chicago in 1893, competing with the World's Fair on Sundays, they hired the big tent of Forepaugh's three-ring circus and packed in twenty thousand who reached from the shavings of the arena to the top with its slung-back trapezes. The showmen plastered billboards with "Ha! Ha! Ha! Three Big Shows. Moody in the Morning! Forepaugh in the Afternoon and Evening!" There was a difference. The evangel's hour brought the hush of heaven under the canvas. With five other tents, nine halls, two Gospel wagons and a line-up of churches, he made that Fair a tributary to salvation.

All his life through Moody grew with his Gospel. He held to sin's retribution but he talked of heaven rather than hell after Henry Moorehouse, the young preacher, came over from England in 1867 and put the theme of God's love in his heart with the memorable text of a dozen sermons on "God so loved the world." He ceased trying to defend the Bible, admitting there were things he did not "profess to understand." He accepted the Book, saying "There is as much reason to say that the sun is worn out as to say that we have got beyond the Bible."

Jonah and the whale were as true to him as Fulton and the Clermont. He had his meeting in Detroit raptly intent upon his dramatic drive of Elijah aloft in his chariot of fire. And he had the Yankees of New England chuckling appreciatively over this version of the Flood: "They would say to one another, 'Not much sign of old Noah's rainstorm yet.' They would talk it over in the corner grocery store. I tell you what—before the world got as bad as in Noah's day there must have been corner grocery stores."

As for the old doctrines, common sense applied what he found in Scripture. "If I have sinned I must die or get somebody to die for me—that is where the atonement of Jesus Christ comes in," he said. "God looks over His ledger and says: 'Moody, your debt has all been wiped out by Another.'" He disposed of "election" with the words "Whosoever will let him come." With Wesley he believed conversion instantaneous. "A man may be a thief one moment and a saint the next," he declared, "vile as hell itself one moment and saved the next."

Belief was mandatory with him; unbelief was the "damning sin of the world." His demand was urgent; he lived in the constant expectation of the final judgment. "I don't think the time is far distant when the Lord will return," was the way he put it again and again. But he never allowed any hysterical excitement or morbid manifestation. He dominated the deeper waters. His audacious bluntness even vanquished the skepticism of erudite Boston. And his impregnable calm banished all fear of a panic when part of his tabernacle roof fell in at Fort Worth, Texas.

Moody loved children and horses, a good joke and a good meal. He was a great neighbor and ever a Samaritan. He was sure of himself and people trusted him and did what he told them to do. He believed God answered his prayers —including one for a barrel of flour when times were hard in early Chicago and another to save a liner sinking under him in mid-ocean; he believed God inspired his preaching, made his decisions and guided his every project. He felt that God's will halted his work at Kansas City in

November, 1899, and at home on his death-bed at North-field in December he spoke like a sentry on post: "I'm not going to throw my life away. I'll stay as long as I can, but if my time is come, I'm ready!"

Dwight Lyman Moody might have been a captain of finance or of industry. Instead he was captain of his own soul and Field Marshal of the million souls he led marching with him home to God.

## CHAPTER XVII

## TORCHBEARERS ON THEIR OWN

Sowing in the morning, sowing seeds of kindness,
Sowing in the noontide and the dewy eve;
Waiting for the harvest, and the time of reaping,
We shall come rejoicing, bringing in the sheaves.
                    KNOWLES SHAW, 1834–1878.

WHEN Moody's mortality was laid under the snow on Round Top at Northfield there stood by the graveside one to whom his mantle might have descended. Not that Reuben Archer Torrey was unworthy to wear it, not that his labor was undeserving, but that none have come afterward of like stature to fit it, like soul to blaze under its folds. Torrey, who had stepped into the breach and carried through the unfinished task at Kansas City, who for a decade had led in Chicago the training of evangels as Moody would have them be, Torrey was foremost of all the successors of the straight-Gospel preacher.

He found his Sankey in Charles M. Alexander, the Tennessee singer, to whom the Moody Bible Institute taught the art of revival music, and together they went over the world to places where Moody had been and to places he had had no time to reach, the Antipodes, the Orient, besides America and Britain, and they mobilized their tabernacle thousands under the new century's rubric of "Get Right with God."

Both had served apprenticeship with Moody and Sankey and inherited their direct-dealing tactics. But now Moody was dead, Sankey was singing alone and the revival itself had passed the peak of high spirituality and was levelling toward commoner courses. Trite slogans, convert counts, calculated publicity, herd lip-Gospelling, mob-singing, hero-worshipping of self-centered revival rangers, and churches looking for members that did not come when the shouting was over—all this was gathering like an avalanche to crash down upon America in the name of evangelization.

It was a transitional age in the life of the nation, a time of material and emotional expansion yet growing sophistication which challenged ingenuity to keep pace with a volatile people. Good men and honest, broad-minded yet deadly in earnest, their conviction their message, bore lone torches over the land. Others, starting sincerely, set off pyrotechnics in eagerness to burst barriers and extend themselves with their missions.

Dr. Torrey and his immediate contemporaries changed the rigging a bit but steered the Moody Gospel ship pretty close to the old seaway the while flamboyant sails were being hoisted. The father of Dr. Torrey was a banker who was ruined in the panic of 1857, a year after the birth of the son, but recouped and was able to pay the youth's card and racing losses at Yale without a reproach. Young Torrey's conscience, however, almost drove him to suicide. Moody arrived in New Haven in time to spoil a legal career and make a minister of him.

Bible in hand, Torrey stalked the young woman who had been his frequent dancing partner. Two hours of importuning and she knelt and forswore the waxed floor forever. His first preaching was tremulous, with fright and

~ B. FAY MILLS ~

not feeling, and Niagaras, of sweat and not tears, ran down his face and neck. A pastorate in an Ohio nest of infidelity made him a bold fundamentalist of the "whole Bible from cover to cover" and provoked a three-year revival all his own. It was highly successful. A poker game was suspended while he led in prayer in a saloon. The next day the boss of a rival bar-room indignantly protested the discrimination and Torrey promptly set things right with another praise service.

He founded the "Open-Door Church" in Minneapolis and thence graduated to the Moody sanctum sanctorum in Chicago where not a Sabbath got by him without new names written in heaven. In 1898 he was with the army "eating, drinking, breathing dust with the soldiers," and in 1899 by the side of the evangel chieftain up to the moment when the command fell to him at Kansas City. A week of supplication at Chicago in 1901 prayed down a world-wide revival. Dr. Torrey took the commission and chose Alexander his lyric lieutenant.

They were a contrast to the prototype preacher and singer, Moody the gruffly domineering, Sankey the ingratiating. Dr. Torrey, graceful of gesture and movement for all his portliness, attained domination with perfect suavity and induced agreement with his positivism. His close-trimmed white beard enhanced either beneficence or solemnity of mien. Alexander bent over no organ. Tall and long of reach, he was the amiable upstanding chorister who lifted people out of themselves in their singing.

Alexander was on his feet when he sang and his sensitive, long, thin smooth face mirrored the feeling borne by the tender "Tell Mother I'll Be There" or the exultant "Yes, There Will Be Glory for Me." After twice girdling the globe with Dr. Torrey, he teamed up with M. B. Williams and finally with Dr. J. Wilbur Chapman. It was Alexander that laid down the lines for the modern revival singer, for his life span stretched out of the old way into the new. He was singing for Moody in pitting salvation against the World's Fair midway in 1893 and by 1907 he was working with Charles H. Gabriel who forthwith tuned up as bard extraordinary to William A. Sunday.

The singer was born at Meadow, Tennessee, on October 24, 1867. He went from Maryville College to the Moody Bible Institute, where he was of the first crop from the Gospel seed that was planted. From tent chorister he rose to be master of music in the Moody Sunday school of eighteen hundred. He learned how to handle the crowd. And the crowd was attracted to him. He was always his half of any evangel combination.

Once in New York a voice from the gallery called for the hymn "He Will Hold Me Fast." It was a new one with music by Robert Harkness, ranking composer of twentieth-century revivalism, and Alexander had to sing it over and over till the audience learned it. Then he dared anyone to stand forth and sing it alone, promising a copy of the song as the guerdon. A colored man rose and rendered it perfectly. Alexander asked him if he were a Christian. He was and his name was Charles Alexander and he hailed also from Tennessee. That is why the revival was on the front pages the next morning.

Alexander's last campaign was in Detroit but the World War found him at Northfield bearing a message in song for wounded hearts and torn souls, "a heavenly minstrel singing blithely to his fellow-pilgrims here below." He had perfected his system—the solo that cued in with the preaching, the choir that served as a Grecian chorus in advancing the sacred drama, the congregational singing that achieved universal participation with handshaking and unison after this side then another, the men then the women, had sung. And when he died in 1920 this was the system he bequeathed to be adapted by the rollicking revival of Billy Sunday and Aimee Semple McPherson. Reuben Torrey, however, remembered the old days when in Alexander's passing he said: "Charlie is still singing, singing as he never sang on earth."

Within the time and tradition of Moody belongs one other great singer who was also a far-travelled evangelist, Knowles Shaw, the Campbellite Boanerges and Baptizer, whose "Bringing in the Sheaves" is still a Sunday school stand-by. Butler County, Ohio, was taking its religion from log churches and woodland camp meetings when Shaw was born there in 1834 and particularly susceptible to the world-end alarm of the Millerites. His dying father gave him a violin and told him to prepare to meet his God. A happy-go-lucky carouser and popular fiddler for neighborhood reels and quadrilles, he lived by his bow till one night the parting parental warning recurred to him and never again did he call "Sache the center." Instead it was "Come, kneel at the altar."

For days, lying on the floor wrapped in a blanket and fed bread and milk by a much-concerned mother, he battled it out with the Devil. George Campbell himself happened along to the Flat Rock (Indiana) Church and wrought the conversion. Knowles Shaw was dipped in the river. He married and tinkered with sewing machines and clocks for a living out in Missouri till in October, 1858, this jack of all trades, musician and poet ascended the pulpit with most of his learning comprised in the Bible. The fiddle went with him and together they set religion to music in Ohio, Illinois and Michigan, Indiana, Kentucky and Iowa, Tennessee, West Virginia and Texas. They paused often at small towns but big places also heard them —like Quincy, St. Louis, Memphis and Dallas. Twenty stands netted two thousand two hundred thirty-six for the Lord and Shaw made sure of them by thorough immersion. In June, 1879, when he was killed in a train wreck in Texas, his personal register had recorded eleven thousand conversions.

In his prime he was six feet four inches of ungainly genus homo with flowing red hair and chin whiskers. While preaching or singing he swayed like a tall pine in a storm, his long beard streaming like the tail of a comet. Versatile as a trouper, he would convulse his audiences with laughter by mimicry, pantomime and grimaces and then baptize them in tears while he stood in memory by the death-bed of his little girl and repeated her "I'm going home, dear father, and after a few years more you'll follow me." His sentiment ran freest in music and old hymn books preserve it in his "Shining Ones" and "Lambs of the Upper Fold."

In those flourishing days of religious receptivity evangelists could streak about the country and double on one another's tracks without a lean spell or a junction point. They had no such confraternity as now foregathers at Winona Lake, Indiana, no centralized plotting of circuits. Each took his chance. None starved. No wonder their number was legion. A few had biographers, usually enthusiasts raising an Ebenezer for what happened in one place, but most of them would now be nameless except for renown handed on by the word of mouth of the people.

Everyone remembers when the holy lightning struck his part of the landscape and who pulled it down from the heavens. Everyone volunteers his candidate for canonization, one way or another. If collected in one volume with only a paragraph apiece, the revivalists of the past fifty years would form a book that would dwarf an unabridged dictionary. There were E. P. Hammond, whom children loved,—his recital of the "Charge of the Light Brigade" converted a veteran of Balaklava and thrilled Rochester, New York; Sam Small, the ex-slave of Methodist memory; "Drummer Tom" Osborne and his plaintive rendition of "Sowing the Tares"; James McGranahan singing "Sometime We'll Understand" and "I Shall Be Satisfied"; Frederick Harrison, the "boy preacher," who collared the hesitant and dragged them over the pewtops; and Joseph Weber and his "tornadoes" whirling through sin from Ohio to Maine—in a calmer moment he wrote the words and music of "Can a Boy Forget His Mother."

These itinerant preachers loomed large to all who heard them. Their greatness is beyond the measure of the men and women who found their faith through them. They are recorded here as representative of their brethren. And may all of them find eternity exactly what they preached it to be!

The lesser lights still twinkled but, as the revival matured and attained larger-scale organization, it tended to gravitate toward personages of widely acknowledged distinction. They reached the top by pulling on their own bootstraps or tugging at another's coat-tails. Sam Jones and B. Fay Mills developed original technique; J. Wilbur Chapman earned his spurs with Moody, and Rodney (Gypsy) Smith drilled with the Salvation Army. William A. Sunday began as apprentice to Chapman.

Sam Jones was a lawyer in Georgia before the Methodists redeemed him from rum and in the pulpit he never forgot how to plead with a jury. Colloquial horse sense, every-day comparisons, misty-eyed pathos and hearty humor were stock in trade with him. And he never neglected Sam Jones in any of his sermons.

He is quoting a boastful blade of St. Louis: "Who will pay attention to Sam Jones? If I want a drink of whisky, that is none of his business; if I want to curse, if I want to sin, it is none of his business." Now he answers this hypothetical braggart: "I don't like to say such a thing in public, but I want to tell you, you are lying like a dog! It is my business and everybody's business to see that everybody else does right. ["Amen!" from the southeast corner of crowded Music Hall.] It is the business of your poor, sad-eyed wife and your sweet little children who may follow you to a drunkard's grave." [Redoubled "Amens" from the corner.]

He figures the liquor license yield to the city as twenty cents a head on the population and declares the people sold to the demon for two thin dimes apiece. Then—it is 1895 —he makes this unerring prediction: "I tell you the day will come when there will not be a saloon in this town!"

Professor E. O. Excell, music master for Jones, leads the six thousand in "Where is My Wandering Boy Tonight." Dry eyes are scarce and handkerchiefs are out. The drooping mustaches of the preacher accentuate his momentary sadness. In spite of his prophecy he admits that the idea of driving out whisky this moment is "chimerical."

Now as to some of the Commandments, again he is interlocutor. "Sam Jones," he asks himself, "did you ever cuss and did you ever steal?" He pleads guilty; he also was "jubious" and he stole the peace of his home. "There's no manhood in it," he cries, "it can do nothing but debauch you now and damn you hereafter. Rise and say tonight— 'I've sworn my last oath, boys, I've sworn my last oath!'"

Hordes of foreigners don't like the American Sabbath. Jones anticipates the hundred percenters by telling the blasphemers to go back where they came from. "Ain't that right?" he asks the people. "Yes, that's right," from the steadfast southeast corner. He hurls their acquiescence back at them, saying "Yet right here in this town the godless element care no more for the Sabbath than the goats of Georgia or the cattle of Texas. Woe to America whenever we abolish our Christian Sabbath!"

Another night he is lambasting the racetrack, deriding "bum sports" and advocating "thoroughbred men as well as thoroughbred horses." Still another night he is thundering that man and the church have "stabbed the conscience to death" and invoking God to come down and "dig up the conscience in every man's bosom." Every night he calls on the people to stand with him and pledge quittance of sin and, God helping, the leading of a better life. "Now while we sing, come give me your hand and let's settle it!" All the trail needs now is the sawdust.

In one year alone the recording angels chalked up twenty thousand for Sam Jones. His revival began in the Auditorium at Memphis, Tennessee, in 1881, hit its stride at St. Louis in 1895, and had no diminution in popularity to the day of his death in 1906. Rough-boarded tabernacles were whacked together for him all over the South. Camp meetings met just for him. Ten thousand at a time sat within sound of his voice. In five weeks at Cincinnati three hundred thousand heard him in Music Hall. He pitched a huge tent in St. Joseph, Missouri. Brooklyn and Washington acclaimed him and Chicago was overwhelmed. Eighteen special telegraph wires, run into Farwell Hall, carried nine thousand words a night to newspapers in distant cities while compositors were setting up column on column for the Tribune and the Inter-Ocean. Sam Jones was preaching to an aggregate circulation of two or three million.

Be it said for Jones he made news and he was news without being over much if at all aware of it. B. Fay Mills, however, planted himself with his revival on front pages of extra editions the day he arrived in a city marked for blasting and blessing. He would breeze in three hours ahead of schedule and dramatically declare that "the work of Jesus can't wait; it must be begun right now!" No city editor could ever resist him. Too much circulation was at stake, for Mills had had every denomination lined up months in advance of his coming. He was the great expectation. His entry meant stopping of presses.

The Mills machine was already running smoothly with the city divided into districts, each ruled by a complete set of committees on every detail from devotion to dollars, all radiating from central committees and all converging toward huge union meetings. Every pastor, deacon, organist, choir singer and sexton was enlisted. Merchants and manufacturers, men of every business and profession, not forgetting the overworked purveyors of the printed word, were supplying grease for the gearing.

Whether it was Jersey City, Utica, Rochester, Syracuse, Albany, Columbus, Cincinnati or Chicago, all the master engineer had to do when he got there was stand out where he could be seen at the main power-house, grip the salvation lever and move it notch by notch day after day till full speed spun on the indicator. Then he hated to let go of it. He would often ask his ministerial aides and sponsors if any one of them dared stop the work of the Lord in his city. One up-State New York Methodist brother had the courage to stand up and say that the contracted period had ended and that he would carry on his own revival thereafter. At the end the harbinger of holiness would accept gifts from the appreciative. No account had to be rendered on that score. Collections paid all other costs.

The harvest was all his—five thousand seven hundred converts in six weeks at Cleveland, eight thousand in forty-five days at Cincinnati, three thousand in three weeks at Chicago—because he counted in all who had been garnered at the "district meetings" in co-operating churches—forty-five such feeders were in Cleveland and seventy-one in Cincinnati. One so reckoned, though saved on the outside at Utica, is still resentful toward the mathematics of Mills.

Mills was never alone. He had his retinue. Lawrence Greenwood of West Somerville, Massachusetts, had an ambitious downy beard and a seraphic voice when at the age of twenty-six he joined Mills as a soloist. At one stage of his evangelistic career, which began in 1885 and extended into the new century, Mills had for singer and chorister George C. Stebbins, the peer of Bliss, Sankey and Philip Phillips.

Stebbins was a veteran of the baton. He helped train the Chicago contingent for the Peace Jubilee in 1872 in Boston where seventeen thousand singers and three thousand musicians assembled. He directed music in Tremont Temple and thence went to Northfield to enter the service of Moody, leading choirs of one thousand voices. It was he who wrote the music for Fanny Crosby's "Saved by Grace" and "Jesus Is Calling," for Frances Havergal's "True-Hearted, Whole-Hearted, Faithful and Loyal" and for James Edmeston's "Savior, Breathe an Evening Blessing."

At Cincinnati, Mills had an able pulpit lieutenant in J. Wilbur Chapman, then on leave from the big Bethany

Presbyterian Church in Philadelphia in which John Wanamaker was Superintendent of a Sunday school of three
thousand. Unquestionably Chapman learned from Mills
how to put the revival on a big business footing and passed
the sublime system on to William A. Sunday to develop to
its perfection.

But Mills was no Aladdin of tabernacles, no cost-plus
entrepreneur of wholesale salvation. From the present per-
spective he was a novice experimenting in rudimentary
method. Though he announced that nothing could be accomplished except by means supernatural, he had more
printing of posters, tickets and pledge cards than any other
soul salvage promoter.

Ironclad pledges were exacted from choir singers and
ushers whose pasteboards had the stamp of a time-card.
Admission was free and no collections were taken till the
last day but tickets were issued and treasured by the
throngs that received them. Especially effective were those
reading "For Men Only," "For Young People," and "For
Mothers." Every morning bill-posters were slapping up
colorful fresh tidings and street cars bore Gospel guidance
alongside their signs of destination.

"Good cheer" services, noonday prayer meetings and
"mid-week Sabbaths" were among the innovations. Secular
concerns would halt in the consecrated hours and the word
"Closed," countersigned by Mills, would flare in the windows of stores, offices and factories. It was good business.
Mills told his people to be appreciative of this co-operation
by Catholics, Israelites and infidels with their Protestant
brethren and to patronize them. The whole city would re-
volve about his revival.

The evangelist himself, however, was superior to his
mode of compelling a hearing. Two thirds of his sermons

persuaded Christians to live up to their religion. In the others he pleaded for the irrevocable gift of men's selves to the ideal best that was in them—"because it is right, for no man can be a genuine Christian if his motive be only to escape from hell."

"There is no earthly knowledge pointing out to me the mercy of God," he used to say at the crux of one of his best sermons. "I might study geology all of my life and yet not find the Rock of Ages, mineralogy and yet not find the Pearl of Greatest Price. Astronomy does not point out to me the Star of Bethlehem. Biology does not explain the reason of my existence."

Here came a pause. Then a tremulous appeal for silent prayer while the soloist queried in a minor key "Where Will You Spend Eternity?" Another pause. More intense suasion to voiceless supplication. "O God, be merciful to *us* sinners!" Mills had identified himself with every individual conversion taking place around him. The choir burst into the pæan of "Jesus Saves."

There Mills stands in his triumphal moment. His spacious histrionic mouth that has been pouring a rapid, fervent flow of eloquence seems on the verge of speaking again. His eyes glow with a mystic light. His head tilts to lift his countenance just enough heavenward—the angle crosses that nose of the Cæsars and loses itself in thick curly hair. His broad upper lip quivers. "It is necessary to give ourselves to God," he is saying. "I have no use for mechanical contrivances or machinery in this matter of conversion. It is the work of the Holy Ghost."

But all who want prayers requisite to timeless assurance must stand up and let the Lord and His people and His particular Servant see exactly who they are. The flying squadron of "workers" swoops down the aisles and darts

among the pews pressing cards upon the seekers of redemption. It is a simple promise—"I desire henceforth to
lead a Christian life"—and dotted lines await the name
and church preference. A thousand signatures in one night
is no marvel. Mills spares his wrist from the handshakes.
The fluttering of kerchiefs in a Chautauqua salute signals
the victory, the hail and farewell to the great Gospel
visitant.

Mills finally broke with the old-time revival. This New
Jersey Presbyterian, born at Rahway in 1857 the son of
a preacher and heir to the Tennent tradition, rejected the
fall of man and the atonement, renounced the literalness
of hell or heaven or of the personality of God or the
Devil. Chapman, his college-mate at Lake Forest, sadly
turned away from him and let him go on alone urging all
who heard him "not to wait to be wafted into an un-
merited heaven of oriental splendor but to make a paradise here among the joyless children of men." Upon this
foundation he established his "Los Angeles Fellowship"
to which he dedicated the rest of his life.

The super-revival moved forward without him, its destiny being shaped by men steadfast in the faith funda-
mentals the while their vision encompassed majestical
means for quantity production. But while they were
emulating the Napoleons of beef, oil and steel in creating
their soul-saving combination, one great independent upheld the simpler revival tradition.

On a Saturday afternoon in 1874 Moody and Sankey
drove out from London to a gypsy camp in Epping Forest. The sweet singing of a lad of fourteen, the son of a
tribal lay preacher, touched the heart of Sankey. Laying
his hand on the head of the gypsy boy, he said—"May
the Lord make a preacher of you." Fifteen years later

he met the answer to that prayer when Gypsy (Rodney) Smith came to America. In 1928 he was here on his twenty-fifth voyage of evangelization. He had survived the whirlwind of the tabernacles, the siege of the cities and the material expansion of the most eminent of the Fordizers of salvation.

He is still the straight, broad-shouldered, compact, swarthy little man of other years. The heavy mustache that once was jet black is mottled with gray, but that is the only sign of age. His rich baritone has all the old volume and power. "There is a Fountain Filled with Blood" is his favorite and it is the hymn of his Methodist conversion. A Gypsy Smith service is an alternation of singing and preaching. He has always pointed what he was saying by slipping into interludes of appropriate song. Camp meetings have rallied to him and soldiers behind the lines in France heard that gypsy sing.

On his first trip to America he crowded the Nostrand Avenue Church in Brooklyn for three weeks and five hundred took a stand for the simple religion he sang into their hearts. At Cincinnati rejoicing was mutual when he visited a camp of his nomadic kindred. In 1891 he became a permanent figure of the Ocean Grove (New Jersey) Camp Meeting, the largest Methodist Gospel ground in the world which is operated like a Wesleyan heaven with gates shut on Saturday night and not even a milkman allowed to intrude upon the Sabbath. In 1892 he had a bigger crowd at Ocean Grove than met for a bishop. "I am going to lift up my Lord," was his text and it brought three hundred to their knees.

In later years he ranged from Boston to Denver, took in New York and Washington, coursed over the South and the West, and crossed the line into Canada. His Gospel wagon traversed the British Isles and he circled the world. All the way through the years he has been the same warm-hearted, frank persuader of men to be decent, to examine themselves and render account to their God.

As a lay-preacher, a graduate Salvationist, he is hardly original in thought. He uses the terms of a self-educated man that common people understand and yet won him success at Harvard and in a Fifth Avenue drawing-room in New York. He is dramatic without being theatrical, he is urgent without resorting to hypnotic compulsion. He is saving of words as well as of souls; he talks as if he were cabling at a dollar a word. This is Gypsy Smith, still a torchbearer on his own.

CHAPTER XVIII

## THE LAST AWAKENING

From sinking sand He lifted me,
With tender hand He lifted me,
From shades of night to plains of light,
Oh praise His name, He lifted me!

Words by CHARLOTTE G. HOMER.
Music by CHARLES H. GABRIEL.

MATURED in the crucible of the experience of its
modern masters, the American revival discarded
obvious crudities of method, adapted itself to
changing mental and emotional responsiveness and synthesized the elaborate, sweeping strategy of mass evangelization. The close of the first decade of the twentieth century witnessed the consummation. A national idea and
objective were put to work for a universal inculcation of
the religious incentive. Uniformity of thought and feeling
and action made a people malleable. They were ripe for a
new experience in spiritual togetherness and the revival was
ready for them.

It began in Boston where the Great Awakening under
Whitefield reached its meridian in 1740. And, from present portents, the unparalleled mobilization of evangel man-
power and legions of Italy in 1909 constituted what may
be rightly termed as the Last Awakening. In calm serious-
ness and with rational control this culmination of the evolution of the revival justified its ambitious magnitude by

revitalizing, refilling, and reconsecrating the one hundred sixty-six churches that sponsored it voluntarily. To their one hundred twenty thousand members were added ten thousand to fifteen thousand more.

These conversions were not mere handshakes and overnight affairs. They were not the bestowal of independent grace upon lone-coursing souls. Every one that was counted meant a seat filled in a church. The total outlay for the three-weeks campaign was twenty thousand dollars. For the minimum of ten thousand actual church accessions that meant a cost of two dollars apiece or a virtual assessment of only a little over sixteen cents upon each of the one hundred twenty thousand original church members.

Compared with what happened to the big revival in subsequent years, the Boston result was definitive and intrinsic rather than inconclusive and transitory. Instead of a grandiloquent revivalist walking off with anywhere from ten thousand dollars to thirty thousand dollars for himself alone, the Bostonian churchmen stayed within the bounds of true New England common sense and made every cent count. And yet not for a moment were they scrimping with talent or parsimonious toward the size of the job.

A phalanx of sixty first-string evangelists and choristers with Dr. J. Wilbur Chapman, the preacher, Charles Alexander, the Gospel singer, and Robert Harkness, the revival pianist, holding down the center at Tremont Temple, conducted a day and night campaign in all of the Protestant churches of the city and the suburbs within a dozen miles' radius. Commander Evangeline Booth came in person and Colonel Adam Gifford led the Salvation Army's full local strength out into the streets in co-operation with the efforts going on in the edifices. At the end, Dr. A. Z. Conrad, pastor of the Park Street Church—at old Brimstone Corner—

as Chairman took the whole revival to Mechanics Hall, then the largest auditorium in the city. The climax welded the work into a perfect whole.

City editors performed a heroic task in getting the widespread story covered. "District men" had standing assignments on the simultaneous revivals in Brookline, Cambridge and Watertown, Everett, Malden, Melrose, Medford and Stoneham, Somerville, Newton, Quincy and Lynn. The city staffs were heavily drawn upon for the churches inside the city limits. For twenty-one days the "lead" on the first page "broke" to inside layouts of "follows." Features in "boxes" and pictures dressed up the arrangement.

It might have been a little difficult to have tried converting some of the copy-readers and make-up men. And a few of the reporters were worn a bit ragged. One of them, asked in the lobby of Tremont Temple if he was a Christian, misunderstood and answered—"No, I'm just a newspaper man."

The newspapers were under no other compulsion than imperative public interest, however. The revival was a "good story" in the parlance of the press, the sort any editor prefers to print. In the first place, here was a strong company of interesting men who naturally made news. Among the three-score collaborators with Chapman were such as John Elliott, a veteran of Moody's Chicago battle of 1893; James O. Buswell, from the lumber camps of the Northwest, and A. W. Spooner and Charles T. Schaeffer, who illustrated their sermons with lightning pictures in chalk or charcoal.

Albany Smith, the son of the Gypsy Smith, dates his own evangelistic career from being a leader of song in Chapman's little army. Among the other singers were Lawrence Greenwood, who, like Chapman, had trained with B. Fay Mills, the twin brothers Ernest and Everett Naftzger and F. M. Lamb. The last two were strong for ornithological allegory, Naftzger specializing in "His Eye is on the Sparrow" and Lamb in "The Bird with the Broken Pinion."

It was Chapman's greatest revival. For fourteen years he was leader of the Winona Lake (Indiana) Bible Conference Movement, the rallying ground of revivalists great and small and the laboratory where their adroit modern system was worked out. When the three hundred seventy-five ministers of Greater Boston invited him, in May, 1908, to be their boss-awakener, he accepted because he saw the strategic value to the future of the revival in concentrating upon large centers of population.

Unlike most evangelists, Chapman had no definite time or place to which to attach his conversion. Born in Richmond, Indiana, on June 17, 1857, he joined the Presbyterian Church in 1876 without any emotional storm and stress. But his first collegiate experience was at Oberlin which was saturated with the memory of Charles G. Finney and later at Lake Forest he met up with B. Fay Mills. They called each other "Bill" and "Fay" and rode the revival wave together till Mills transshipped to Unitarianism. Chapman, out on his own revival, converted a Governor of Michigan in 1903. After that he hooked up with Alexander, who had been with Torrey, and they had acquired an international reputation when Boston asked to be roused religiously.

It was to be the biggest and "thoroughest" revival job ever undertaken. Chapman took his time and made Boston lay ground-work from June till January. The solidarity of the participating churches was brought about by dovetailing of responsibilities within the machinery set up. Seven major committees did the work. Subscriptions from the church members paid the costs. Yankees have been in the habit of wasting neither toil nor money. They had expert assistance in conserving both in the salvation venture.

At this point, reflecting the trend to practicality, the revival was a cold, hard business proposition. Chapman sent his brother, E. G. Chapman, whom Chairman Conrad described as "a business man of rare ability, sagaciousness, suavity and effectiveness," to talk ways and means with those Bostonian bidders for the evangelist's services. A general committee proceeded to line up the churches and put a preliminary $10,000 in the war chest.

In September Chapman himself came and in parley with the parsons told what he would do and how he would do it. Dr. Conrad said that the man was not "arbitrary" but that "God interposed and overruled" and the pervading elements of the campaign were to be "faith and love." He added that "the business side of the Chapman-Alexander meetings was significant and the importance of organization was properly emphasized."

Early in December the Chapman staff specialists were on the scene organizing "personal work" and "publicity" departments. The churches were grouped and evangel teams assigned. The dates were as set—January 26 to February 17—and every pulpit began working toward the now inevitable and unescapable. All Boston, the thirty per cent of alleged Mayflowerers and the 70 per cent of Cunarders (no offense to the White Star Line and the good old S. S. Celtic), was going to be evangelized.

Chapman brought with him some relics of Mills,—the "Good Cheer" and "Mother's Day" meetings and the "opportunity cards" for those impressed by the spirit. He added a "Flower Day" and a "Day of Rejoicing" to exercise the charitable impulse stirred up by the influx of religion. And the cards were handled with a novel ingenuity.

There was no avoiding those cards. The "personal workers," well-drilled in preparation for the attack, were skillfully "planted" with assigned "territory" in every audience. It was a sort of holy espionage. Before a meeting the worker would casually converse with neighbors in his section as if he were one of them and "get a line on prospects." Later, when the invitation hymn was tugging at the heart-strings it was not so difficult to get the dotted lines filled in.

Compared with the garnering sickle of the old-fashioned "inquiry room" of Moody the new card scheme was a tractor-drawn reaper, binder and gleaner. But Dr. Conrad's Committee was strict on the count: cards did not mean converts. The final test of lengthening church rolls was applied and the recidivists did not get added up to the credit of Chapman. Nor was the evangelist preaching or thinking in such terms. The greater revival was on trial with its whole future dependent upon its sound success.

Everything was favorable. New England was evangelistically farrow. Furthermore, the industrial depression following the financial panic of 1907 had made the generality of the people considerate of their humbled souls, amenable to religious persuasion and as eager for divine guidance as their fathers were before them in 1857. They had their hope put into hymns. "From sinking sand He lifted me," they sang over and over, and "On Christ the Solid Rock I stand—all other ground is sinking sand" and "He will hold me fast." Again it was the ancient motive of escape from things as they are to refuge in the security of things yet to be. Chapman preached the way and

Alexander sang it while sixty others echoed them for twenty-one memorable winter days and nights in Boston.

The bell in the tower at Brimstone Corner tolls the hour of noon. Yonder in Tremont Temple three thousand persons on this 27th day of January, 1909, are breathlessly awaiting the opening of Boston's great revival. They fill the floor and the storied tiers of the two balconies up to the dome. All eyes are on the stage—the choir solid-banked in the background, sixty evangelists and choristers seated in the foreground, three men standing out to the front. Dr. Conrad presents Charlie Alexander "of Tennessee and the rest of the world" and Bob Harkness, the Australian pianist and composer. The thunder of applause is Boston's welcome.

Alexander's mellow drawl makes everybody like him. He talks to the three thousand as if to a single mountaineer neighbor. "Have you all books—you there—and there—and up in the gallery? No? Well, jes keep stirrin' things up till you get some. Now all sing one hundred thirty-eight—'My Faith Looks up to Thee.'" His long arms sweep the entire audience into choral unity. That is an old hymn, familiar to all. Now for a new one, at least new to Boston, "He will hold me fast," composed by Harkness. Bob plays his chorus through twice. Charlie sings it alone. Then he leads his people into it. Ernest Naftzger offers a solo—"His Eye is on the Sparrow"—destined to be one of the revival's memories—and the preparation is complete. Dr. J. Wilbur Chapman comes forward without any formalities and begins speaking.

Glasses train his eyes steadily ahead. Deep lines furrow his face from the nose to the corners of the mouth. His expression is one of stored energy. There is no vanity about him. His black hair is close-trimmed. His compact physique stands rooted to the spot and his open-handed gestures are few and far between.

Dignified yet genial, feelingful yet self-possessed, he addresses himself to the task in front of him. He inspires confidence in his ability to accomplish it and concludes with a ringing appeal for the faith and help of others that make the three thousand his firm allies. In the late afternoon is speaking again—at the first of the "Quiet Hours" in the Park Street Church. He is defending his type of revival.

Excitement? Well, how about a political campaign, how about every day on the stock exchange? These are analogies for energized religion. They are accepted. Reaction? Not necessarily—but even if many were swept backward in the aftermath still a few would have been lifted higher to stay. This is the irrefutable logic of the revivalist—just one soul redeemed out of a hundred thousand would cause hosannas in heaven. It is the companion piece to the consolation for a meagerly attended meeting— "Wherever two or three are gathered together in Thy name—" Thus spake the Lord. None can gainsay Him.

Three days are given over to warming up Boston at Tremont Temple. Noon and evening the rendezvous of religion was besieged; the police had hard work to keep a thin lane of traffic moving on Tremont and School streets at the critical hours. Only half of those who came could get in and those who succeeded were the mightiest in fervor. Alexander had one tremendous choir from top to bottom. Chapman had an auditory that hung on his words and unitedly Amened them. On the third day the devotional temperature had reached the simmering point; on the fourth the simultaneous campaign in the one hundred sixty-six outlying churches started up in emulation of the power-house of the Gospel pipe-lines in Tremont Temple.

They all had their night marches, their cumulative exaltation in song, their mighty moments under preaching power, their heart-throbs of tender petition and yielding. On every side the soul-stirring drama was being enacted with countless episodes of deep human interest. But all centered in Tremont Temple, the fountain head of the outward flow and the confluence of the returning streams of saving waters.

Alexander has them "going." Far down the streets the Temple singing can be heard. "What a Savior!" "Is He Yours?" "I'm a Subject of the King of Kings!" the anthems swell. Old hymns mingle with the new in Alexander's book —almost everybody has one—McGranahan's "Showers of Blessing," Lowry's "Wandering Boy," Sankey's "I am Praying for You," Bliss's "Almost Persuaded." Eyes get misty and voices tremulous with "Over the river faces I see, dear ones in Glory looking for me," "Will the Circle be unbroken?" and "Tell Mother I'll be there!" Alexander delivers them, men, women and children, to Chapman, and Chapman, calm, simple, direct—Chapman preaches them into resolution with him. It is the revival at its best. The aisles are filled with the unbroken lines of those going forward to declare the faith that is in them.

Chapman won't rant or scathe or kindle hell or belabor sinners. There is nothing of the picturesque showman about him, nothing of the popular prophet. He is a plain preacher though something of a sentimental idealist. And he is adept at creating an emotional atmosphere. His characteristic method is ancedotal and he gives it immediacy and veritability by dwelling upon "requests for prayer" that flood his mail.

Here is a note just thrust into his hand. "I'll be there tonight. I'm struggling with sin. Say a word to help me." Then a ream of appeals that mourn the inroads of the rum demon. An old soldier asks intercession for the unconverted veterans of the Civil War. Other petitioners locate sin geographically, still others designate relatives in four generations. One would not have believed there were so many widows' sons.

Now the scrawl of Little Annie—"Please pray for my papa to come to Christ. My mama is in heaven." That's pretty pathetic. It dampens the handkerchiefs. The next is unreadable. It is about a couple living together out of wedlock. "Pray that both may not be lost," the evangelist is quietly saying, "but that they may go hand in hand to God." And a hard-boiled reporter at the press table concedes that it is "pretty decent of him."

It is tearful, this revival, but there is just enough control to keep it from being maudlin. When the decisions are made there is an end of weeping. Faces are uplifted, exultant. An old sea captain comes to anchor in the "harbor." Blind Peter Trainer leaves his newspapers by the Old Granary Burying Ground and feels his way into the Temple to share in the "Light of the World." On the tenth of February three thousand men and women shout "I will!" to Chapman's challenge to dedicate their lives to "salvation, sacrifice and service." Two days later two thousand five hundred stand and pledge themselves to live better lives and to "get in line with every decent man who is trying to make Boston better."

Toward the final days a thousand at a time are rising for prayer in the Temple. And in the one hundred sixty-six churches working alongside choruses are pealing the anthems of an awakened metropolis.

Chapman had no illusions, however. "God alone knows the heart," he said. "What I count worth while is that a person shall definitely make his purpose clear by joining the church. You may cry your eyes out and you may sign a score of cards, but that amounts to nothing in itself. I want you to go to the church of your choice."

Whether they joined up or not—and the number that did join was a surprising proportion—those people made great days in the Temple. The "Flower Day" sent blooms to all the shut-ins of the city, and the "Day of Rejoicing" food and fuel to the poor and down-hearted. "Education Day" assembled two thousand teachers and "Mother's Day" brought great-grandmothers along with young matrons with babies in their arms.

Chapman went over to Harvard and received the "regular cheer" in Sanders Theatre from enthusiastic undergraduates. His rescue mission aides, Mr. and Mrs. William Asher, knelt in the snowy streets with outcasts who would not venture near churches. Among others, one known on police blotters as "Jerry the Crook" was converted. Lawrence Greenwood and the Ashers sang and preached while machinery was shut down for them in factories. Four hundred ministers reconsecrated themselves at the behest of Chapman and took the revival spirit to all parts of Northern New England.

Evangeline Booth took a hand, preaching in Tremont Temple. The music of the revival was her theme. She said she could convert folks if she could only get them to sing. That night Colonel Adam Gifford of the Salvation Army took her at her word and led his full strength with banners, cornets and drums down into Scollay Square.

There in the gaudy Theatre Comique, the first motion picture house in Boston, Colonel Gifford brought together for Chapman the "sports" and the "bums," the "out-of-lucks" and the "rough-necks" and the women of the streets. "And his father saw him afar off," Chapman repeated in the story of the Prodigal Son. Mrs. Asher sang the "Mother's Prayer." About fifty prodigals were brought "home." The Rev. Herbert S. Johnson, the "regular fellow" newspaper men liked, welcomed the returned sons and daughters.

On February 17, the group services ended and all converged on Mechanics Hall for the last four nights of the campaign. Ten thousand got in every night and ten thousand came too late to get in. Special trains steamed into both railroad terminals. All New England had caught the spirit. Alexander had a choir of one thousand five hundred and he had the whole crowded hall singing with them. They "gathered at the river" and they held the "ho-o-old" in "He will hold me fast." Bob Harkness got in his opening chords at the piano but after that he might have been playing upon a silent keyboard.

Chapman's closing sermon was on "Jesus of Nazareth passeth by." In his concluding prayer he said "We have all wrought the best we knew how." Boston agreed with him then and agrees with him to this day. All the mechanized framework, all the business calculation had been subordinated to the larger human purpose. The super-revival had had its finest exemplification. But in its own structure, already apparent, lay the flaws of its future. This, indeed, was the last genuine, thorough-going, durable Awakening.

CHAPTER XIX

THE COME-OUTERS

There's a new name written down in glory,
And it's mine, oh yes, it's mine!
And the white-robed angels sing the story—
"A sinner has come home,"
For there's a new name written down in glory,
And it's mine, oh yes, it's mine!
With my sins forgiven I am bound for heaven,
Never more to roam.

C. AUSTIN MILES.

INDIVIDUALIZED religious renewal—the personal
sense of bridging the gulf between man and God, the
personal feeling of tangency to the supernatural, the
personal interpretation of the experience sublime—has
always shaken through the rocking revival sieve originat-
ors of faith. Guided by chapters, verses—even single words
—from the Holy Writ, which has shown itself capable
of infinite connotation, these inspirationalists have
wrought extensions, cleavages and departures from established doctrine and practise. Their aim was greater and
surer spiritual satisfaction. It has led back to the primitive
and it has undertaken further experimentation. In either
direction the revival route usually has been taken.

New Lights and Separatists were winnowed from the
Great Awakening of 1740, still other Lights from the
frontier revival of 1800 and varied divisions were driven
from the Methodist and Baptist communions. The Miller-

ites, come-outers themselves, split up into diversified Adventists. The Mormons were essentially proselytes and so were the followers of Dowie and Pastor Russell. The unsuccessful have been forgotten; the others are now thriving churches.

Not all of the religious innovations have emanated from a revival nor have they been evangelistic. Sects philosophical or psycho-therapeutic in nature, like Theosophy or Christian Science, have stood aloof from the revivalist method in attracting believers. Then there are grotesque cults nurtured by brutish superstition, but they are another story. Their orgiastic rites and colonized subjection to arrant shamanism and necromancy belong to the colorful category of psychopathic phenomena. Only when one has recourse to the revival to gather adherents does it enter into the epic of evangelization. And it intrudes as bizarre byplay almost unbelievable.

The faith born of a revival, however, can be differentiated in this respect: it demands an even stronger revival for its own perpetuation. All it has of apocalyptic discovery, peculiar promise and special assurance is poured into the swift current flowing from the break in the dam. Holiness, and yet more holiness, in fact complete sanctification, drew away from the Methodists the Pentecostal Church of the Nazarene. No Wesleyan revival ever approached the Pentecostalite sound and sentiency, rapture and intensity. The irrepressible rejoicing of the redeemed has drowned out the traffic of cities and shattered rural quietude. A whole new hymnology was required to express it in song. But the preachers have been reminiscent of old-time exhorters like Ezekiel Cooper and Lorenzo Dow.

Making a joyful noise unto the Lord has been blessed with success. Nationally united in 1907 and 1908 with only one thousand two hundred members and two hundred and thirty churches but five hundred and seventy-five unconstrained preachers, the Pentecostalites in twenty years have accumulated about sixty thousand members, one thousand five hundred churches and three thousand expounders of entire sanctification as the consequences of regeneration from Adamitic depravity.

With the preachers double the number of the pulpits and every one a hair-trigger evangel, foe of rum and tobacco and the taint of carnality and herald of the Second Coming that would find men sunk in sin or ready for resplendent robes, there ought to be at least half a million singing that their names are written down in Pentecostal glory if this wicked world lasts twenty years more.

As it is, reconsecrated Methodists, stray Adventists and occasional Baptists, not to mention the hitherto churchless seekers of grace, are being constantly "saved, justified and sanctified" in churches a-tremble and tents straining on guy-ropes all over the country. The results may be generally salubrious, as might be expected of a religion affirmative of happiness. But what could happen may be judged from what did happen when the Pentecostal revival rolled through a village in New Hampshire.

Willing hands helped the evangelist stretch his canvas on the time-honored site across the tracks from the railroad station and bordering the highway that stretches westward toward the Ossipee Mountains. On this spot the soul of Little Eva had often taken its flight and once a hound paused in pursuit of Eliza to wag his tail in appreciation of some meat mischievously tossed to the rickety platform. Between banjo solos, slapstick sketches and ballads and ditties here also medicine had been sold for all the ailments of man and beast—rattlesnake oil for aches and pains, Sioux salve for cuts, bruises and burns and Tuscarora tablets guaranteed to give an elephant intestinal uneasiness. On the same ground wayfaring revivals were welcomed with equal hospitality.

And so in the dark when the first night's preaching was over and the Pentecostal apostle and his acolyte were standing on the settees to blow out the lamps, it was not surprising that an ingenuous trader and a workmanlike blacksmith, both fond of their cups and recently indulging, should insist that the visitants were ministrels and not ministers. Let them be called Tom and Jerry, not their names, of course, but convenient to answer the purpose. Oblivious to warnings of well-wishing neighbors the stragglers burst into the tent and stood there dumbfounded. But they didn't get away. Before morning both were on the road to conversion.

"I'm saved!" Thomas shouted to the stars of those hot August nights of 1915. "And justified and sanctified," Jeremiah supplied the rest of the salvation formula. Now may be they got it all wrong and expected too much, but they were convinced that they could sin no more. For a fact their previously besetting temptation was removed so long as the revival lasted. It was a season of uncommon righteousness.

There was a sister who never wearied of repeating that she was "under the Blood" and done with carnality; a brother who talked in terms of intimacy with his Savior. Even the weekly movies in the hall over the grain store lost patrons who stoutly declared abjuration forever. Perhaps a score of converted were trampling the grass round the altar. They had sufficient incitation to jubilant holiness. Such preachings, such singing would cower the minions of hell and startle the angels in heaven. None scoffed;

everybody helped; all wanted to keep it going. Creeds did
not matter; it was the human drama in that little tent
that counted. Who would be next to go forward?

There are four on the platform. A brawny man of
liberal measure in height, girth and voice, with massive
forehead, bushy eyebrows and tawny mustache—that is
the peregrine preacher himself. The plump, motherly person in the corner with a tambourine in her lap is his wife.
She helps with the singing. Beaming over the top of the
organ, a thin-faced slip of a woman awaits the signal to
start pumping and playing. By the side of his chief stands
the faithful coadjutor, stubby and corpulent, his gray hair
thinning but his countenance radiant with the joy of
shouting, singing and sweating for salvation.

"Number Seven!" The Gospel gunner has opened fire.
His basso profundo blends with the lusty tenor of his
Brother Jonathan and the clear treble of the two women.
"I came to Jesus, weary, worn and sad—He took my sins
away, He took my sins away—and now His love has
made my heart so glad—He took my sins away." The
volume has been gaining. The whole tent vibrates with
the chorus. There's no stopping. One parson alternates
with the other in raising a triumphant "He took my sins
away!" Another hymn—"Then at once all my burdens
rolled away, rolled away, rolled away." And yet another
—"Oh Glory Hallelujah, I am on my way to heaven,
shouting glory, shouting glory all the way!" The tambourine is tapping. The organ swells are wide open. Pentecostal power is come.

Preaching is on. You know your own wickedness. You
know the consequences.—Here the Sister at the organ
nods vigorously and, all smiles, cheerily chants—"Yes,
you're going to hell, you're all going to hell."—And why?

Old Adam, he's in you. Depravity, you were born that way. Now don't you want to be rid of that lower self, shake off that bent to sinning, be reborn in the Spirit, justified by the Faith and sanctified by Grace?

The Blood of the Atonement was shed for you. This is your way out, the only way. "Whosoever will" lets you in. Won't you say "Yes" tonight? The Sister at the organ plaintively sings "Now I'm coming home." There's a stir in the fifth row. Feet are pulled in to permit the passage of the brother. He makes for the front brokenly trying to say what a full heart chokes in the utterance. The big hands of the preacher are on his shoulders. "Pray through, brother, pray through!" The already redeemed gather round murmuring encouragement. Here is a break. The preacher renews the invitation while his aide kneels with the penitent. "One more—just one more—tonight?" But there is no answer and a last chance, given during the parting hymn, yields not a sinner.

The faithful few linger to labor with the new brother. Out on the road on their journey homeward, the villagers stop at the sound of a joyous hymn back in the tent. "There's a new name written down in glory, and it's mine, oh yes, it's mine!" They know what it means. Horace has prayed through. He gets converted at every revival.

August passed. Folks began covering their flowers at nightfall and farmers worried about crops being nipped by a frost. The Methodist pastor, a gentle soul there in the hills for his health, felt a rebirth of Pentecostal religion and opened his warm church to the holy encampment. A strange light gleamed in his eyes. His pews were filled and somehow he thought that this revival mood would last forever. Then came the windup and final thank-offering and the evangels departed leaving the zealous pastor to

carry on with his saved and sanctified recruits added to
his staid congregation. Before snow fell disaster descended.

It started with Thomas and Jeremiah. Cider grew hard
and they wondered if the Holy Ghost would let them
drink it. Then they speculated upon whether entire sanctification would prevent the usual result. Their experiment
was conclusive when late one night Tom and Jerry appeared at the parsonage. That began the backsliding and
by Spring hardly a trace remained of the holiness revival.
The Methodist minister was never the same afterward.
Within a year he died of anemia. The village had reason
to remember the Pentecostalite visitation.

Three years later another evangelist of the same persuasion vainly thundered and pleaded—once barked and
yowled in what he called his "animal sermon"—till at the
end he collected one convert. A terrified boy screamed at
the people that they were all marked for hell but he was
saved, saved, saved from damnation. And his was the last
sanctification among them.

Holiness has been responsible for at least twenty come-
outer evangelistic movements of such designations as "Assemblies of God," "Church Apostolic" and "Church
Transcendent," "Daniel's Band," the "Burning Bush" and
the "Pillar of Fire." Their high altars are scattered
throughout the country, in Indiana, Michigan and Wis-
consin, Kansas, Missouri and Arkansas, Ohio, Tennessee
and the South Atlantic States, Zarepath, New Jersey,
Denver, Colorado, and Oakland, Maine. The zeal of the
members makes up for their paucity. It has given them
strange nicknames. Some are popularly known as "Holy
Jumpers" and others as "Holy Rollers."

The Jumpers—they are brands from the Burning Bush
—invaded prosaic Boston in the early 1900's and the

municipality for the regular rental permitted them to use old Faneuil Hall. Shades of Samuel Adams, Daniel Webster, Charles Sumner, defenders of freedom, well might have recoiled from the hullabaloo in the name of religion let loose in the Cradle of Liberty. Leaping and hopping, vaulting and hurdling in ecstatic measure with shouting and singing, the joy in the Lord pounded like a hail storm on the ceiling of the market stalls below and burst like shrapnel against the floor of the armory of the Ancient and Honorable Artillery above. It was bedlam.

Boston looked on and marvelled. Matinée and evening there was standing room only. The press table—in the line of fire round the rim of the platform—was jammed with reporters. Every day the copy grew warmer. The stories centered upon the master-exhorter, a hatchet-faced lively sprite of a man as agile as a squirrel.

He would begin with comparative calmness and would deliberately create a tense stillness for the sheer delight of demolishing it. There was his discourse on the Flood.

Sedately enough he reads the Scripture. He gets a bit buoyant as he romps about the stage picking up assorted beasts and bugs and snatching birds out of the air, but he stands stock still in impressive solemnity after the gang-plank has been pulled aboard and Noah plants himself in the bow to watch the weather. Noah knows what is coming though an iniquitous world refuses to believe it. Next time it will be by fire; this time it is by flood; and all of the wicked are awaiting destruction. Thunder rumbles and lightning slashes across the clouds thickening overhead. The preacher pauses ominously, holds out his hands and gazes upward.

"RAIN!" he yells and he rockets over the heads of the paralyzed reporters. "Rain—WHOOPEE—rain!" He alights in the aisle, whirls on his toes and springs back to the platform. It is the deck of the ark and he dances upon it. All over the hall his saltatory saints bound into action, pummeling tambourines, cavorting and chanting a rhythmic refrain of his faster and faster flowing strophic phrases.—"Raining all day, raining all night!" "Forty days, forty nights, miles deep of water!" "Deluged, drowned, damned!" "And the old ark a-riding, a-riding, a-riding right along!"

He lurches as the ark strikes on the hard ground of Ararat. "Steady-y-y!" he bawls through cupped hands and the rain revel abruptly ceases. The dove brings back the olive branch and the rainbow arcs the sky. A moment of rejoicing, a few gladsome cries and capers, and a holy hush prevails. Which would you—renounce all worldly things or burn with them in hell? Which would you—jump for Jesus now or jump from the prick of a pitchfork hereafter? This is unsmiling, serious, reverent. Misery or rapture, take your choice. It is for eternity. The invitation hymn is borrowed from the standard revival. "Earnestly, tenderly Jesus is calling" sounds incongruous in this fantastic setting. But it works.

One day an Italian barber made a public bonfire of his combs, brushes, shears and razors. Another day a tall, reedy colored girl dedicated her shrill voice and nimble feet to the Bush that is Burning. Not many in all were joined to the Jumpers, but they were sufficient to show what could be done with resilient holiness, even in Faneuil Hall in the City of Boston.

When not in the air the Jumpers at least stay on their feet. That is more than can be said for the Rollers. At their mildest they hear "inner voices," conversing with God and the Devil; behold "inner visions," getting glimpses of things beyond mortal ken; respond to rhythmic sound and motion, rotating horizontally in an exhilaration regarded as "spiritual." At their worst they mistake orgastic sensation for divine infiltration and by a psycho-physical concatenation of ritualism work up their gyrations to a concupiscent climax.

Not many years ago the citizenry of a New Hampshire village amid the White Mountains tore down a huge barn-like structure, timber for timber, and farmers plowed over the site to obliterate every vestige of what had stood there. It had been a temple of the Holy Rollers. Under its roof unspeakable things had happened, things which had had biological consequences outraging the countryside. At first the cult kept to itself; then its leader, a gigantic Negro, utilized its rites to promote a revival. That was too much for patient endurance.

Led by their chieftain and a band of flutes and drums the Rollers would march in a singing procession with cadence infectious, encircling the village and drawing in both the curious and the susceptible. Back to the barn they swung, stepping like automatons bewitched in a dream. The benches were far apart—a little more than the length of a body—and the space between was strewn with hay. All through the night the wailing music and drum-beat mingled with incantation and incoherent exhorting. The lights went out. The rolling began. And in the morning bewildered novices wondered what had happened. They were the reason for ending it.

A temperate variety of Rollers was still operative at Oakland, Maine, in the Summer of 1928. They have an edifice of anomalous architecture and a long-bearded shepherd who has amazing dexterity in performing on a big drum beside the pulpit. Lay testimony accelerates their revival and the drum reverberates a muscle-twitching rataplan after every contribution.

"I've come here from Belfast," began a volunteer in such a way that one might think he had just pulled in from Timbuctoo rather than the shore of Penobscot Bay. "And the Devil he had a-holt of my coat-tails all the way, he did. Says he, 'Git you back to Belfast!' Says I, 'Git you back to hell.' Says he, 'What be ye about and where d'ye think you're a-goin'?' Says I, 'I'm a-goin' to meetin' in Oakland.' And, Praise the Lord, here I be!"

Thump - thumpa - thumpa - thump, thump - thumpa - thumpa-thump clattered the drum. Tapping feet kept time with it. Half a dozen ejaculations heightened the fervor of the congregation. Another rustic witness of the Word was on his pins.

"Almost lost a calf last year but God saved it," he said. "Poor little critter couldn't git up on his legs. Just lay there tremblin' pitiable. I hadn't no heart to see him suffer so I went to the woodshed to fetch my axe to put him out of his mis'ry. Whilst I was gone my wife she wept into her apron and riz her streamin' eyes to heaven and prayed the Lord to restore that little calf. When I come back that calf was friskin' in the dooryard. And if God can do that for a calf what can't He do for you and me?"

Interrupting the drum's tattoo, an excited woman in the rear of the house shrieked—"Glory to Jesus! I've got that calf now and he's a big fine bull."

Boom, boom, boomalay, boomalay, boom! The drumsticks hit up the jubilation measure. Bodies swayed with the rhythmic strokes. Swifter and swifter grew the syncopation. The pastoral whiskers almost touched the drumtop as the patriarch bent to his task. All of his people where half-singing, half shouting. Testimony bumped out of them spasmodically.

But now a new Roller came forward. The vocal cacophony subsided and the speed of the drummer slackened till finally the tapping trailed away. No rolling this night, and the students from Colby College turned back to Waterville disappointed. Outsiders assured them, however, that the next meeting might be more propitious for rotative religion.

Both the Rollers and the Jumpers react more or less involuntarily to primordial impulses, springs of action quite human, not so deep in the margin of the mind*and nothing mysterious. No special mental effort is needed; indeed it might hinder. In contrast to them, the denizens of Zion, capital of the "Christian Catholic Church" founded by John Alexander Dowie and preserved by Wilbur Glenn Voliva, must have the will to believe that God and the Devil personally are factors in the affairs of an earth that is flat. The Zionites must accept an interweaving of economics, therapeutics and theology along with Ptolemaic astronomy. There is something ratiocinative as well as emotional in their completeness of material and spiritual submission.

It was while Moody was successfully competing with the World's Fair midway in 1893 that Dowie set up business in Chicago. His faith healing got off to a tremendous start. In 1895 he was arrested a hundred times for violating ordinances and he paid twenty thousand dollars in fines and legal expenses, but the publicity of his martyrdom was worth a million. He was aware of it through long previous experience. As a child—he was born in Edinburgh on May 25, 1847—he was thrilled to discover the meaning of his names, John, "Grace of God," and Alexander, "Helper of Men." As a youth—in Australia—he achieved a corner in light by buying up all the lamps and kerosene on the market when the Adelaide gas works blew out.

From Edinburgh University he returned to the Antipodes a preacher, took a fling as a political reformer, decided clerical stipends were unholy and stepped out on his own as an evangelist depending on "free-will offerings" that made salaries insignificant. Puny and weak, he "went to the Lord" and waxed stout, hale and vigorous. From this experience he evolved his "ministry of healing" which he tried out in London and imported to Chicago. Forthwith he became "Elijah the Restorer," established the church in which he pontificated, built round it Zion City with its bank, press, industries, and schools spreading over six thousand acres on the shore of Lake Michigan where he ruled like a rajah.

His rapidly increasing followers adored him, obeyed him unquestioningly and paid their tithes with their homage. For was not the "General Overseer" of Zion also "the Messenger of the Covenant, Elijah the Restorer and That Prophet of whom Moses spake, all one and the same person, Elijah III"? In his official pronouncement, published in his "Leaves of Healing," Dowie said:

"The Declaration that we are that person is either what those peculiar theologians, . . . the Chicago Press, declare it to be, a Great Blasphemy, or it is a Tremendous Fact of the utmost importance to the whole world. We have not assumed it. It has been imposed upon us by God Himself. Had we been deceived in this matter, then God would have deceived us. That is an impossibility."

Calculating hypocrite or self-deluded adventurer, he was an imposing figure of forceful personality, an ecclesiastical and financial autocrat, this anti-medicinal

healer by faith. Stern when he spoke ex cathedra, his countenance could light up with beneficent smiles or easily
melt into inordinate weeping. The speech of his strong,
clear voice was now ornate and impressive, now coarse
and grotesque. His physical endurance and mental agility
were extraordinary. Next to his gorgeous array of sacerdotal vestments, his prophetic beard was his greatest pride
of adornment.

Intoxicated with prospering fanaticism, Dowie denounced all who would not accept him and governed his
kingdom with a rod of iron. Business got so big that he
mechanized healing. Applicants for cures filled out slips
which were put through a praying machine and came
out stamped with the minute of registration in heaven.
"Prayed for and healed, corns and bunions, of Simeon
Smith, May 10, 1901, 3.27 P. M. John A. Dowie." That
was a receipt. There was no comeback. When Dowie's
daughter, Esther, died of burns from an overset alcohol
lamp in 1902, he is said to have attributed the tragedy to
her use of a liquid which he had forbidden.

Ambition, love of power and self-confidence overcame
everything for him till the Fall of 1903. It was then that
Zion City tried to annex New York. The Chosen went
up against Jericho but their trumpet blast and shout
availed not against the walls of the Citadel of Sin. Waves
of laughter repelled them.

Eight special trains brought Zion's thousands of holy
warriors, with surpliced choir, brass band and the Zion
Guard of eight hundred tailored like a Balkan army but
carrying holstered Bibles in their belts instead of weapons
more belligerent. Already preparatory artillery had laid
down a barrage of twenty tons of tracts and sappers had
constructed a tank in Madison Square Garden for divers

duckings of hostages. General Elijah was ensconced in palatial headquarters at the Plaza. Zero hour was three o'clock on the afternoon of Sunday, October 18.

Madison Square Garden could hold no more, not even at a Democratic National Convention at the pivotal ballot. Police reserves held back the crowds for blocks. Here was an enemy eager to be shot at. Singing serenely, the white-robed choir slowly mounted the platform and arranged itself in tiers in the background of Elijah, the prophet resplendent. Awe and admiration held the audience spell-bound. The last chord of the music receded as to a vast distance. There was a moment of expectant silence. In that moment victory paused upon the banner of Zion. And then flapped its wings like a buzzard and flew away. For Elijah opened his mouth.

Something snapped in the brain of that man. He suddenly regarded everyone in front of him as a mocker, a persecutor, an enemy. From self-adulation, in defense of his apostolic personality, he plunged into a seething torrent of defiling invective. Foul epithets and horrendous imprecations spouted from a visage fiendishly distorted by rage uncontrollable. The effect was immediate,—titters, guffaws and then an avalanche of laughter.

That kicked the pedestal out from under Elijah. The rest of the show was anticlimactic. Hundreds swarmed to the exits. Elijah was frantic. He bellowed to the police to stop the exodus but they only smiled. As one old sergeant said to a reporter—"We can kape them out but we can't kape them in." The Zion Guard interposed shoulder-shoves and straight-arms but were swept aside by the impact. And the little pot-bellied prophet knew he was defeated.

For the rest of a tumultuous week hilarious throngs

crammed the Garden. Disgruntled and vindictive, Elijah gave them all they were looking for. He was beside himself. A great city made merry over the antics of a madman. In retrospect it is pitiable. Night after night he performed, now lifting the skirts of his cassock and dancing a jig, now crawling on all fours, leering through his whiskers and snarling "Stinkpot!" at the collective adversary. It was a one-week stand. After that for a few days Dowie reviled empty seats and got casual mention in the papers. He decamped three hundred thousand dollars "in the red."

The New York revival ruined Dowie. It undermined his faith in himself as a manipulator of men. Cunning and desperate, he hung on till 1905 when Voliva denounced and deposed him. His people turned against him but cleaved to the cult he had found and hailed his successor. He died in delirium two years later.

Contemporary with Dowie though widely differing from him in message and method was Charles Taze (Pastor) Russell, a millennialite who, unlike William Miller, would not confess misreckonings but patched them over with amendatory prophecy. He had something in common with Joseph Smith, Jr., the Palmyra excavator, inasmuch as he discovered himself to be the prophet scheduled from the days of Daniel to come forth in the 1870's. The kindest thing to be said of him is that he evidently believed in himself and his life-long exhaustive search of the Scriptures to rectify and confirm that belief is the evidence of apparent sincerity.

Be all this as it may, Pastor Russell was head and shoulders above Dowie and Smith in that he was the cleverest propagandist of the age and a business man par excellence. His evangelizing, such as it was, consisted of free lectures illustrated with vivid and quaint stereopticon slides of heaven and earth from the creation to the millennial end. But from the outset of his independent ministry in Pittsburgh, where he was born in 1852, he kept the presses spilling out tracts, pamphlets, books and continuous periodicals. And his critics alleged that the profits, invested in lead, asphalt, turpentine, coal and coke ventures, yielded him millions of dollars. This has been warmly disputed.

He located his plant in Brooklyn where it is still an emporium of mail-order religion, competitor of every old-line church and disrupter of home-town parishes. The firm is the International Bible Students' Association, successor to the Watch Tower Bible and Tract Society. Saving its customers both time and money, it furnishes more citations of Scripture than all of its rivals put together.

It seems that "Gentile Times" began in 606 B. C. and ended in 1914 A. D., the World War being "nation rising against nation," the Belgian starvation the "famine" and the influenza the "pestilence" fulfilling the Biblical prophecy. Meantime Christ had returned in 1874 and had been laboring in preparation of the vineyard since 1878, the very year Pastor Russell ascended his unique pulpit.

Since 1914, it is averred, the world has entered the new era of a thousand years during which, at the proper time, the Lord will take over direct sovereignty with the Russellites as His special assistants to give all sinners a chance to repent. At the termination of this period the wicked will be annihilated and the holy will dwell in peace forever more.

One must be patient and bide the Lord's time. For instance, the dead were supposed to start rising in 1925, Abraham, Isaac and Jacob first and then from the most recently deceased back to Abel. And it is declared that "millions now living will never die." As yet no graveyard is known to have been disturbed except to receive accessions. Still, one cannot be sure about those Hebrew patriarchs. No other signs of the "Golden Age" have been reported in the newspapers, such as the cessation of marriages, births and deaths. To the contrary, vital statistics continue to accumulate.

And yet Russellism flourishes. When the Pastor died in 1916, his broadcloth mantle was picked up by Joseph F. (Judge) Rutherford, one-time Missouri lawyer of surpassing eloquence and prescience, who has put Russell's magic lantern on the shelf and gone in for the greatest radio hook-ups in the history of evangelization.

No President of the United States ever had such a command of the ether as Judge Rutherford assumed for an hour and a half when he spoke in July, 1928, over a chain of ninety-six stations. In January the Dodge Motor Car Company paid forty-two thousand dollars for an hour's use of forty-seven stations. This gives some idea of the cost to Judge Rutherford, the foe of organized Christianity as the churches of the Antichrist, to broadcast his oratory. It could not be ascertained whether the outlay was borne by the International Bible Students' Association, by the judge himself or by a friendly philanthropist.

In this formidable array of assorted come-outers, one meek, unselfish character is deserving of mention, another Elijah, Francis Schlatter, an Alsatian immigrant. Sometimes in jails, sometimes in asylums, when he was loose he roamed about barefoot, bareheaded in all kinds of weather preaching the love of God and peace among men, laying on hands to cure the maimed, the halt and the blind. He would take no money and often went hungry. He would accept the gift of cheap gloves and, having once worn them, would give them away as possessed with his gift of healing. At the height of his career in the nineties he disappeared and never was seen again. He left this penciled note to one Alderman Fox of Denver: "Mr. Fox—My mission is ended and the Father calls me. I salute you. Francis Schlatter. Nov. 13."

# CHAPTER XX

## CORYBANTIC CHRISTIANITY

Brighten the corner where you are!
Brighten the corner where you are!
Some one far from harbor you may guide across the bar,
Brighten the corner where you are.
> Words by INA DULEY OGDON.
> Music by CHARLES H. GABRIEL.

WINONA LAKE is the symbol of a business that has arrived. It is the practical and spiritual headquarters of the full-fledged twentieth-century evangel preacher and Gospel singer, tabernacle builder, advance agent, publicity and advertising expert, and committee organizer. Barnstormers no longer count and come-outers cannot make a scratch on the graphs charting seasonal and regional progress of the wholesaling of salvation. Nothing is left to chance. Routing and booking and returns are absolutely assured. For the American revival of religion has eliminated waste, competition and barren ground and has stabilized the big industry of redemption.

It is the year 1916. The better minds are in council. William Jennings Bryan has sanctified the circumambient Indiana atmosphere with an address on "Faith." Now the Rev. William Ashley Sunday, D.D., purveyor extraordinary to the great national diversion of taking delight in damnation, is expounding for the benefit of the mantled brethren. His text is Second Chronicles 18: 13—"As the Lord liveth, even what my God saith, that will I speak."

"These are the words of a Man of God who didn't put on his glasses and look into the pews to see who occupied them before he announced his text," says this Ajax of the tabernacles. "This fellow's name was Micaiah."

Micaiah, be it remembered, was a prophet of bad news that had a habit of coming true. King Ahab of Israel had him locked up but that did not prevent Ahab's foretold defeat in battle and the dogs from licking his blood. Dr. Sunday continues to expatiate on Micaiah:

"His sermons were not written on the head of his barrel of flour. His preaching did not hinge on what he had to eat. The condition of his cellar had nothing to do with his liberty in the pulpit. He was not afraid of getting canned for taking dead aim at some influential sinner on the front seat.

"He was a six-cylinder preacher. A patch on his coat didn't make him think he was not called to preach. His only anxiety was to please his God. He didn't care a hang about the kind of success that can be set down in numbers.

"Micaiah was a preacher who put it across. The traffic cops lifted their hats to him and stopped everything while he made his lordly way across the streets."

That was Micaiah. This is Dr. Sunday:

"People don't get mad because I preach the truth. But I make them so blamed uncomfortable that they never feel the same afterwards when they are doing wrong.

"The Arrow of God [first used by Edwards, Rev. J., 1735] is on the wind. It will find you where you hide behind rich tapestries, whether you clothe yourself in sealskin and silks, ride in limousines or hoof it, in bank or drawing room, even in a coal-mine or the cabin of a loco-motive."

Micaiah and William, there they are at Winona together. The one has been jovially jigged a few thousand years from the Book to a latter-day pulpit. The other is in the midst of the most lucrative year any evangelist ever had. It was a war-profit year for the country, neutrally selling shoes and shells, beans and bayonets for the millions who were getting shot at for the sake of Christian civilization. It was on the eve of the Liberty Loan "drives" to pay for a glorious adventure in pure altruism. Micaiah never had such pickings.

There were no "patches" in Billy Sunday's fur coat. He did not have to worry about the contents of flour barrel or cellar. Traffic "cops" did make way for his "limousine." But, unlike his beau-ideal of a prophet, he had a concern for numbers which his pot-shots at "influential sinners" only increased. Every campaign—Omaha, Syracuse, Trenton, Boston, New York—culminated in the statistics of success. Instead of any danger of his being "canned," welcoming parades hailed him wherever he went and farewell collections would put a strain on adding machines. At the end of the route he probably could have matched remunerations with many a captain of industry and come out ahead.

Always he has started with a bang. His first day in Omaha brought out twenty-eight thousand people who chipped in $3,024.51; in Syracuse thirty-five thousand poured $2,217.04 into the chiming pans; in Trenton thirty-one thousand scraped together $1,110.45. One haul of the Gospel net at Syracuse drew in two thousand six hundred converts.

The Trenton record is typical: total attendance in the

seven weeks, eight hundred twenty thousand five hundred; accounted converts, sixteen thousand seven hundred forty-five; collection for current expenses, $29,661.14, for charity, $3,598.73, and for William A. Sunday himself—$32,-358.03. This foots up to $65,617.90. Thus the cost to the community of each "trail-hitter," whether he tracked any sawdust on to a church aisle carpet or not, was $3.91.

Boston's church members paid an average of sixteen cents apiece for the Awakening of 1909. Chapman, Alexander and sixty other Class A-1 preachers and singers as well as all sundries stayed within $20,000. And at least ten thousand were added to the churches. In seven years the rate had jumped from $2 for certainties to $3.91 for uncertainties. The business of redemption had reached the peak of expansion and expensiveness and had become shoddy.

Still Dr. Sunday insists that he has always split his personal gratuity seventy-thirty or fifty-fifty with his staff of ten or a dozen—including Homer ("Rody") Rodeheaver, trombonist, chorister and "Mister Bones" of the troupe—and, though he steadfastly refuses to give an accounting or to answer strictures on the subject of how well it pays to serve the Lord, his intimate friends declare that he tithes his income and have no doubt of his generosity and sense of stewardship. What he did with $44,000 rendered unto him in Pittsburgh is between him and his God. Some day while he is balancing up with his old crony, Saint Peter, a probate court will disclose to a curious world what profiteth a man to jazz up Jesus, syncopate salvation and capitalize corybantic religion for the multitude.

So long as he is still on earth and able to shout "SAFE!" as he slides to the home-plate of acrobatic grace, he will be defiant. He is not a bit sensitive about his gate receipts.

He squares off and raucously roars a two-fisted challenge.

"Come up here if you want to charge me with being a grafter," he says. "But get your picture taken first, for your wife won't know you when I get through."

"Don't sing 'Jesus Paid It All' and then drop a nickel in the collection plate," he admonishes as the coins rattle in tabernacle dishpans. "A bushel of nickels will lead a gang so close to hell that one can smell the sulphur!"

No "Hear the Pennies Dropping" of sweet Sabbath School memory for him. It takes units of substantial denomination to click the turnstiles of his heaven. And he gets them. Before he was half through his Philadelphia campaign in 1915 the collections amounted to over $43,000, and as in all two million three hundred thirty thousand people heard his one hundred twenty-two sermons, it is only fair to assume that they got their money's worth.

If Billy Sunday has an income of over $100,000 a year it is the inevitable fruit of the promoting ability of the greatest salesman of salvation ever on the road and not necessarily because he might be mercenary. Aside from living well and dressing nattily, he probably does not give much thought to the accumulation of wealth. His wife, "Ma" Sunday, to whose discipline he is submissive, looks out for his interests in dealing with pious business men. His pride is in the size of his tabernacles, the count of his converts and in being a self-made man. He accepts his reward as a matter of course. He feels it is coming to him.

Something that happened the day after his own conversion in 1886 explains his attitude toward money. He was playing right field on Adrian ("Pop") Anson's famous Chicago baseball team of the National League. Detroit was at bat with two out, a man on second base and another on third and two strikes, three balls on the hardest hitter. The ball was a liner. Billy ran ahead of it and beneath it, nailed it and rolled with it under a team of horses. When he came up with the ball in his hand, Tom Johnson, former Mayor of Cleveland, put $10 in his hand and told him to buy the best hat in Chicago, saying—"That catch won me $1,500." Asked by an old Methodist minister in later years if he took the ten, Evangel Billy replied—"You bet your life I did!" And there's a cheer every time he tells the story.

His whole evangelism is fielding for the Lord. His coaching entertains the bleachers and his grandstand plays take the crowd off its feet. And when it comes to the donation —who wouldn't loosen up for the man who won the game of ten thousand lives for God?

According to one computation—Billy is hazy on dates —he will be sixty-five years old on November 19, 1928. But he is still the wiry, close-knit, springy athlete of twenty years ago. His hair keeps that part in the middle, his eyes their twinkle and flash, his smooth, lean jaw its aggressive angle. The repertory changes only to conform to locale. It is a sort of travelling reservoir. There is really nothing spontaneous about his gymnastics, lingual and otherwise. The flow of speech and stage business is switched on and off at will. It is just Billy Sunday's way of brightening up the straight and narrow path.

The acrobatic feats and characteristic slang, repeated over and over, are sufficiently shocking, when a novelty, to jar people in their seats and make excellent publicity. The main point with Sunday, however, is the dramatization of his own personality with its virile, militant masculinity, its utter familiarity with the "man in the street" and with the God he brings down among "common folks" as the Biggest Fellow and the Best Pal. He puts vernacular into the mouth of Jesus. He buttonholes God in prayer. And he chases the devil around a stump. This is verisimilitude. The crowd has something to hear, something to see, something it is capable of understanding.

Here is the tabernacle. Never mind how it came or what preceded it. That is another story, though a story which makes possible all which follows. Ten—sometimes twenty —thousand are tightly packed on the wooden benches under the stoutly-timbered low roof. There's a smell of fresh pine. The sawdust-strewn aisles all center before the platform, twenty or thirty feet square, with a sounding board like a huge inverted sugar scoop hanging over the only furniture, a plain pulpit desk and kitchen chair. At one side another platform holds the piano—Bob Mathews is already running his fingers over the keys—and the choir of anywhere from five hundred to one thousand. Just behind, though not out of range, is the space for reporters and parsons, the latter soon to be stigmatized as "mutts, stiffs and deadheads."

Quarter past seven. Homer Rodeheaver is on deck with his megaphone and trombone. Yes, it's "Rody" of the Rodeheaver Company, publishers of the song books used exclusively in the Sunday campaigns, the same Rody who is genial now and an hour hence will be melting pathos itself as he diminishes the cadence of "Just As I Am Without One Plea" and "Lord, I'm Coming Home" with such emotional effect that the "trail" will be jammed.

"Rody" drips good cheer and under-the-skin fellowship yet he is the personification of self-possession. The choir responds to his slightest motion; the tabernacle throng obeys like an army. First he tries out the old hymns that everybody knows—"Jesus, Lover of My Soul," "Glory to His Name," and "Coronation"; then the Billy Sunday revival obbligato blazes away—"Floods of joy o'er my soul like the sea billows roll since Jesus came into my heart" and "Brighten the Corner Where You Are!" There never were such choruses "this side the Golden Shore." All voices are one voice.

Billy Sunday arrives. He is exactly five minutes ahead of time. His people are ready for him. No preliminaries, he wades right in "doping it out for the Lord," "Soaking it into Satan," and he is prepared to "stay on the job till hell freezes over and then use skates." He rams a charge down the barrel of a figurative blunderbuss the while he is barking—"And then I loaded my old Gospel-gun with ipecac, rough-on-rats, buttermilk, rock salt and whatever else came handy, and the gang has been ducking and the feathers flying ever since!"

He introduces the devil for comic relief, spice and snap. "This old Devil," he rasps, "has been practicing for six thousand years [Fundamentalist chronology] and he has never had appendicitis, rheumatism or tonsilitis. If you get to playing tag with him, he'll beat you every chip."

Billy crouches on the platform, knocks on the floor and shouts an invitation for the Devil to come up and take his medicine. Billy admits his own fearlessness and when the bid to Beelzebub is not accepted the audience shares with the champion the delight and satisfaction manifest in his victorious smile and conquering pose. Cheers ring for the tower of physical strength and spiritual righteousness whom the Boss of Hell dares not meet in combat.

This is no gentle Galahad going a-grailing; it is a Jack the Giant Killer gunning for Fiery Griffins. He isn't standing there and merely talking about sin and sinners. His occasional pensive moods are statuesque. The rest of the time he is in action, now stalking his game, now impersonating the characters of this tremendous one-man drama.

He "snuffs the coke" or "jabs the needle" and lops over the pulpit. His snoring can be heard all over the tabernacle. He gulps poison, writhes in agony and stiffens out dead on the floor. Up he springs, both feet on the chair or one foot on the chair and the other on the pulpit, shouting—"Break away from that old bunch of the damned!" He leans precariously over the edge of the platform, jaw thrust out, trigger finger pointing at the composite human mass, and snarls—"You old hypocrite!" He grips his frail pulpit and leans back beaming—"Ha, ha, old skeptic, I've got you beat!"

Look out, Goliath! David William Sunday D.D. is stretching a stone in his sling to "knock your block off." "Come on, Naaman, it's up to you to jump seven times into Jordan! Hold your nose, shut your eyes! Ee-yow! You've stubbed your toe on the brink. Oo-ee, a big sand-fly biting between the shoulder-blades!" In and out the seventh time, stamping, spluttering, shaking the water out of his ears. But—Naaman William Sunday D.D. does a handspring and lands with legs wide apart and shoulders arched back—"My flesh is made whole, my leprosy is healed!"

No posture is impossible for this versatile go-getting Gospel gymnast. Squatting on his toes, his knees brushing the floor, his fingers flicking the green carpet for balance, for a split second he is the man who is "no better than a four-footed brute."

Deathbed repentance—waiting for the undertaker—Billy bends over the soon-to-be-a-corpse and shows him how the embalming fluid will be pumped in. "Burning the candle of life in the service of the Devil and then blowing the smoke in God's face—pfouff!" The light is out.

In the prize ring with the Devil—the knockout blow—
the slow count, eight, nine, ten and "OUT!" On the Mara-
thon race to heaven the runner, Billy in the rôle, without
an understudy in the world, lunges prostrate at the goal.
The greatest base-stealer in old-time baseball knows how
to slide.

A callow youth is sneaking into a brothel. He climbs
the stairs and on the top landing recoils from the girl he
has bargained for—his own sister! This was stunning at
Dartmouth College. It shivers every audience. But Billy
is sparing of horror and prefers to evoke more laughter
than tears. Once in a while he is startling. There was the
night in Philadelphia when the press section fled precipi-
tately as the chair suddenly became the jawbone of an ass
in the hands of Samson William Sunday D.D. and whizzed
over the heads of the scribbling Philistines.

Hell—his coat comes off and he drags it after him—
hell—"You bet there's a hell, not Hades but H—E—double
L with fire and brimstone! It's not furnished with modern
conveniences and they won't serve you booze on a tray."
He is through with the coat for the remainder of this
session. One leg is straightened out behind him, there's
a straight line from the top of his head to his heel. One
fist on the other knee is taking punishment from the other
fist pounding in his words like a pile-driver. Sweat streams
from his face. And the voice that was hoarse from the
outset is now strained to the cracking point.

Dogmatic? The chair resounds with a blow that would
skin any other knuckles. "This is a chair!" The desk rocks
under the impact of another swing. "This is a desk!" Out
flies his watch and he waves it. "This is a watch!" Hell is
just as definite, as actual as his anthropomorphic God and

Devil. And "Modernists" are "theological crooks, the same kind of roughnecks who crucified Christ, dosing the churches with spiritual poison and doomed to roast in the hell they don't believe in."

This is no radical revolutionary of religion. He is an anti-evolutionist troglodyte of conservatism. John Wanamaker and John D. Rockefeller, Jr., have sat by him and endorsed him with something more than their presence. A poll of the religious press a few years ago resulted in fifty-six votes for him, forty-three qualified, and twenty-eight against him. Only two Baptist papers opposed him, and none of the Methodist and Presbyterian. The Lutherans were stoutly hostile, but if there's no sawdust on their soles on Judgment Day, that's their lookout.

Sunday's hell, however, is not the lurid pit of McGready's conjury or Finney's blast-furnace. He is more concerned with the sorrows of this life that waste it out to an inglorious end. His deathbed scenes are among his calmer best and his mimicry and pantomime of hell on earth rival the theater he so roundly berates. Besides, he is aware how far hell will "get across." He can drop his slang and antics and speak crisp Anglo-Saxon straight from the shoulder or scale heights of Ingersollian oratory. Then what he is saying is shot through with a social dynamic.

Fear of eternal punishment is not to be compared with Sunday's stirring call to fathers and mothers to save their children from the pitfalls of modern society. Warning of perdition might leave young men cold but Sunday's taunting demand that they be not found cads or cowards in the big game of life sets their red blood coursing. Volunteers from gray-beards to youths not yet shaven, grandmothers to girls in their teens troop forward to enlist in the fight against the cussedness of a wicked world.

The broadsides from the platform do not seriously offend more than a negligible few. The guilty are convinced that their neighbors are just as bad or worse, exalt the accuser, admire his unintimidated audacity and applaud. The vast majority heartily agree with the railing against their peccadilloes, readily accede to the need for forgiveness and the help of God for noble living here and a heavenly reward hereafter. That is what kicks up the sawdust.

The choir turns from the rhythmic lilt of syncopated hymnology to the yearning strains of the old-time invitation hymns. "Rody" signals the soft-pedal volume and the soul-pulling cadence. And the hand that stopped liners hot from the bat is equal to a handshake a second for half an hour. First Billy reaches out from the platform. Then as the line troops by faster and faster, a trap-door lets him down to a thrust-and-take level. No time to kneel, just shake and keep moving. That seals it with God and the Reverend Billy. This is high-speed salvation. There's propulsion behind it. The herders are pushing. In New York seven thousand of them were trained for the job. All this is a triumph of organization.

"To hell with the twentieth century!" That is a peal of antediluvian thunder from the pulpit of William A. Sunday. But his show would not go in any other century and it had to wait for this century's business genius and acumen to get started. In a nutshell, it is religion C. O. D.

The originator is not so original. He is the last of an experimental line—Mills, Chapman, Sunday—an inheritor, borrower, improvisor, improver. Hundreds have attempted to imitate him. It is impossible, for in himself he is the consummation.

Born in a log cabin near Ames, Iowa, the son of a soldier who gave his life for the Union, he spent his early years in an orphans' home. In all he was seven years in big league baseball and a credit to the game. His conversion at a Salvationist street meeting in Chicago made him a better man and a better ball-player. Then he became an evangelist and apprenticed himself to Dr. J. Wilbur Chapman as advance agent and general utility man. In the winter of 1895–96 Chapman went back to his Philadelphia pastorate and left Sunday on his own. The young evangel's first stand was in Garner, Iowa. From then on no knight of the road ever accumulated such an itinerary.

In 1898 at Oneida, Illinois, he took on a singer. Churches could not hold his crowds and his first tent, a three-pole affair, was pitched at Hawkeye, Iowa. Often he would be roused by gales at night to tighten the braces and sit on the guy-ropes. A blizzard at Salida, Colorado, wrecked the tent and he turned to tabernacles. The first seated one thousand at Perry, Iowa, a town of three thousand, that in three weeks came through with a five hundred and fifty dollar free-will offering to the man whom the local press extolled for his "extensive vocabulary, striking impersonations and mastery of the situation."

In these early days Sunday was planting men in pews for a fact. Six weeks in Burlington, Iowa, landed two thousand five hundred. In a voice that would carry half a mile he shouted "Farewell, fellow-sinners, I'm free of your blood!" At Columbus, Ohio, nine thousand church recruits were credited to him in two weeks after his departure and twelve thousand in the course of six months. But this was before the recording angels caught the writer's cramp. By this time the technique was complete for the salvation sieges of cities.

Bookings had to be made a year or two in advance and there had to be unanimity among the churches in assuming spiritual and financial responsibility. The evangelist was never to be left holding the bag. Guarantors signed up and got receipts in the shape of shares to be treasured as mementoes of what happened to their town. At Bangor, Maine, in 1927, two thousand five hundred dollars in cash down was said to have been required. But no guarantor has ever had to forfeit a cent. Billy has always raised the expenses as well as the customary parting tribute. He can do it because the audience is contracted for, the goods are standardized and advertised and the customers are thoroughly canvassed.

Here is a line-up of Sunday's pre-campaign committees: directors, executive, building, ushers, personal workers, entertainment, dinner, business woman, nursery, decorating, shop meetings, church and religious association officials. Dwight L. Moody would not be bothered with committees, but he has been left far behind in another era.

Sunday sends on his experts to train the choirs, ushers and personal workers, bind the bargain, build the tabernacle, lay the wires. A month of prayer-meetings—Pittsburgh had four thousand one hundred and thirty-seven—and Billy arrives like a triumphant Cæsar and takes full command.

With him is his retinue,—physical trainer, secretary, chorister, leaders of outside meetings and "Ma," mother of his four children, now grandmother, and balance wheel of the outfit. "My work is sitting on the safety valve," she says. A wardrobe trunk keeps a dozen fashion-plate suits in perfect press, not a frock coat in the lot, all in the mode of the man of business.

That is what he is, a man of business. He is putting on a sales campaign for Jesus Christ and he is going to make it snappy. The enterprise is like marketing automobiles or biscuits. There's a system and it has superlative efficiency. This is the successful American of the twentieth century. "Other preachers use a tackhammer," he says, "but I use a sledgehammer." No wonder he shakes the cities that ring through the nights with the singing of his lively songs and wake up of mornings to see what he has said splashed all over the front pages of the newspapers.

The gregarious herd dotes on him. He appeals to its prejudices and social strivings and plays upon its vindictive and sentimental moods. Adroitly adjustable, he can save any situation. There was the night in 1917 when he asked all who had registered for the draft to stand up. The response was pretty thin. He called for all who would have liked to register if they could. Ten thousand patriots leaped up cheering. And there was his memorable visit to Dartmouth College amid the deep snows of that winter. Only the eve of the biggest football game of the year could compare with it. Billy staged a potpourri of headliners from his repertory, the student body and many of the faculty marched to the front of Webster Hall and wrung his hand and united in a hearty "Wah-Hoo-Wah for Billy Sunday!"

That is to be expected of modern college men who idolize their football coach. It is not many years since Dartmouth's coaches were whispered to have received more for three months than the president got for a year. Anyhow, no gridiron mentor in the country would have worked for the twenty-five dollars a week paid to instructors of English at Dartmouth in the Year of Grace 1916. But then, as with Billy Sunday in contrast to other preachers, it is a question of productivity. And the mob— or the alumni—decides.

The religious rabble delights in the mirror of its moronic

mediocrity. The "man in the street" hates those who are his intellectual superior and adores the mind that works as his does but has the wit to glorify banalities. The plebeians follow their hero because of his oneness with them that renders them, in his eyes and theirs, stalwarts of the truth marching arm-in-arm with God and commissioned by Him to confound and condemn all who disagree with them. "The man who sneers at revivals," says Billy Sunday, "spits in the face of Christ."

Regardless of whether his stock in trade is factitious, Sunday is a deliberate vulgarian. Ranting, gesticulating, cavorting, he revels in portrayals of dereliction and lewdness that for downright rottenness almost surpass the acts themselves, he goads the dull passion of demos for self-righteousness and he drags down the most revered name of the ages to the level of a hail-fellow-well-met.

"Well, Jesus, I don't know how to talk as I would like to talk," Dr. Sunday is praying. "I am at a loss as to just what to say tonight. I wouldn't dare stand up and say that I didn't believe in you. I'd be afraid you'd knock me in the head."

"O Lord, we had a grand meeting last night, when the crowd came down from Dicksonville (or what was that place, Rody?) Dickson City, Lord, that's right. It was a great crowd." That is another fragment of chumminess and here is the acme of intimacy:

"Well, Jesus, I'm not up in heaven yet. I don't want to go, not yet. I know it's an awful pretty place, Lord. I know you'll look after me when I get there. But, Jesus, I'd like to stay here a long time yet. I don't want to leave Nell and the children. I like the little bungalow we have out at the lake. I know you'll have a prettier one up there. If you'll let me, Jesus, I'd like to stay here, and I'll work harder for you if I can. I know I'll go there, Jesus, and I know there's lots of men and women in this tabernacle tonight who won't go."

That goes with his crowd and jibes with its mentality. For is he not a Reverend and a Doctor of Divinity? Chapman preached the sermon when Sunday was ordained a Presbyterian minister at Chicago in 1903. When the theologians pressed too hard with their queries, Billy would say "That's too deep for me" or "I'll have to pass that up." But his fundamentalism was unshakable. In conferring the divinity degree upon the Reverend William on June 13, 1912, Dr. R. M. Russell, President of Westminster College, at New Wilmington, Pennsylvania, declared: "We count it an honor to Westminster that she did this thing. In many institutions it is customary to bestow the honorary degree of Doctor of Divinity upon those who are more noted for their knowledge of 'the traditions of the Scribes and Pharisees' than for their knowledge and practical use of the Bible itself."

Consequently the multifarious "man in the street" has for a genuine boon companion a Reverend Doctor who, though admitting he knows as little of theology as "a jackrabbit knows of ping-pong," is out to "administer digitalis instead of oyster soup." The crusader emerges. He must have targets. Sunday's best bull's-eyes have been the devil and rum. During the World War he damned the Germans; since then it has been the Bolsheviki. In the summer of 1928 he concentrated upon Governor Alfred E. Smith of New York, the Democratic candidate for President of the United States.

He may be an egotist and a braggart, but the herd worships a man who makes it believe he is being persecuted and is fighting an insidious foe with his back to the wall.

"That dirty, stinking bunch of moral assassins," Billy
Sunday addresses the liquor interests, "everything they
say about me is a dirty, stinking black-hearted lie. I'll fight
them till hell freezes over and then borrow a pair of
skates." There is no reply from the deadly enemy, but that
makes no difference. In 1926 he threatened to run for the
Presidency on a "to hell with booze" platform. He changed
his mind in 1928 and took the stump against Smith. It
paid.

He spoke at the Ocean Grove (New Jersey) Camp-
Meeting Auditorium on "Crooks, cork-screwers, boot-
leggers, whisky politicians; they shall not pass—even to
the White House." A collection of four thousand five
hundred dollars was turned over to him.

It would almost seem that the services of this self-
appointed mouthpiece of Jehova were for hire. There is
no question that tempting offers have been made, one of
the most transparent nature coming in the summer of
1928.

Mayor Harry A. Mackey of Philadelphia, who was manager of the campaign that produced the votes but failed
to get William S. Vare into the United States Senate, was
faced with the exposure of bootleg corruption of his police
force from top to bottom. At a mass meeting in the Arch
Street Methodist Church where both were speakers, the
Mayor asked Dr. Sunday to step in and give the city "a
great spiritual revival" in the "present crisis." The evangelist said he would give the invitation serious considera-
tion. One can visualize the Vare machine "hitting the
trail" in a body.

Another solicitation was to conduct a series of revival
meetings in the mining district of West Virginia in 1922.
The Rev. Dr. Stephen S. Wise, speaking to the congrega-

ton of the Free Synagogue in New York City, denounced the project in these terms:

"I have never come upon a more offending and loathsome instance of the attempted prostitution of the Church. We all know what it means—that he [Sunday] is to use all the power of his eloquence and personality to lead the men back to work under conditions just as unjust."

Saying that he hoped Dr. Sunday would not accept the invitation, Rabbi Wise declared that, if he did, leaders of the Church and Synagogue would go to West Virginia and "point out the truth to the men, that they are not to accept injustice and wrong and starvation as the will of God, but that the will of God is that there shall be justice in the world and that men are always and in every way to strive for it."

Cornering the devil in Maine or throttling John Barleycorn at Ocean Grove would seem to be more expedient, if less lucrative, than holding a revival in Philadelphia or in West Virginia with a political aim in one and an economic motive in the other.

Dr. Sunday knows his own business, however, and critics have never got very far with him. Of course, he has had detractors and traducers, but they are not impressive. There was one Alfred Sheldrick, disgruntled over being deprived of the post-card concession in the tabernacles. He said Billy acquired his habit of calling people polecats, rattlesnakes and jackasses from the Rev. M. B. Williams, who was Alexander's partner at one time. Such terms could hardly be copyrighted.

In the December 26, 1914 issue of the "Truth Seeker," an agnostic periodical which would have to be considered partisan, Franklin Steiner called Dr. Sunday ". . . the greatest hypocrite and mountebank before the American public . . . not only a professional liar but an unblushing literary thief." He was referring to an address delivered by Dr. Sunday before old soldiers at Beaver Falls, Pennsylvania, on May 26, 1912, as almost identical with Colonel Robert G. Ingersoll's Decoration Day speech in the Academy of Music, New York City, May 30, 1882. The evidence submitted was the Beaver Daily Times for Monday, May 27, 1912. Dr. Sunday's reply to the charge, carried in a special dispatch to the New York Times from Philadelphia on January 30, 1915, said:

"If I stopped to heave rocks at every yellow cur that barked at my heels, I'd be throwing stones all the time. It's the same old low-down flock of booze-hoisting infidels, the same old crowd of free-thinkers that try to start something wherever I go. You can tell the whole dirty bunch to come on. I'm here, and I'm giving hell the best kind of a run I know how."

He added that people constantly sent him clippings for use in preparing sermons and that he utilized "some good stuff." All preachers, he said, prepared their sermons in this way and it was not his fault if he used something of another man's. Some might regard the explanation as a little lame, but it must be remembered that Dr. Sunday was having a strenuous time in Philadelphia as disclosed by a suit for $1,754 brought against the Sunday Campaign Committee by Colonel Charles Keegan, who rented his home there to Billy and his party, for damages to the house and furnishings.

Colonel Keegan's claim, as published in a special dispatch of May 11, 1915, from Philadelphia to The New York Times, alleged that furniture was smashed, walls were gouged and more than a hundred beer, whisky, cordial and champagne glasses disappeared. Six doors were

off their hinges, he averred, a big jardinière was broken
and patched together, the piano stool was smashed, a
marble dog was gone and a big toe of the statue of a
young lady was broken off. Also listed as missing were two
sets of Haviland china, six oil paintings, nine bath towels,
three table covers, ten napkins, thirteen pillow-cases, seven
sheets, a wicker armchair, five embroidered silk scarfs,
three silk curtains, a Turkish rug, five books, a silver-
plated syrup jug and a shade on the front door. The
broken articles specified included eight chairs and a lounge.

"It's false from beginning to end," "Ma" Sunday said.
"It's a good thing the two dozen whisky glasses and thirty-
eight beer glasses are gone, if they are gone, for nobody
will get liquid damnation into their systems by them any
more."

The retort might be considered appropriate, if a bit
inconclusive, but still one might pertinently inquire why
the evangel band was housed with the paraphernalia of
Dr. Sunday's booze-devil.

This was only an incident in a great career, however.
The super-salesman of salvation is pachydermic to all cen-
sure. He is secure with his masses.

"Well, no matter whatcha think about the man himself," that unforgettable "man in the street" would say,
"y' gotta take ya hat off to him—he gits the dough an'
he gits the people to do what he says an' hit the trail an'
cough up just the way he wants 'em to."

Billy Sunday is in a strong position. He is virtually
immune. For how can one question the motive or attempt
to impugn the sincerity of the most productive evangelist
America has ever known? Tens of thousands of men and
women will rise and declare that he has renovated their
lives and given them a hope for eternity. Of course they

are grateful and they have expressed their gratitude in a practical way, the only way they knew.

And he has accepted their offerings. What of it? Is not the servant worthy of his hire? No price can be set on a soul. So what boots this temporal reward when compared with the treasures laid up in heaven? This is unanswerable. Billy Sunday has probably asked the Lord for more reservations in the mansions yonder than any other interceder for the wayward children of men.

# CHAPTER XXI

## CONTINUOUS PERFORMANCE

Take my life and let it be
Consecrated, Lord, to Thee;
Take my hands and let them move
At the impulse of Thy love . . .
Take my feet and let them be
Swift and beautiful for Thee . . .
Take my lips and let them be
Filled with messages for Thee.

> Aimee Semple McPherson's favorite hymn.
> Words by FRANCES HAVERGAL.
> Music by WILLIAM J. KIRKPATRICK.

AIMEE SEMPLE McPHERSON—each name is meaningful and all taken together express a career and a character unique in this world since the first disobedience of Saint Paul's high injunction for women "not to teach, nor to usurp authority over the man, but to keep silence in the Churches." Aimee, the beloved, was perfectly mated with Robert Semple, the six-foot Scotch-Irish evangel who converted her. Aimee, the beloved, bereft by death of her partner, tried domesticity with Harold McPherson, a grocer. Aimee, the beloved, forsook kitchen and husband that the Lord might speak through one of the rarest masterpieces of His sculpture.

Dedicated before she was born, consecrated one snow-bound day in Ontario at the budding age of seventeen, enshrined in her own sanctuary in the bloom of her woman-

~ AIMEE SEMPLE MCPHERSON ~

hood before she was thirty, behold the Priestess of the Foursquare Gospel, the healer by Faith, the Impresario of the now splendorous revival of America anchored at last on a permanent location. Gone are the halcyon days of itineracy. Going are the over-night rough-hewn tabernacles. Fading is the glory of pulpiteer masculinity. A continuous performance, seven days a week, year in and year out, with standing room at premium in a Cathedral of Evangelism, flows from the wand of the radiant daughter of the sun. And great is the guerdon laid upon her altar.

Sister Aimee, "that's *her*," as the emancipate Corn Belt connoisseurs of California climate and cult murmur as a buxom white-clad figure wafts itself amid a bower of roses under the delicate tints of intermerging lights to the centre of the marvelously set stage of Angelus Temple. The soft curves of those shoulders and arms and hips are hiding muscles of steel that strained on tent ropes not so many years ago and now bend ever so slightly to the task of quadruple arm-linked baptisms. Luxuriant red-gold hair billows over her forehead, tumbles back and is caught in coils above the nape of her comely neck. The flash of her eyes instantly anticipates the parting of her full red lips in a winsome smile or their curving and conforming with her gentle yet strong features in an expression of sweet solemnity.

Every movement of her plump physique, every gesture of her graceful hands, every tone and cadence of her mellow voice is appealing, beckoning, attracting. Femininity prophetic has stepped out of Eden.

This Eve is not the petite, frail, please-protect-me type. She is rich-blooded and complete like the first mother after nibbling on the apple. Yet she is not Amazonian. Her daughter, the child of Semple, is not quite so tall as she. Her son, the offspring of McPherson, stands a head higher. Save in sentiment, she is not maternal. Rather she seems the perennial bride-to-be. And love is her lure to wholeness in faith. She has been called the Mary Pickford of revivalism. Every devoted heart in her presence is hers by mental projection, hers for dedication to the Spirit of the Foursquare Gospel, the Sovereign of Angelus Temple.

The tax records of Los Angeles in September, 1926, showed the value of the temple property at Echo Park, half way between the city and Hollywood, to be six hundred twenty-eight thousand, three hundred ninety dollars. It belongs to Sister Aimee. Loyal to her are fourteen thousand adherents and two thousand juvenile members. She says she now has four hundred twenty-three branch churches in different parts of the world and that a new one is being built every day. Can anyone believe that this could be accomplished by a pinch-faced, wan, sad-eyed, wapper-jawed, slab-sided, long-skirted holy woman, virtuous because no man ever looked upon her with the eyes of desire? It is more plausible that the achievement is due to the fact that the inspirative message was borne by a warm and beautiful creature enhanced by an aura of intriguing mystery.

Apart from her personality, which, after all, has its parallels in other kinds of endeavor, Sister Aimee's sole contribution within her chosen field lies in making the most of modern methods, inventions and ingenuities—lighting and scenic effects, the radio and the craft of the motion pictures—and evolved by experiment her own combination adapted to the service of theatric evangelism.

Mediæval mystery plays, heaven and hell on the wheels of the York and Towneley, Chester and Coventry Cycles of Fifteenth Century England, the Victorian Cantata, the present-day vaudeville turn, band concert and organ recital, and touches of Max Reinhardt pageantry mingle upon the Sunday stage of Angelus Temple. Sister Aimee is all at once playwright, producer, director and star performer with the rest of the cast harmonized in a choral, instrumental and histrionic background to set off her stellar rôle. Scenery painter and property man execute her ideas. Electrician and scene-shifter, band-master and organist obey her guiding signals. The "bill" changes every week and it is a show of constant surprises.

Angelus atmosphere unites the art of Greek temple with the mechanical features of a Keith-Albee stage and the devices of mass communication. Corniced and arched, parapeted and domed, the fane bows into a circular front with many doors of crystal glass. Silvered radio towers rise above the roof, superimposed like a gigantic half watermelon upon the white walls of cement overlaying a frame of riveted steel. It is built "to stand till the Lord comes." A siding of electric railway from Los Angeles accumulates a long string of trains that bring the devout and the curious out to the daily services and wait to take them back to the city, and the parking area for automobiles looks like the environs of the Yale Bowl as the whistle blows for the kickoff in the football game with Harvard.

Angelus capacity is five thousand, three hundred. Less than a third of the throng straining against the ropes of the traffic line can get in. When the last eager cohort jams through and the doors swing shut, the other thousands range around the woodland about the glowing edifice and listen to the loud-speakers roaring under its eaves.

Earlier batches from the lifted ropes have been taken in hand by competent women ushers garbed in snowy purity, and led to the banks of seats along the seven aisles which, like the sticks of a fan, are joined at the front. The later increments have filled the two balconies, upheld by stout columns rooted in the floor and supporting the border of the vaulted dome, sky-blue, flecked with fleecy clouds and dotted by gleaming stars, reminding one of the rotunda ceiling of the Grand Central Station in New York City. Eight stained-glass windows, thirty feet high, depicting episodes in the life of Christ, pierce the two walls between the balconies and the platform.

Every eye is focused forward. Beneath the rose-hedge fringing the platform on each side of the pulpit desk, the Silver Band of the Temple is pouring out patriotism to the tune of "The Stars and Stripes Forever." Those in the near rows can see the wicker chairs with the electric call buttons and telephone on one arm by which the *dea ex machina* will operate the pending performance. Behind it and above it, like a balustrade of heaven, the hundred choir seats are tiered. Flanking the hallelujah gallery stands the great organ, the pride of Sister Aimee, the triumph of reed and pipe and power that even Roxy might envy. And then the baptistery,—it is disclosed to view on Thursday nights when brawny youth and shrunken age alike are dipped in the clear-rippling waters shaded from the spotlight by palms on the grassy shore.

Most of the audience are coastal emigrés from the Middle West, giving rein to a lifetime of repressed emotion, struggling with inferiority complexes, flocking to Sister Aimee after varied experimentation with new thought or raw food, baths internal or external. They may have frigidaires at home, but their minds are essentially back with Joshua when the sun stood still.

The musical waving of the Stars and Stripes flares to a

finish. A bell rings. Two seraphic maidens carry to the stage a banner with the words "SILENT PRAYER" in letters reminiscent of the signs in proscenium slits announcing the "Ten Tumbling Sweeneys." Again the bell, and the prayer is over. Ladies are requested to remove their hats. Footlights glow from the floral marge as scenery slides into place—perhaps the California conception of the Holy City with battlements and colonnades, Moorish minarets and Oriental towers, all powdered with dust of gilt and mother-of-pearl, erotic blooms and familiar fronds, perhaps a rocky headland with a practical lighthouse flashing its beacon across the waves of dancing blue.

A spectral voice from the clustered horns of the loud-speaker overhead gives warning of the choir's approach attired as angels or as mariners, depending on whether the setting is celestial or nautical. The great room throbs as the organ bursts into pealing "Love Divine, All Love Excelling" or "Sailing, Sailing Over the Bounding Main," as the dramatic context dictates. And the winged host of heaven or the natty sailors and sailoresses sing their way onward to their seats.

Last of all comes Sister Aimee, an armful of roses deep red against the soft whiteness of her becoming dress that has all the simplicity of a deftly adapted Parisian mode. Once, as a tent healer, she affected something like a nurse's costume. But now it is different. She clings to white and the fabric clings to her. It is said that her lingerie is the most expensive afforded by the shops of Los Angeles. Even so, why shouldn't she be beautifully arrayed for the service of her Lord?

She places her roses on a stand of carved teakwood, arranges her corsage of orchids and kneels between her son and daughter. She arises and presently is speaking into

the microphone upon the pulpit desk—"Angelus Temple,
KFSG, Sister Aimee Semple McPherson talking!"

Now everyone must shake hands with at least four
others and say "God bless you!" That is "ketching the
Temple spirit," as Sister says. Lights out in the auditorium, vari-colored floodlights on the stage, the organ
lilting a joyous hymn, Sister is swaying on tiptoe with a
cornetist on her left and a trombonist on her right, her
voice is lost in the exultant volume but her whole supple
body animate with the movement of the music.

She seizes a tambourine, flutters it aloft and steps high
as she pummels it. "All the tenors sing 'Amen,'" "All
the sopranos," "The altos—the basses." She trips into a rollicking ditty, punctuated by the tambourine, "Amen, amen
amen. A-men, A-men. Amen, amen, amen—AMEN!'
Her facility with the tambourine recalls an earlier phase
of her evangelism symptomatic of holy rollerism, in her
tent revival of July, 1919, in the Bronx of New York
City. Then her methods were crude as well as vigorous and
her rhythmic thumpings and shaking of the timbrel induced a contagion of saltatory hysteria.

The organist takes a bow. The applause is a foretaste of
the waves of enthusiasm that will greet each number of
the program. If the stage is set for Paradise, there's the
contrast of Perdition, the saved souls in white, the hell-
bound in black, music to match and conflagration for a
climax. If it is for the sea, a grim pirate brig sinks a
merrily sailing pleasure craft, a merchant galleon goes on
the rocks, and Christopher Columbus emerges from the
lighthouse to lend his booming baritone to "Sail On, Sail
On!" Sometimes Crusaders gallantly bear cross and standard down the aisles to strike a tableau on the stage. Or an
old salt in oilskins plays "Listen to the Mocking Bird" and

"The Old Oaken Bucket" on a tin whistle. Sister Aimee is uniformed now as an admiral, now as a traffic officer mounted on a motorcycle with gauntleted hand upraised as she cries— "Stop! You're speeding to ruin!"

Such "acts" are curtain-raisers for the sermon but the preaching also has scenic, pantomimic and musical illustration. Sister needs material assistance for her ingenuous homiletics. Platitudinous sentimentalism saturates her exposition of the Foursquare Gospel. Her trite phrasing of sterotyped metaphor, her melodramic ventures into the pictorial and her dull lapses into the vernacular would die of desiccation on the lips of any woman unlike Aimee Semple McPherson. She gives them reality and force and makes them live by her utterance, by her intimacy with the five thousand, three hundred "Sister-conscious" people in front of her. Impulsively she rushes toward them with outstretched hands. "Oh, say, folks, you know I think God is—oh, say, I think He's just simply wonderful, don't you?" It's irresistible.

"Oh, will you follow Him? Oh, men and women, this is brought to a show-down!" She is giving her altar-call. "Now please, don't any one go out. Don't move. Give me my chance. You want to go to heaven, don't you?"

Heaven is a glorious place where angels eternally strum their harps round a Great White Throne and its antithesis is the still bubbling bottomless brimstone lake. You're a saint or a sinner, one or the other, no half-ways, and the consequences are your choice.

"Those of you who want to go to heaven—who want me to pray for you (*Aimee, the beloved, praying for me, for me, even me!*) put up your hands. In Section One.—In Section Two.—In the first balcony.—In the second.

"Now those who have your hands up, STAND UP!

Now those who are standing, MOVE FORWARD! Now you who up here in front, KNEEL at the altar!"

She sweeps to the microphone and ecstatically murmurs that "crowds, great crowds, are coming." On Thursday night the sound of splashing in the close-up of the Jordan will be borne over the ether and Sister will shout "Oh, what a happy funeral!"

But if they don't come fast enough, if one more heroic effort is needed to get them started, Sister Aimee sinks to her knees and with arms and countenance uplifted implores presence divine in a tingling torrent of supplication till sobs blend into hallelujahs and the redeemed, weeping, "talking in tongues," shadow-boxing with the Spirit, choke the aisles in a rush to gather as near as they can to the hem of her stainless garment. Such tumults of emotion are seventh heavens to her.

Two thirds of her votaries, however, are won by healing, and if they keeping on piling up discarded crutches, wheel-chairs, casts, braces, straps and stretchers in the foyer, the Temple will have to erect a museum annex as big as the Smithsonian Institution. A bust of poor old bygone Elijah the Restorer and a model of the prayer-machine of Zion might have a niche in the Hall of Antiquities.

For every Saturday night demonstrates the ultra-modernity of Angelusian psycho-sanative art. Every case is a "cure." Preliminary interviews assure that. Sister Aimee just lays on her velvet hands and prays, but her energetic assistant, Brother Smith Wigglesworth, imported from England along with his *magum opus*—"Worthy Words from Wigglesworth" or "Tidbits for All on the Word of God"—Brother is downright pugnacious. He exorcises all manner of ills and vigorously propels into action limbs that have not moved for years. He is only one assistant. Always there are five thousand, three hundred others, not to mention the organist, the choir, a couple of symphony orchestras and a brass band.

Pleading eyes, reaching hands, yearning hearts and a vast hall full of people intent upon realizing the miracle of faith. "I Need Thee, Oh, I Need Thee!" they sing. "What a Friend We Have in Jesus!" and "Sweet Hour of Prayer." Then, ever so softly, the organ tenuously touching distant reeds:

> Oh, touch but the hem of His garment
> And thou too shalt be free,
> His Saving Power, this very hour,
> Shall give new life to thee.

Yesterday, today and forever! "I believe, oh, I believe" rings the glad cry of the healed. And the organ rumbles into the deep diapason of "Rock of Ages." This is the technique perfected in the Dreamland Arena of Balboa Park at San Diego where the sea phase of Sister Aimee's evangelism appealed to the Naval Base when she was heading towards Los Angeles. It traces back to humble beginnings at Corona, Long Island, and Jacksonville, Florida, in 1918-19.

Sister Aimee's first attempt was more direct. She plainly told the Lord in prayer that He was able to heal the bowed down, twisted and supposedly rheumatic young woman standing at the chancel rail of the Swedish Methodist Church of Corona. Amid a resounding refrain of "Praise the Lord!" the joints straightened, the arms were lifted up and the feet felt their way once more.

There was more to it in Florida. A youth offered himself with an arm, said to have been broken in three places, rigidly strapped down in bandages. While the crowded tent prayerfully joined their mass hysteria to his desire to be healed, the little choir at the rear was singing:

A little talk with Jesus makes it right, all right,
A little talk with Jesus makes it right, all right,
In trials of every kind, thank God, I always find,
A little talk with Jesus makes it right, all right.

Sister served as interlocutor in the conversation. "Brother, don't you believe Jesus can heal that arm?" "Yes, I believe He can." "Lord, heal his broken arm, just now, and we will give Thee the glory." Pause. "Brother, take off the bandage. Straighten the arm. Jesus tells you to. The Devil is keeping you back. Let Jesus have His way. Now lift it!" Up it went with a "Glory to Jesus and His Servant Aimee!" And the future of the healing half of the Foursquare Gospel was sure as determined woman could make it. Many "cures" were reported in Montreal in 1919–20. San Diego witnessed multitudes that made the crutch pile grow from dawn till starlight. The Avenue to Angelus was paved with those crutches.

More than delight with the show, more than admiration for the producing preacher of charm and beauty, it is gratitude that guarantees unwavering loyalty to this absolute queen of the pulpit and weighs down the collection plates laid upon her Bible.

In a single day five thousand dollars was raised for Sister's new automobile when the three thousand, five hundred dollar car of the year before was getting "positively shabby." The faithful unhesitatingly chipped in seventy-five thousand dollars for the broadcasting of their belief. That was casting bread upon the air because of the "radio collections" which arrive daily by mail. The "Foursquare Monthly," edited by Sister, brings in a goodly income. Often it is specified from the pulpit that nothing less than five-spots will do. What are the totals? Sister says the books are open in the six-story office building adjoining the Temple and an elaborate "social service" organization is functioning there.

Her plant is the last word in the Rotarianizing of evangelized religion. The Sunday school has one hundred fifty-seven classes. Typewritten sheets of as many as three hundred names at a time are read over the radio which also carries calls for wandering boys to go home to mother. The Foursquare City Sisters maintain day and night telephone vigil to synchronize "organization" with "service." They will tell anyone what time it is or give deathbed calls instant response. "The lights of the Temple are never out," says Sister Aimee, "and prayer has never ceased within its walls since it was opened, January 1, 1923, men praying all night and women all day in two-hour shifts."

Non-believers insist that Sister Aimee has gained no distinction as a distributor of charity among impecunious followers and that she has lived like a Princess of the Pacific. They further allege that on her trip to the Holy Land a few years ago she was attired in the latest fashion and traveled in regal style. But the Templars gave her a welcome home that would have gladdened the heart of Cleopatra.

Until May 18, 1926, Aimee Semple McPherson was idolized or criticized in only a very small part of this planet. She was hardly known beyond the bounds of Southern California. What happened between that day when she disappeared while bathing at Ocean Park, Santa Monica, and January 10, 1927, when all resultant charges against her were dismissed in the Superior Court of Los

Angeles County upon the motion of District Attorney Asa Keyes, *made* Aimee.

Her alleged kidnapping, her trial, and the linking of her name with that of her former radio operator, Kenneth G. Ormiston, constitute a climax in her life. Everything in her career, guided by the efficient management of her ex-Salvationist mother, Mrs. Minnie Kennedy, had been pointed and built toward such a climax. A sudden coup was all that was needed no make her a world figure and what happened certainly had the desired effect. She may have connived at the affair for the realization of the zenith of her ambition or she may have been pushed into it by the force of circumstances.

The probability is that just as William Ashley Sunday is beyond mere monetary corruption, Aimee Semple Mc-Pherson is superior to common carnal temptation. Of course she is cognizant of her charms. She is not stupid. But sex is only part of the mental, physical and nervous composite of a human being and is not to be stressed any more than any other natural impulse. Aimee, the beloved, is supremely aware that her whole alluring self must be preserved intact for the idealized possession of the mind's eye of her multitude. Indeed, she has put her prudence into words: "The absurd, insulting insinuation that I, pastor of a mighty church, editor of a Christian magazine, mother and member of a Christian family, should topple the whole by running away with a former employe!" But though only the press of Los Angeles took note of her dropping from sight, the newspapers of the entire country printed columns about her after she "emerged from the desert" and foreign correspondents cabled the accounts abroad. It was not wholly a matter of insinuation, insulting or otherwise. It was a Page One story. And this was exactly what Aimee had to have.

District Attorney Keyes branded the exploit a hoax but concluded that the fabrication of a kidnapping yarn was not within the scope of judicial action. Whatever it may have been, it certainly was indicative of Aimee's lifelong skill in the utilization of circumstance, a skill which sometimes goes by the name of opportunism. The facts of her parentage and career explain the woman and give a clue to possible motives.

She has written two autobiographies, one about 1920–21, entitled "This is That" and the other in 1927, captioned "In the Service of the King, The Story of My Life." These abound in roseate clouds of adjectival intimation but contain surprisingly few specific details. She lets her father go without a given name and gives her second marriage one hundred and fifty words without mentioning who or what the other contracting party was. She omits her age, but in a recent interview she said: "Why, I don't mind telling how old I am; I was born in 1892." Never mind the month and the day. The Lord has it in the Book of Life.

Her ancestors were Methodist and Baptist preachers. Her father was a "choir leader who loved to sing." His name was Kennedy. Her mother is said to have been a Salvation Army lassie and is regarded by many as the real architect of her daughter's amazing fortunes. Before her birth on their farm near the village of Ingersoll, Oxford County, Southwest Ontario, the parents "prayed for a baby girl who would some day preach the gospel."

An only child, she was physically vigorous and experimenting. In school she was an elocutionist, throwing herself into various rôles with abandonment. She tried to tell her schoolmates what they should do and how they should do it. Her early mental development was in a religiously-saturated family atmosphere and when in high school she met with the evolutionary theory her doubts were immediately and violently expressed. Never intellectually attentive, she was even then emotionally explosive to such ideas as reached her. She seemed to have had no formal schooling beyond the age of fifteen or sixteen, but how ready she was to "tell the world" is revealed by her in her article, signed "Perplexed Schoolgirl" and published by *The Family Herald and Weekly Star* in Montreal.

Aimee's conversion—it was typical of the small-town revival—came at the age of seventeen in Salford, Ontario, under the magnetic pleading of Robert Semple, a handsome, athletic young giant of Scotch-Irish Presbyterian stock. She was and is of a strongly sensory rather than a rational nature. Mingling love with religion, she and Semple married, and set out to evangelize the Orient together. He died of fever in Hongkong and a month later (in 1910–11) her daughter was born in an English hospital there. On the voyage to San Francisco, Aimee discovered her objective power of appeal when the passengers raised a cash subscription for her.

While engaged with her mother in mission work at Chicago in 1917, she married Harold McPherson, a grocer. She says it was "with the understanding that I should go back to the Lord's work if ever the call came." The Lord drafted her in 1917 after her son, Rolf McPherson, was born. McPherson obtained a divorce at Providence, Rhode Island, on April 21, 1921, on ground of extreme cruelty, charging that Aimee "threw a fit" when up against domestic work. His mother, Mrs. Annie McPherson, characterizing Aimee's kidnapping story and trial as "a huge publicity stunt," said in a newspaper interview at Providence on September 29, 1926:

"I gave Aimee her first money to start her evangelistic career. That was when she was my daughter-in-law, living with my son. My friends engaged with her in this spiritual work, starting in a little room in East Providence. Gradually her influence grew until she managed to procure a tent in Providence. Here Aimee held her first public revivals. With the aid of my money, she travelled all over the country, becoming richer and more influential. She left my son two years before he filed his divorce suit."

Aimee does not mention anything like this but sets a melodramatic scene in a hospital (not located) where she lay "dying from a general breakdown." Prayers for healing were met by a firm heavenly voice saying—"Will you preach? WILL YOU GO?" She yielded and got well and with a baby in each arm went back to Ontario where she tackled a mountain of dirty dishes in a tent revival at Kitchener. It was at Mount Forest, she adds, that she pitched her own tent and first preached the Foursquare Gospel. One may believe her or her ex-mother-in-law or attempt a synthesis of both versions. Every great life has its difficulties for the biographer.

Newspaper files corroborate Aimee's appearance with a tent in the Bronx in 1919, after her experience at Corona, Long Island. She herself records the development of "faith healing" on a Southern trip which bore special fruit in Florida. She veered westward and was preaching in Los Angeles in 1920. There she received the gift of a bungalow, where she made her headquarters and worked out the Angelus Temple idea while she accumulated a following at Philharmonic Hall and at Balboa Park, San Diego. But it was the proximity of Hollywood and the rise of the radio which helped her to fashion her "modern line" of evangelism. By 1926, with the aid of her mother, she had a practical and profitable proposition on a sound business basis. Only one thing was lacking—something to bring her forth as a national figure.

On May 19, 1926, the Associated Press, under a Los Angeles dateline, carried this dispatch: "Aimee Semple McPherson, founder and pastor of Angelus Temple here and widely-known evangelist, who was reported to have drowned late yesterday while swimming in the surf at Ocean Park, is still missing here today after an all-night search." Note the magic words "widely-known evangelist." Her fame was not so far-flung as to give her more than a stick of type in Eastern newspapers the next morning. But the handwriting was on the fence.

Mrs. Kennedy expressed the conviction that her daughter had drowned, and a Coast Guard cutter sent down deep-sea divers, one of whom, Ed Harrison, lost his life. It was established that Aimee's clothes were found on the beach by her secretary, Miss Emma Schaeffer. Kenneth G. Ormiston, former radio operator at Angelus Temple, appeared at Los Angeles on May 25, denied having seen Aimee, went to San Francisco on May 28 and vanished.

Search was conducted at Bouquet Canyon, near Saugus, California, on the basis of a note saying: "Help. They took me to a cabin in Bouquet." By June 4, search was abandoned at the beach. Memorial services for Aimee had been held at Angelus Temple, "ransom" demands had come frequently and false clues were run down. Then on June 23 the story cracked wide open in an Associated Press dispatch from Douglas, Arizona, as follows:

"Aimee Semple McPherson, missing Los Angeles evangelist, was brought to a hospital here today in an exhausted condition. She related a tale of having been kidnapped by two men and a woman at Ocean Park, California, on May 18 and held a captive in Mexico for five hundred thousand dollars ransom.

"James Anderson, an American, said he found Mrs. McPherson in a state of collapse at Agua Prieta, across the border . . .

"Mrs. McPherson said she escaped while her captors were away from the Mexican shack in which she was held."

Type began talking for Aimee all over the United States. Her mother started to join her. On the same train was Deputy District Attorney Joseph Ryan with instructions from District Attorney Asa Keyes to investigate the alleged kidnapping "to the bottom." Mr. Keyes observed that fifteen thousand dollars had been collected at Angelus Temple for a memorial to Aimee, that a reward of twenty-five thousand for her safe return had been twice offered and withdrawn. R. A. McKinley, a blind lawyer of Long Beach, later drowned, was named as the go-between. On June 23, however, Governor Abelardo Rodriguez of the Northern District of Lower California, was positive, because of his border police watch, that Mrs. McPherson had not been in any part of Lower California since her disappearance on May 18.

Aimee braced up at the Douglas hospital, detailed her adventures and offered five hundred dollars reward for the location of the hut from which she said she escaped. With her mother and two children she entrained for Los Angeles. At Tucson, B. H. Greenwood, City Building Inspector, boarded her car and said he had seen her on the streets of Tucson four weeks previously. On June 26,

Aimee had a triumphant welcome home to Angelus Temple where, fresh, lively and good-looking as ever, she told her heart-rending story.

On July 1, she crossed the border at Douglas and made a futile search for that hut. The next day the County and Federal Grand Juries at Los Angeles took up her case, the Federal inquiry involving alleged tampering with a letter from McKinley, the blind lawyer, to Mrs. Kennedy to conceal Mrs. McPherson's being alive till after the Temple had raised thousands of dollars.

J. F. Tena, Collector of Customs for the Agua Prieta District, told the County Grand Jury that it would have been physically impossible for Aimee to have covered the territory she said she had and to have crossed the border without being seen by Mexican line riders. Aimee was subpoenaed and the telegraph wires began to hum.

After backing and filling for a month, the Grand Jury finally got it straight that Ormiston and a woman, known as "McIntyre and McIntyre," had occupied a cottage at Carmel, California, from 4 A. M. May 19 to May 29. Affidavit from the ex-radio man declared the lady was a "Miss X" who should come forward and clear Aimee's name. The only "Miss X" to show up was Mrs. Lorraine Wiseman-Sielaff, arrested on a bad-check charge, who said Aimee offered her five thousand dollars to pose as "Miss X" and paid only two hundred dollars. Aimee accused Mrs. Wiseman-Sielaff of trying to blackmail her.

Warrants were issued on September 17 for the arrest of Aimee, Mrs. Kennedy, Ormiston and Mrs. Wiseman-Sielaff on charges of "conspiracy to defeat justice," specifically, "perjury, subornation of perjury and preparation of false documents." Two days later Aimee appealed from her pulpit for a "devil fund" to fight her case and the following month staged at the Temple a "March of the Martyrs," a tableau portraying Biblical scenes reviewing the "history of persecution."

Meantime a third death had occurred in the case, in the suicide at Los Angeles of Dr. A. M. Waters whom Mrs. Wiseman-Sielaff had named in connection with procuring a "Miss X." Then, on the kidnapping angle, the stenographer of the now dead blind lawyer, McKinley, said that Aimee had asked her to continue the work of producing one of the villains and she had dug up a Long Beach character whose photograph Aimee had "recognized."

At the preliminary hearing Judge Carlos S. Hardy of the California Superior Court tesified to his belief that Aimee had been kidnapped and made a distinct impression. A dispatch to the *New York Evening Post* from Los Angeles on September 5, 1928, quoted Judge Hardy as admitting that he had received two thousand, five hundred dollars as a "free will offering" which Angelus Temple leaders insisted upon giving him for legal advice.

Aimee refused to allow her fingerprints to be taken for comparison with prints made at the Carmel cottage. A fire in her Temple destroyed papers and photographic negatives relating to the case. Still there seemed to be sufficient evidence on which to bind the three women defendants over, on November 3, for trial in the Superior Court for criminal conspiracy. Aimee issued a statement declaring her faith in God and disavowing the feminine apparel and letters found in Ormiston's trunk at a New York hotel.

Ormiston was located on December 10 at Harrisburg, Pennsylvania. After various dickerings, he finally surrendered to District Attorney Keyes. On January 1, 1927, Ormiston named a "Seattle nurse" as the "Miss X" of

Carmel. She never materialized. On February 14, his wife, Ruth Peters Ormiston, divorced him in Los Angeles on ground of desertion. No reference whatever was made to the McPherson case, according to reports of the Associated Press.

The charges of criminal conspiracy against Ormiston and the three women were dropped on January 10, 1927. In moving dismissal, however, District Attorney Keyes insisted that the evangelist had not been vindicated and maintained that she had left Los Angeles on May 18, 1926, in Ormiston's automobile bound for the Carmel cottage and that she had perpetrated a disappearance hoax. In conclusion he said: "Reputable and reliable witnesses have testified sufficiently concerning the so-called Carmel incident and the so-called return from the so-called kidnapping adventure to enable Mrs. McPherson to be tried in the only court of her jurisdiction, the court of public opinion."

But words did not hurt Aimee. In the trial she found an important asset for her trade, a live Devil,—Asa Keyes, and she dramatized him as such, to his personal and official embarrassment. She is unquestionably an artist. The loyalty of her followers was stimulated by the charges against her and between May and January the membership of Angelus Temple increased by about a thousand.

She did well by the publicity attendant on the court hearings, warming up the copy by appearing attractively in the limelight and by finding frequent occasion to shout "LIE!" at the prosecutor or at an opposing witness. Among the syndicated newspaper serials of her life which appeared at that time, one, under her own signature, was in the *New York Evening Graphic,* a tabloid well-known for its vivid handling of the cases of "Peaches" and "Daddy"

Browning, of Alice and Kip Rhinelander and of Ruth Synder and Judd Gray.

"Did I go from my pulpit into the arms of a paramour?" she asked in *The Graphic* of October 20, 1926. "On God's word I did not. They bear false witness against me. But Father forgive them, for they know not what they do!"

That was just the trouble. "They" did not know what they were doing. But Aimee did. If there is any doubt upon that score, witness the fact that she started an evangelical tour of the country the moment the case ended. And in the Fall of 1928 she told the Foursquare Gospel to Europe, pausing in Paris to say a *bon mot* for the city before entering upon her conquest of the British Isles.

Great crowds greeted her at Dayton, Ohio, on February 1, 1927. They had been reading the papers. She had the Chicago Coliseum in tears on February 8. By way of Washington, she reached New York on February 18, and there were big collections at Glad Tidings Chapel in West 33d Street where she assailed drink and the Devil, praised the prohibition law and talked of the "sin of the city" and the "hearts of gold underneath." She also spoke a kind word at Texas Guinan's Three Hundred Club early one morning and the genial Tex asked her guests to "give this little woman a big hand." They gave it.

Aimee went to Florida on March 3 but did not stay out of print long. In April and May (1927) she was writing up the Ruth Snyder-Judd Gray murder case for the *New York Evening Graphic*. She was in the headlines again in July when her mother accused her of "scheming" to mortgage the Angelus Temple property for personal gain. A settlement was made in August leaving Aimee in full control, with a board of trustees on which was her secretary, Miss Schaeffer.

Aimee Semple McPherson may wander far and build ten thousand children-churches, but her heart will always be with Angelus Temple. She says she is waiting for the Millennium when Jesus Christ will come and take and use that edifice for His very own. One wonders if even then she would leave the stage.

## CHAPTER XXII

## FUNDAMENTALISM TO THE FORE

Hallelujah! Thine the glory,
Hallelujah! Amen!
Hallelujah! Thine the glory,
Revive us again!
WILLIAM P. MACKAY.

B ELIEF in the Book, howsoever it may be interpreted
or accepted with paradoxically diverse varieties
of literalism, has always been the prime requisite
of any plan of salvation. Before being reborn one must
believe. To escape being damned one must believe. For
refuge now and heaven hereafter one must believe. Having believed, one must lead others to share the belief and
the experience it affords. So germinates the perennial
American Revival.

Every evangel stands like an angel in the way, like the
angel that dealt with Balaam and his long-eared mount,
pointing to the only Truth and the only Light. Turn
about and don't look back. Remember Jonah, remember
the wife of Lot. The Book is the guide and the Word is
infallible. On such premises disagreement is impossible.
It is useless to argue with a Fundamentalist. That is one
reason why the revival survives.

Any text can be applied at any time in any part of a
world fashioned and populated in six days and now less
than six thousand years old. Quibble with this and a hun-

dred other texts are available to back it up. All that has
come to pass in the latter days was prophesied and there is
nothing new under the sun that is not in the Book. Prohibition of alcoholic beverages in the United States of America,
for instance, has been supplied with Scriptural foundations, though one Fundamentalist group recently looked
askance at something that happened at the marriage feast
of Cana.

Some evangelists, it is true, have called upon men to
be reconciled to the Son of the Father, but many have
warned of the wrath of a Jehovah that must needs be
propitiated. The thunders of Sinai crashed one night over
a New England hamlet. A two-hundred-pound son of the
soil went out from the revival meeting palsied with fear and
at midnight awoke a neighbor by shouting under his window: "Bonesville is a-goin' to be destroyed before morning!" The reply was emphatic. "No it ain't. Go hum
and go to bed." And a safe and sane sunrise cleared the
storm. In the same village, and also within the memory
of this generation, the citation of a Biblical mandate to
confess sins brought to the altar a weeping man and woman
who regaled a crowded and interested house with the story
of their adultery. The burden was cast upon the Lord
while the community listened in. It is the only thing remembered of that revival.

A primitive faith naturally has primitive expression,
which the revival only emphasizes, such as Pentecostal
power, speaking in tongues and divers emotional and physical manifestations. Evangelism among those Negroes who
still possess a racial naïveté demonstrates these elemental
traits.

The pastor is likely to be a lay preacher who had dropped
a hoe to wrestle it out with the Lord by his lone in the

~ JOHN ROACH STRATON ~

brush to assure his "call." He will have to know as much
Bible as any brother or sister in front of him and he will
have to be able to hold his own with them in singing the
free melody of their communal song. He will have assistance; his people come because they want to be saved or
because they want to save others. Not even a church row
can withstand a revival; at least there is a truce till the
season is over.

The prophets of old never spoke with a greater wealth
of imagery than that which rhythmically rose and fell while
the kerosene lamps swung with the swaying shoulders in
a little Virginia meeting house packed from pulpit to
door. Oh, how the plagues descended upon Egypt! Pharaoh slapped at flies and scratched for fleas. (The Scripture had it lice but fleas were more familiar along the
Old Dominion shore.) Frogs leaped and hail rattled and
swarms of locusts clouded the sun. "O Pharaoh, let My
people go!" Darkness fell over the land and the angel of
death visited the cradle of the first-born wherever the
blood was not sprinkled on the door. "Ah, Pharaoh, he
let God's people go!" "Hallelujah!" shouted a sister.
"Hallelujah!" shouted a brother. "Old Pharaoh, he let
God's people go!"

Then the Pillar of the Cloud and the Pillar of the Fire
led those people on. On through the wilderness. On
through the deep Red Sea with the fishes swimming in
the water both sides along. Coming through, coming
through! Till the Lord set their feet upon the shore. Then
Moses, he stretch out his hand and the waters close behind.
Pharaoh's horses, Pharaoh's men all swallowed up in the
deep Red Sea. And then God's children sing!

Standing on the bank of the deep Red Sea these first
children of the Lord on High sang with the Israelites

the joy of their deliverance. A shrill soprano led off and a chord of resonant harmony caught the second bar. "Keep the Old Ark A-Movering, Keep the Old Ark A-Movering Right Along, 'long, 'long!" Such music the stars did hear when the world was young.

And now who will go through the water? Who will go through the fire? Who will be counted with the people of the Lord? The preacher prophesies with Isaiah as he exhorts, kneels at the foot of the Cross as he pleads. He weeps and his flock weeps with him. He implores and the brothers and the sisters repeat his words. A tall youth wavers in the aisle, his eyes wide open, his forehead wrinkled in perplexity. Strong arms seize his and press him to the altar. "Pray through, brother, pray through!" But he can't pray. The words won't come. "Mourn him up, chillun, mourn him up!" Low crooning gradually rises to a rolling chant. Again that soprano—piteously— "It's Me, Lord!" Again the choral unison—sobbing— "Standing in the Need of Prayer!"

"Oh, Lord!" It's the penitent. The Spirit has taken him. And how he prays! What he won't do no more! "Oh, Lord, let me in!" Open the Gates of Glory, a sinner has come home! The jubilation shout carries on into "I Want to be Sitting in the Kingdom to Hear Jordan Roll!"

All this is simple and understandable. Rudimentary religion, spontaneously conceived, experienced and transmitted, is close to the spirit of the minds that made the Holy Writ. Quite different is the synthesized religion which deliberately uses Scripture to serve its purposes. For to be pure a faith need not necessarily be primitive.

There is no quarrel with the Traditionalist. It is he who takes the offensive and calls names, identifying Modernists with "infidels," "materialists" and "anarchists." To him it is sinful to exercise the critical function for the rationalizing of faith. He alone can be right. All who disagree are damned. And most of the damned maintain an exasperating indifference.

Once in a while the zeal of the Fundamentalist encroaches upon what others might consider intellectual freedom. Even then the defensive side is more curious than outraged. There was the cross-examination of William Jennings Bryan by Clarence Darrow during the Scopes evolution trial at Dayton, Tennessee, in July, 1925.

Question: Do you claim that everything in the Bible should be literally interpreted?

Answer: I believe that everything in the Bible should be accepted as it is given there.

Question: But when you read that Jonah swallowed the whale—or that the whale swallowed Jonah—excuse me, please,—how do you literally interpret it?—You believe that God made such a fish, that it was big enough to swallow Jonah?

Answer: Yes, sir. Let me add—one miracle is as easy to believe as another.

Question: Perfectly easy to believe that Jonah swallowed the whale?

Answer: If the Bible said so.

Both Mr. Bryan and Mr. Darrow were interested in the first cause and the final goal; the one was positive and the other frankly did not know. A few days afterward Mr. Bryan went where there is no controversy and where lawyers and Chautauquans, scientists and theologians stand a chance of being corrected. Conceptions of creation and destiny all become relatively insignificant across the bourne of the infinite and the eternal.

None will question the integrity of true religion which

men live as best they know how. None can presume to dispute the authenticity of a belief without affronting the faith by which men may humbly walk with their God and bravely pass from this existence.

But when self-anointed prophets arise in this Twentieth Century and curse it for lacking universal agreement with their peculiar—and privileged—view of the relation of God and man, the case is altered.

The Rev. Dr. John Roach Straton, D. D., pastor of the Calvary Baptist Church of New York City, has taken the witness stand in court with a Bible in his hand and sworn that he was a "Prophet of God," that Satan was an entity and that he had seen evidences of the Devil in Calvary Church.

The occasion was his prosecution of Charles L. Smith, President of the American Association for the Advancement of Atheism, who had been indiscreet in communications with the minister concerning religion, birth control, evolution and various moral questions. That was their own affair. But the evidence as to what had occurred in the Stratonic evangelization at Calvary Church constitutes a public record of what militant Fundamentalism stands for in this day and generation.

Defying and denouncing the tree ancestry, nebular and solar vagaries and Scriptural inexactitude of the Modernists as responsible for an age of immorality and irreligion, Dr. Straton has restored what he apprehends to be Biblical Days at Calvary Church with Hebraic creationalism, Ptolemaic astronomy, simplified Scripture, healing by faith and speaking in tongues under the baptism of the Holy Ghost. All-night prayer-meetings are the yeast of his continual revival.

In one of these nocturnal convocations the pastor's son,

Warren, at the age of nineteen had his first contact with the "power of heaven." It came after a long session of concerted supplication. Let him tell of it: "Suddenly I was conscious of the power of the Lord. I started to sing, I guess, and pray, and the more I prayed the happier I became. The Lord took my voice, and I magnified Him as loudly as I could."

This experience has been shared by hundreds among the throngs whose hallelujahs cheer on the preacher's thin-lipped invective against card-playing, cocktail-drinking and dancing, evolution, modernism and Clarence Darrow, novels, plays and nude art, horse-racing, dog-racing and prize-fighting. And in between seasons of prayer and preaching, all in the same ecstatic, not to say hysterical, mood, this church, whose pietistic fulminations have resounded throughout the country, intersperses demonstrations of holy healing. Olive oil and a dash of vinegar, according to an experimental reporter of *The New York Times,* comprise the ingredients of the ceremonial emollient applied in the exorcism of human ills. The credence of the devotees has a categorical basis: if the Apostles could do it, so can John Roach Straton, their heir and successor.

Success has stirred the ambition of the tall, gaunt, long-faced inheritor of a halo. The members of Calvary Church —a rebellious few have quit the fold in protest against the pastoral practices and preachments—have ratified his plan for a two-million, five-hundred-thousand-dollar, fifteen-story edifice containing an auditorium to seat three thousand five hundred and three hundred and fifty apartments, one of which will be reserved for the Prophet who will see to it that there is no drinking of intoxicating beverages on the premises. Besides this, the Doctor had bought a hotel and land at Greenwood Lake, New York, for a sum-

mer centre of his evangelism that will rival Winona Lake
and Ocean Grove and prevent vacationists from "saying
good-bye to God" during the annual and customary two
weeks of what used to be recreation.

These projects made headlines in the newspapers and
Dr. Straton is decidedly not averse to such notice. In fact,
he has made it unsafe for city editors to neglect the covering of Calvary Church. That was why the front pages
blossomed out one summer morning in 1928 with his pulpit attack on Governor Smith of New York as "the dead-
liest foe in America today of the forces of moral progress
and true political wisdom."

Dr. Straton was on the hustings of the Presidential
campaign. A repercussion of publicity, comparable in
its results with Aimee Semple McPherson's bold stroke
in May, 1926, made him a national figure. The Governor
helped by challenging him to a debate in the pulpit.
The pastor preferred Madison Square Garden. The bubble
grew so big that it burst. But John Roach Straton suffered no loss of prestige with his people. On the contrary,
they probably accounted his exploit as another victory
for Fundamentalism.

Dr. Straton and his wife have sponsored another remarkable evangelical career dedicated to the faith that
is fundamental. As often happened in the camp-meetings
of the frontier in 1800, the Voice is heard speaking through
a child. The present prodigy is Uldine Mabelle Utley who
at the age of sixteen has been preaching, visioning, poetiz-
ing and healing for five years. Since 1924, accompanied
by her father and mother, a manager, a tutor and a secretary, she has travelled about the United States, sometimes addressing audiences as large as fifteen thousand.

When she was eleven years old, Uldine had a vision of

a rose which has since served as a symbol in her work. In 1924 she started a monthly magazine called *The Rose Petals of Sharon*. She writes editorials, stories and poems and conducts a "Happy Hearts" column. Everything is based upon her amazing knowledge of literally accepted Scripture.

Her New York début, in June, 1926, followed the testimony of Mrs. John Roach Straton who said that she had been suffering from a severe pain in her side and that the girl removed it by prayer. Moreover, Mrs. Straton attributed her baptism by the Holy Spirit to the young prophet, declaring that under the experience she fell to her knees and wept in gratitude and humility before the Lord.

In the Fall of 1926 an attempt was made to stop Uldine's preaching on the ground of the employment of a minor, but investigators of the Society for the Prevention of Cruelty to Children reported no cause for action against her sponsors. Soon thereafter she lectured before a hundred parsons at the weekly meeting of the Baptist Ministers' Association. They listened for almost an hour, applauded and unanimously adopted a resolution thanking her for her "message."

Uldine is athletic and vigorous, a beautiful girl with smooth blond hair and large blue eyes. A natural orator, she speaks in a clear, high voice that carries to the fringe of a large audience. Her sermons and prayers are extemporaneous and she is never at a loss for words.

Her father was a motion picture operator and her mother was taking tickets at the theatre when Uldine was born at Durant, Oklahoma, on March 16, 1912. As a small child she was attracted to the theatre and wished to be a dancer and moving picture actress.

"I was first stage-struck at the age of seven," she has said. "I used to write love stories and imagine myself playing the rôle of heroine in them."

On her way to a dramatic rehearsal at the age of nine in Fresno, California, Uldine turned aside to attend a revival service of Aimee Semple McPherson. It is not clear whether she was converted upon that occasion. Whenever and wherever it was, this is how she describes it:

"When the speaker asked all those to come to the platform and pray who wanted Jesus, I felt I wouldn't be able to breathe unless I went. I heard a woman say—'There's another one of those silly girls who hasn't any idea what it's all about.' I'll admit I didn't understand everything the preacher said, but I knew I wanted Jesus."

She was just eleven when she preached her first sermons, a series of five, at Sanger, California. Her fame spread and, in December, 1923, a group of men asked her to conduct a five-day campaign at Oakland. That was her first venture on the revival road.

She has preached in tents and churches and one day, in the Summer of 1927, she went out from her canvas bethel in New York City, mounted a sandbox in the shadow of the Treasury Building at Wall and Nassau Streets and soon attracted a large white-collar throng out for the noon hour.

Her methods of preaching and her vocabulary, simple at first, have shown evident development. As to her mental progress, a *New York Times* report of her sermon on the topic "Adrift" in her tent at Brooklyn in the Summer of 1928, quotes her as follows:

"Many people suppose God used to be, but are of the opinion that He is not so necessary to human life in these modern times. They seem to suppose that God has really

diminished in power and everything is left up to man
to do the best he can. But the God who is now is just the
same as He used to be, and there are many in every age,
no matter how busy they may be, who recognize His
power in all His works."

In an interview in *The New York Evening Post* on
August 30, 1928, she said: "I am reading a lot nowadays,
but everything of a religious nature. Not theology, no,
because somehow I don't seem able to get through long,
learned theological books yet. May be later, when I'm
older. I read discourses—discourses on various things, you
know."

Uldine Utley's assertion that Christ is speaking through
her is like that of Krishnamurti, the foster son of Mrs.
Annie Besant, who declares that the World Teacher uses
him as His mouthpiece. Her confidence is perfect. Her
fundamentalism won't hurt anybody. But one can imagine the use to which it might be put by others when
John Roach Straton says:

"While the Modernists have played traitor, I believe
it is part of God's scheme to send this prophetess as a rebuke to them."

Prophet and Prophetess! A mantle is bestowed upon
Uldine. This is of a piece with the consecration of the
son of the Prophet who lay prone on the floor of Calvary
Church at an all-night prayer-meeting "uttering unin-
telligible words and singing beautifully."

The Levites must be girded for the battle against Modernism. Even killing is only a casual incident in the holy
warfare. It was another Reverend Doctor who fired the
pistol, an incongruous utensil of a pastoral study even in
Texas. And a week after J. Frank Norris, champion of
Fundamentalism, had shot D. E. Chipps, a wealthy lum-

berman, in the Summer of 1926, the outdoor Baptist Tabernacle of Fort Worth was crowded with ten thousand zealots to hear that parson preaching on "Jesus Only."

He is another tall, thin man. Despite the gray at his temples, he has a boyish, dreamy, sensitive face. It is hard to think of him as a slayer. The throng on the serried wooden benches might or might not have been mindful of the murder as it greeted him with a burst of applause. This is the man who in fourteen years has made the Fundamentalist revival pay till he has acquired a following eight thousand strong that can never get enough of it. Like Aimee Semple McPherson, he has his own private radio broadcasting station and his own journal, the weekly *Searchlight,* which has supplemented his pulpit attacks upon sinners in high places and his exposition of hell-fire religion for the edification of the multitude. After the courts had freed him in the Chipps case without the spectacle of a dramatic trial for which he had asked several of his flock to put up one thousand dollars apiece to bolster up the Cause, *The Searchlight* increased from sixty thousand to sixty-five thousand in circulation and Norris had dreams of its reaching a million. Since then, however, the press of the country has let him down. Only Texas knows he exists.

But there is one Elementalist of whom the world is very much aware. His specialty is college students of both sexes. President Hibben exiled his cult from Princeton and the students' magazine of Oxford demanded its expulsion from that University. The man is Dr. Frank N. D. Buchman, "Soul-Surgeon," and his purity process called "washing out," is known as "Buchmanism." Both have been characterized as the bane of many a campus.

The system is applied at "religious house-parties" of students at which personal faith is discussed and group confession of intimate sins is encouraged. "Conversions" result under the intense emotional strain that is engendered. The self-revelations run the gamut of pruriency, incontinence, nymphomania and onanism. Distraught young minds suffer acutely under the self-inflicted torture and from the excruciation of others which eggs them on.

Against whatever "relief" some of the subjects may be said to have experienced, must be set the shattered nerves and warped minds of the others. In one fine old college in Virginia a student lingered for days on the verge of madness till a sensible alumnus, called in for the purpose by one of the faculty, succeeded in restoring the youth's mental balance.

Dr. Buchman is not without prominent supporters. Dowager Queen Marie of Rumania has been interested in his work, and several years ago he spent three weeks at the royal palace in Bucharest at her invitation. In England, Harold Begbie told in his book, "Twice-Born Men," of his backing Dr. Buchman. Formerly a Lutheran minister and for a time a missionary in India, Dr. Buchman derives his income from the gifts of those to whom his "soul-surgery" appeals.

One other to venture into this field deserves mention along with Dr. Buchman, though their methods and patients differ. It is the Rev. Samuel M. Shoemaker, Jr., the young rector of Calvary Episcopal Church in New York City, who operates a "soul-clinic" in connection with evangelism. He has written a book entitled "Children of the Second Birth" in which he trenchantly asserts that "Park Avenue needs conversion as much as the Bowery" and tells of his meeting in which people are "born again."

Matters which belong in the psycho-analyst's laboratory are now being dragged out in an epidemic of "public confession," in the name of religion to effect conversion. Opinions of the effect of this method upon the individual confessors may differ, but its social implications raise another question. As a form of evangelism it must be considered in its social aspect also.

But whether the Spirit is invoked by John Roach Straton in Calvary Baptist Church or Uldine Utley in a tent to heal the body and inspire the soul, whether regeneration is contingent upon the confessional mode of Frank Buchman or Samuel Shoemaker, Jr., the proponents and the adherents will seek to justify themselves by the Book. J. Frank Norris, as a true Fundamentalist, probably would not hold the Seventh Commandment a whit more inviolable than the Sixth. The defense is grim. So sayeth the Book. The Book must be believed as it is.

To be critical is to sin. To engage in unbiased—hence uninspired—research is heresy. Things have not changed. As it was in the beginning is now and ever shall be. But what was in the beginning? The Word. That suffices for the Fundamentalist revival.

# CHAPTER XXIII

## RATIONALIZED RELIGION

Blest be the tie that binds
Our hearts in Christian Love;
The fellowship of kindred minds
Is like to that above.
JOHN FAWCETT, 1739–1817.

SYNDICATED revivalism, capitalized at one hundred million dollars, starring William Ashley Sunday and Aimee Semple McPherson on a national circuit of palatial tabernacles equipped up-to-the-minute with essential paraphernalia, has been proposed by a man of business if not spiritual vision. One vaudeville concern is reliably reported to have offered Dr. Sunday ten thousand dollars a week to grace its boards. That acceptance has not yet been obtained is beside the point. Dr. Sunday and Mrs. McPherson would not have received such attention if they had not qualified in their own way.

This is the ultimate. The glory of the old revival has departed. No heaven-called amateurs need try to break in. It is strictly professional now, a cold, calculated commercial proposition with immeasurable cash returns for the principals and spiritual dividends of less than one per cent. for the evangelical Churches of America.

Dr. Sunday's campaign in New York City in 1917 cost more than three hundred and fifty thousand dollars, raised by one hundred and twenty thousand dollars in free-will offerings and by gifts of wealthy underwriters. Of the sixty-five thousand to seventy thousand "trail-hitters" only two hundred could be traced to church memberships. His Pittsburgh run footed up to about ninety thousand dollars and three thousand one hundred and seven "converts," very few of them permanent, at the rate of twenty-eight dollars and ninety-six cents apiece. Dr. Sunday is generally believed to be a millionaire and men like the Rev. Charles L. Goodell, head of the Commission on Evangelism and Life Service of the Federal Council of Churches, have expressed the belief that he is worth many times a million.

At the flood tide of high-power revivalism, 1914–1917, the churches with the aid of a charitable public were spending twenty million dollars a year for the purported saving of souls by one thousand evangelists, great and small. The campaigns cost the communities an average of five thousand dollars, but Dr. Sunday and other star performers came higher, all the way up to one hundred and fifty thousand dollars.

Since then the large Eastern centres of population have contrasted costs and results and have become wiser—the promoters of the revival game say "wickeder"—and the remnant of two hundred and fifty salvation sellers concentrated at Winona Lake have turned to charting their courses in the religiously febrile and fertile South, Southwest, West, Middle West and Northwest. The East can go to hell without benefit of the chance to crash the gates of heaven with a handshake and a free-will offering. And Sister Aimee has a lien on the Pacific Coast.

Winona is not waning yet. It has just closed up ranks and shifted tactics. This country is going to be worked to the last collection at the end of the sawdust trail. The little army keeps on drilling. Homer Rodeheaver has his

Gospel Singing School and Dr. Sunday is second in command to Charles R. Scoville in the preaching phalanx. Tex Rickard could take lessons from them all.

But the days of cyclonic pressure are numbered. The legerdemain of the big man of holy medicine and his manipulative entourage repels the intelligent and won't go with the herd the moment its bellwethers scent staleness and lead a stampede to fresher diversion. Already, responsible leaders of that Church which was born of the pure fire of the Wesleyan revival are speaking their mind.

"We have permitted professional evangelism to organize their campaigns too largely upon a commercial basis," says Bishop Adna W. Leonard of the Methodist Episcopal Church. "Their desire to secure money has been as pronounced as their eagerness to see men and women saved from sin. How often it is said that there is need for a revival in order that people may be solicited for funds 'while their hearts are warm and tender.'"

The Rev. Joseph L. Berry, Senior Bishop of the Methodists, classing mass interdenominational revivalism as "high-pressure evangelism," declares that it is now "a thing of the past." He adds that six hundred evangelists are idle in America and that there is little demand for their services.

The Rev. William E. Biederwolf, an evangelist who has done worthy work ever since he began in Jerry McAuley's New York mission, aptly observes that "if the evangelist is getting too much money it is because somebody else is guilty of giving it to him" and voices a plea for the itinerant who goes underpaid or not paid at all. The adjustment is now in the making.

Aside from the mercantile, not to say predatory, aspect of the situation that has come about since Sam Jones admitted getting thirty thousand dollars a year back in the nineties and since B. Fay Mills and Dr. J. Wilbur Chapman laid the groundwork of the modern technique perfected by William A. Sunday, emotional conversion, as a mode of becoming a Christian, is being challenged by thinking men of the Church.

Attacking emotional evangelism as sentimentalism and a waste of religious feeling, the Rev. Dr. Willard L. Sperry, Dean of the Harvard University Theological School, has said in New York City pulpit of the Rev. Dr. Harry E. Fosdick:

"Stirring up religious feelings for the pleasure received from them should be accounted spiritual unchastity. In active evangelism not one person out of ten who is profoundly stirred actually does anything about it; the nine merely have their feelings stirred and do nothing. The effect on the nine is as insidious in its way as taking opium.

"Emotional feeling is the driving, energizing power in human life, but sentimentalism is like racing the motor of your automobile with the clutch out. It gets nothing done and the man who is thus stirred, but does nothing, loses in the end the power to do. This sentimentalism is a stumbling-block in the way of religion."

If the traditional aloofness of Harvard from the revival as a way of getting religion should detract from the force of Dr. Sperry's utterance, corroborative testimony given at the Auditorium of the Ocean Grove (New Jersey) camp-meeting ground of the Methodists should be considered. Speaking on August 14, 1928, at the end of a week during which "twice-born" men and women had been discussed and many conversions had been made, the Rev. J. M. M. Gray, pastor of the Elm Park Methodist Episcopal Church of Scranton, Pennsylvania, said:

"Conversions at evangelistic meetings are nothing more

than emotional outbursts which are merely natural responses of the nerves to outside stimulus."

Naturally, the statement caused talk at Ocean Grove. No one desires to admit to himself that the most sacred influence in his life was born of susceptibility to emotional contagion. Everyone likes to feel that he was particularized by the Lord. His prayer was answered. Grace came to him. This is the essence of mysticism, man's direct and immediate apprehension of God. It accounts for sudden and complete conversion evolving a "new world" for a "new man." It would be presumptuous to attempt the demarcation of the supernatural in such an experience.

But when mechanical means are deliberately employed to induce crowd hysteria and auto-hypnosis, when the rehearsed and transparent artifices of the professional wholesale saver of souls come into play, then there need be no hesitation in plainly stating that it is a wanton profanation of feelings humanity has believed hallowed. And if the motive of financial gain be mixed with that of self-aggrandizement, such conjury with mass emotion takes the color of delusion and imposture.

The revival itself merits no sweeping indictment because it has been diverted from its original purpose or exploited for profit. The very nature of its organic growth parallel with the progression of secular business genius made the results inevitable. At the same time the revival, the sincere and the specious alike, has failed in its intention. The Protestant Churches are barely keeping pace with the increase in population. Submitting conclusive statistics in support of this fact, the Rev. Charles Stelzle, President of the Church Advertising Department of the International Advertising Association, declares the churches are slipping in growth and warns of stagnation.

The churches are well aware of their plight. Some of them still look to the revival as a way out. For instance, the Northern Baptist Convention voted in June, 1928, to set aside the year beginning May 1, 1929, for "world-wide evangelism" and called upon all denominational organizations to co-operate in the campaign. Most of the churches, however, as represented in the Federal Council of Churches of Christ in America, are coming to the view that the method of the revival is outworn, unsound and costly and that it is productive of transitory and unfruitful emotional excitement. Instead of being a quickening force, the revival has been found to have a reaction that leaves the churches in a slough from which they must struggle to recover.

To fill empty pews is the everlasting problem. This the revival has not been doing. Accessions mean more than material prosperity; they are the sustaining power of faith. It is not possible to get too many members. The Rev. Dr. George E. Heath has more than two thousand in his College Avenue Methodist Church in Somerville, Massachusetts,—a notable personal achievement—and he is out for more, for he is a church builder. Numbers mean social, mental and spiritual expansion. That keeps them in the church. The question is how to get them.

"Visitation evangelism" is the answer of the Federal Council of Churches and the major denominations are arrayed behind it in an effort which promises to supersede the tabernacle twisters. Public meetings and public repentance are discarded. Forensic fireworks and mass emotional incitation are dispensed with. Lay volunteers marshalled by pastors carry the appeal direct to the individual in his home. Possibly someone remembered that Dwight L. Moody was converted and won to church membership while wrapping up shoes in the store where he worked.

The new road to religious fellowship has been success-fully tested. In four years, since 1924, one hundred and fifty-eight thousand one hundred and nine persons have passed over it into active and lasting church membership and in the Winter of 1927–28 campaigns of a week's dura-tion brought in ten thousand forty-two in New York City, six thousand four hundred and sixty-nine in Pitts-burgh and six thousand three hundred and thirty-two in Philadelphia. In the Fall of 1928, Columbia University, in co-operation with the Greater New York Federation of Churches, provided a course in this kind of evangelism for about fifty young clergymen and teachers who in turn will give instruction till eventually thousands of others will qualify for participation in the campaign planned for the following Winter.

The Rev. Dr. A. Earl Kernahan, a Methodist minister of Somerville, Massachusetts, who has directed the experi-mental development of the plan thus far, will apply it during 1928 in Greater Boston, New York City, Syracuse and Albany, Philadelphia, Pittsburgh, Harrisburg and Nor-folk, Cincinnati and Youngstown, Covington, Kentucky, Detroit, San Francisco, Seattle and Portland, Oregon. Church Federations throughout the country will be in charge under the general supervision of the Federal Coun-cil's Commission on Evangelism, headed by the Rev. Charles L. Goodell.

Under this plan, lay committees, working under men and women devoting their lives to the work, begin a cam-paign with a community canvass to ascertain church preferences. There is no proselyting. The visitors of the various churches, in pairs, go to the homes where their faith has been indicated as the natural choice, if any, and in quiet, earnest, personal interviews seek to implant or restore Christian convictions. Conversion or reconsecration is always decisive. It means uniting with the Church. It is a rationalizing of religion.

The students in the evangelism course at Columbia will have twelve weeks of intensive study of the psychology of the personal approach, manner of presentation and persuasion. Dr. F. H. Laflamme, Field Secretary of the New York Church Federation, declared the cost of the new system infinitesimal as compared with the old way and predicted the end of barnstorming by emotional revivalists. He cited the elaborate campaign on old-fashioned lines put on two years ago by the three Moravian Churches of Staten Island.

"The campaign lasted nine weeks, they got fifty-three conversions, and it cost twenty-five thousand dollars," he said. "Last year the same three churches adopted the modern method of sending visitors, two by two, to the houses, and they obtained one hundred and six conversions for four hundred and fifty dollars."

He added that the new evangelism was not only more economical but also more effective than the old, saying: "We find that, taking it on a six-months basis, eighty per cent. of Mr. Sunday's conversions relapse but eighty per cent. of ours remain faithful."

"We find it more effective to send our visitors two by two," he concluded. "For one thing it is following the New Testament precedent. For another, it doubles the chances of success. For if the personality of one visitor should prove uncongenial to any particular person, he can slide imperceptibly into the background and his companion can come forward."

Another "visitation" idea being carried out in 1928 is

that of the non-sectarian Men's Church League, led by the Rev. Dr. J. Campbell White. This calls for the enrolling of "one million witnesses" in the churches each of whom pledges himself to bring at least one person into church membership.

It has been calculated that if the two hundred thousand Protestant ministers in this country should persuade one person a month to become a member of the church, the year's total accession would be two million four hundred thousand. Friendly calls and man-to-man talks on the real meaningfulness of Christianity would be the means. It appears plausible. Like the visitation method, it sensibly would move in the direction of something permanent as against the transient emotionalism generated by the eagle-eyed, over-night-and-gone exhorter.

The worked-up revival doubtless will pass. Outside the Winona Lake group, about six hundred intinerant evangelists are still active. But they can see the signs of the times and are revising their pulpit practices. One can simply declare himself a Christian to satisfy many of them and one can forego wallowing through a spasm of sentimentalism. Perhaps a few of the more adaptable heirs of Elijah will come out of the tabernacle and qualify as experts in organizing and piloting card-indexed visitation campaigns. There should be at least a decent living in that.

The decline of the roaring revivalist as a type is largely his own fault. At his worst he has disgusted people of intelligence with his crudities and vulgarities. At his best he has not sufficiently considered the social and intellectual needs of mankind, forgetting that to receive religion implies a mental as well as an emotional process and an understanding of one's relationship with the Christian community. To such neglect can be traced the impermanence of his work which, more than anything else, has caused the churches to turn away from him.

For the churches themselves have more ways of offering their message today than any of their supernumerary spokesmen ever had. The preacher of the metropolitan congregation stands before a microphone and rural folk a thousand miles away hear his sermon as well as the singing of his choir and the music of the organ. The religious use of the radio, already indispensable, has a future limited only by the need for men to gather together in order to sense true participation in the worship of their God.

Soon the "talking film" will bring to all the churches, regardless of location, a wealth of pulpit oratory and Biblical drama. It is planned to record sermons of noted clergymen synchronized with screen pictures of them. Famous choirs will be similarly filmed with their song. A group of actors is to be sent to the Holy Land to make "talking motion pictures" of twenty Bible stories in their historical background. As with the radio so with this art— it is bounded solely by the cause for which man erected churches.

And yet with all the devices for the almost universal transmission of things heard and things seen, the churches have not more to offer today than was borne out from Judaea two thousand years ago by men who were called evangelists. They tasted death that the Word might live. After them have come others likewise called. Even in the New World, generation to generation, they have risen. And with them must be numbered some who were unworthy of their name, since they presumed to preach of One they said had sent them.

Of the true and the great who have evangelized America

let it be remembered that they lived for nothing else. They lifted up their voice to save their people. And they believed whatever they preached, whether hell or heaven, damnation or saving grace. Edwards, Whitefield and those stalwarts of the Wesleyan fire—Asbury, Cooper, Cartwright of the Western circuits; Miller of the Advent; Swann and Knapp in the Baptist Jordan; Finney, Nettleton and Shaw; Moody the last of the Giants of God and Sankey the Singer of the Soul—they and all who in faith and works deserve to stand beside them preached repentance to a nation, made it better, brought its people closer to their God.

The end is not yet. So long as stands the ancient sacrifice, a broken and a contrite heart, the voice of the true evangel will not cease. With drum-beat and trumpet it shall be heard in the city street. Among the free hills it shall be heard in the wayside pulpit. It shall be heard till none is left to cry unto heaven—What shall I do to be saved!

# BIBLIOGRAPHY

ABBOT, LYMAN—"Life of H. W. Beecher."

ASBURY, HERBERT—"A Methodist Saint, The Life of Bishop Asbury."

ATKINSON, REV. JOHN, D.D.—"Centennial History of American Methodism."

BACKUS, ISAAC—"A History of the Baptists in New England"; "A History of New England with Particular Reference to the Baptists, 1724–1806"; "An Abridgement of the Church History of New England, with a Concise Account of the Baptists in the Southern Part of America."

BARNETT, REV. WILLIAM—"Life and Times of Finis Ewing."

BAXTER, WILLIAM—"Life of Knowles Shaw, the Singing Evangelist."

BEECHER, REV. LYMAN—"On Revivals," in the Christian Observer, Vol. 28, P. 537.

BENSON, LOUIS FITZGERALD—"Christian Song. The English Hymn; its development and use in worship." "The Hymnody of the Christian Church."

BETTS, REV. FREDERICK W.—"Billy Sunday—The Man and His Methods."

BIEDERWOLF, WILLIAM E.—"Evangelism"; "Evangelistic Situations."

BLISS, SYLVESTER—"Memoirs of William Miller."

BLIVEN, BRUCE—"Sister Aimee, Mrs. McPherson (saint or sinner?) and Her Flock," in the New Republic, Vol. 48, Pp. 289–91. Nov. 3, 1926.

BONAR, A. A.—"Nettleton and His Labors."

BOUTELLE, ELDER LUTHER—"Sketches of the Life and Religious Experiences of Luther Boutelle."

BRADFORD, GAMALIEL—"D. L. Moody, A worker in souls."

BROWN, ELIJAH P.—"The Real Billy Sunday."

BROWN, JOHN ELWOOD—"In The Cult Kingdom."

BRUCE, W. L., D.D.—"The Psychology of Christian Life and Behavior."

BUCKLAND, REV. A. R.—"Selected Sermons of George White-field."

BURR, ANNA ROBESON—"Confessions and Confessants."

CAREY, W. A.—"B. Fay Mills," in The Arena, Vol. 33, P. 593.

CARTWRIGHT, PETER—"Autobiography." Edited by W. P. Strickland.

CHAUNCY, REV. DR. CHARLES—"Seasonable Thoughts on the State of Religion in New England."

CLEVELAND, CATHERINE C.—"The Great Revival in the West, 1797–1805."

COLBY, JOHN—"The Life of John Colby."

COMSTOCK, SARAH—"Aimee Semple McPherson, Prima Donna of Revivalists." Harpers, December 1927, No. 931, Pp. 11–19.

CONANT, WILLIAM C.—"Narratives of Remarkable Conversions and Revival Incidents."

CONRAD, A. Z.—"Boston's Awakening."

CUMMING, I. A. M.—"Tabernacle Sketches."

CUYLER, REV. THEODORE—"Autobiography, Recollections of a Long Life"; "A Thirty Years Pastorate of Theodore Cuyler —By His Congregation."

DANIELS, W. H.—"Moody, His Words, Work and Workers."

DAVENPORT, FREDERICK MORGAN—"Primitive Traits in Religious Revivals."

DENISON, REV. F.—"The Evangelist; Or Life and Labors of Jabez S. Swan."

DE VOTO, BERNARD—"The Chariot of Fire, An American Novel."

DEXTER, BYRON—"Wanted; A New Messiah." From American Mercury. October 1926, Vol. 9, No. 34, Pp. 233–241.

DIMOND, SYDNEY G.—"Psychology of the Methodist Revival."

DOW, REV. LORENZO—"History of a Cosmopolite Etc." and appended to "Journey of Life" by Peggy Dow, his wife.

DU BOSE, HORACE M., D.D.—"Francis Asbury, a Biographical Study."

DUFFUS, ROBERT L.—"The Hound of Heaven," in American Mercury, April 1925, Vol. 5, Pp. 424–432.

DWIGHT, TIMOTHY—"Life of Edwards."

DWYER, JAMES L.—"Elijah the Third," in American Mercury, July 1927, Vol. II, No. 43, Pp. 291–299.

EARLE, A. B.—"Winning Souls."

EDWARDS, JONATHAN—"Narratives of Surprising Conversions"; "Thoughts on the Revival of New England in 1740."

EGGLESTON, EDWARD—"End of the World."

ELLIS, WILLIAM T., L.L.D.—"Billy Sunday, The Man and His Message."

FINLEY, JAMES W.—"Autobiography."

FINNEY, CHARLES G.—"Autobiography"; "Revival Lectures"; "Memoirs."

FLANIGEN, J. R.—"Methodism Old and New."

FRANCIS, JOHN JUNKIN, D.D.—"Mills Meetings. Memorial Volume."

FRANKLIN, BENJAMIN—"Autobiography."

GALLAHER, JAMES—"Western Sketch Book."

GILLIES, REV. JOHN, D.D.—"Memoirs of George Whitefield."

GOSS, CHARLES F.—"Echoes from Pulpit and Platform."

HAWTHORNTHWAITE, SAMUEL—"Adventures Among the Mormons."

HILL, ROWLAND—"Life, Anecdotes and Sayings."

HOLMES, JOHN HAYNES—"New Churches for Old."

HOOD, REV. EDWIN PAXTON—"The Great Revival of the Eighteenth Century."

HUMPHREY, A. G.—"Revivalism Examined."

INSKIP, JOHN—"Autobiography."

JAMES, WILLIAM—"Varieties of Religious Experience."

JONES, REV. SAMUEL PORTER—"Thunderbolts."

KNAPP, JACOB—"Autobiography of Elder Jacob Knapp."

LANPHIER, JEREMIAH—"Alone With Jesus."

LONGAKER, T. C.—"Some Counterfeit Religions."

LOOMIS, H. JR.—"Rvival of 1858–59," in the New Englander, Vol. 3. P. 79.

MACLEAN, J. KENNEDY—"Torrey and Alexander."

MATTHEW, T. S.—"Good News for Sinners." From New Republic, Vol. 49, Pp. 71–2.

McCORMICK, ELSIE—"A Prophetess of Doom," in American Mercury, October 1926, Vol. 9, No. 34, Pp. 233–241.

McNEMAR, RICHARD—"The Kentucky Revival."

McPHERSON, AIMEE SEMPLE—"Foursquare" in Sunset, Vol. 58, P. 14, February 1927. "In The Service of the King. The Story of My Life."

MILLER, WILLIAM—"Evidences from Scriptures and History of the Second Coming of Christ about the Year 1843 and of His Personal Reign for One Thousand Years"; "Sermons"; "Lectures."

MILLS, BENJAMIN FAY—"God's World and Other Sermons."

MOODY, WILLIAM R.—"The Life of Dwight L. Moody";

"Founders Day Address in The Mount Hermon Alumni Quarterly," March 1927, Vol. 25, No. 3, Pp. 81–85.

MUNGER, HIRAM—"The Life and Religious Experiences of Hiram Munger."

NEEDHAM, GEORGE C.—"Recollections of Henry Moorehouse."

NEWELL, REV. DANIEL—"The Life of Rev. George Whitefield."

NORTH HEMPSTEAD, LONG ISLAND, TOWN OF—"Records."

OTTMAN, FORD C.—"J. Wilbur Chapman—a Biography."

PARKER, REV. THEODORE—"Sermons."

PATTERSON, REV. A. J.—"Discourses on the Revival of 1857."

PHELAN, MACUM—"Handbook of all Denominations."

PHELPS, REV. A. A.—"Purity and Power, Or the Seven P's."

RANKIN, HENRY WILLIAM—"Northfield, Mount Hermon, and Chicago."

REED, CHARLES—"Facts on the Great Revival of 1857."

RILEY, ISAAC WOODBRIDGE—"The Founder of Mormonism; A Psychological Study of Joseph Smith."

ROBERT, PHILIP I.—"Charles Alexander."

RODEHEAVER, HOMER—"Song Stories of the Sawdust Trail."

ROOSEVELT, THEODORE—"Winning of the West."

RUSSELL, PASTOR CHARLES TAZE—"The Divine Plan of the Ages. Studies in the Scriptures." Originally "The Millennial Dawn."

RUTHERFORD, J. F.—"The Harp of God, Proof Conclusive that Millions Now Living Will Never Die."

SANKEY, IRA D.—"My Life and Sacred Songs."

SHOEMAKER, REV. SAMUEL M.—"Children of the Second Birth."

SIEGFRIED, ANDRÉ—"America Comes of Age." Chapter 3, "Religious Aspect."

SIMPSON, MATTHEW—"The Life of Bishop Simpson."

SMITH, JOSEPH—"Times and Seasons"; "Journals."

SMITH, RODNEY (GIPSY)—"Autobiography of Gipsy Smith"; "Real Religion" (Sermons).

SOUTHEY, ROBERT—"Life of Wesley and the Rise and Progress of Methodism."

SOUTHOLD, LONG ISLAND, FIRST CHURCH SOCIETY OF—"Records."

SPEER, WILLIAM—"The Great Revival of 1800."

STEBBINS, GEORGE C.—"Reminiscences and Gospel Hymn Stories."

STELZLE, CHARLES—"The Passing of the Old Evangelism," in World's Work, December 1927, Vol. 55, No. 2. Pp. 195–202.

# BIBLIOGRAPHY 373

STONE, ELDER BARTON W.—"Autobiography."

STUART, GEORGE R.—"Methodist Evangelism."

SUNDAY, WILLIAM ASHLEY—"Sermon-Food for a Hungry World," in Christian Century, Vol. 42, Pp. 1471–73. November 26, 1925.

THOMPSON, CHARLES L.—"Times of Refreshing."

TORREY, REUBEN A.—"Why God Used D. L. Moody."

TRACY, JOSEPH—"The Great Awakening."

TYERMAN, REV. L.—"The Life and Times of Rev. John Wesley"; "Life of George Whitefield."

TYLER, BENNETT—"Memoirs of the Life and Character of Rev. Asahel Nettleton."

WALLINGTON, NELLIE URNER—"Historic Churches of America."

WATERBURY, REV. J. B., D.D.—"Sketches of Eloquent Preachers."

WEISS, JOHN—"Life of Theodore Parker."

WELCOME, ISAAC C.—"History of the Second Message."

WHITE, JAMES—"Sketches of the Christian Life and Public Labors of William Miller."

WHITEHEAD, JOHN, M.D.—"Life of John Wesley with Life of Charles Wesley."

YOUNG, BRIGHAM—"Journal of Discourses."

G. C. L.